U-31-n

Geographisches Institut
der Universität Kiel
ausgesonderte Dublette

Inv.-Nr. B 3169

Geographisches Institut
der Universität Kiel
Neue Universität

Landscape and Settlements

National Atlas of Sweden

Forsmark in northern Uppland; uplifted coastline, Walloon ironworks and nuclear power

Landscape and Settlements

SPECIAL EDITOR

Staffan Helmfrid

THEME MANAGER

Department of Human Geography,
University of Stockholm

National Atlas of Sweden

SNA Publishing will publish between 1990 and 1997 a government-financed National Atlas of Sweden. The first national atlas, *Atlas över Sverige*, was published in 1953–71 by *Svenska Sällskapet för Antropologi och Geografi, SSAG* (the Swedish Society for Anthropology and Geography). The new national atlas describes Sweden in seventeen volumes, each of which deals with a separate theme. The organisations responsible for this new national atlas are *Lantmäteriverket, LMV* (the National Land Survey of Sweden), *SSAG* and *Statistiska centralbyrån, SCB* (Statistics Sweden). The whole project is under the supervision of a board consisting of the chairman, Sture Norberg and Thomas Mann (LMV), Staffan Helmfrid and Åke Sundborg (SSAG), Frithiof Billström and Gösta Guteland (SCB) and Leif Wastenson (SNA). To assist the board and the editors there is a scientific advisory group of three permanent members: Professor Staffan Helmfrid (Chairman), Professor Erik Bylund and Professor Anders Rapp. A theme manager is responsible for compiling the manuscript for each individual volume. The National Atlas of Sweden is to be published in book form both in Swedish and in English, and in a computer-based version for use in personal computers.

The English edition of the National Atlas of Sweden is published under the auspices of the *Royal Swedish Academy of Sciences* by the National Committee of Geography with financial support from *Knut och Alice Wallenbergs Stiftelse* and *Marcus och Amalia Wallenbergs Stiftelse*.

The whole work comprises the following volumes (in order of publication):
MAPS AND MAPPING
THE FORESTS
THE POPULATION
THE ENVIRONMENT
AGRICULTURE
THE INFRASTRUCTURE
SEA AND COAST
CULTURAL LIFE, RECREATION AND TOURISM
SWEDEN IN THE WORLD
WORK AND LEISURE
CULTURAL HERITAGE AND PRESERVATION
GEOLOGY
LANDSCAPE AND SETTLEMENTS
CLIMATE, LAKES AND RIVERS
MANUFACTURING, SERVICES AND TRADE
GEOGRAPHY OF PLANTS AND ANIMALS
THE GEOGRAPHY OF SWEDEN

CHIEF EDITOR	Leif Wastenson
EDITORS	Staffan Helmfrid, Scientific Editor
	Margareta Elg, Editor of *Landscape and Settlements*
	Ulla Arnberg, Editor
	Märta Syrén, Editor
PRODUCTION	LM Maps, Kiruna
SPECIAL EDITOR	Staffan Helmfrid
TRANSLATOR	Michael Knight
GRAPHIC DESIGN	Håkan Lindström
LAYOUT	Typoform/Gunnel Eriksson, Stockholm
REPRODUCTION	LM Repro, Luleå
COMPOSITION	Bokstaven Text & Bild AB, Göteborg
DISTRIBUTION	Almqvist & Wiksell International, Stockholm
COVER ILLUSTRATION	Claes Grundsten/N

First edition
© SNA
Printed in Italy 1994

ISBN 91–87760–04–5 (All volumes)

ISBN 91–87760–30–4 (Cultural Landscape and Settlements)

Contents

Mankind and the Landscape   6
TORSTEN HÄGERSTRAND

Patterns in the Cultural Landscape   10
STAFFAN HELMFRID

Ten Thousand Years in Sweden   12
BJÖRN BERGLUND, STAFFAN HELMFRID, ÅKE HYENSTRAND

Landscape Research— An Interdisciplinary Science   18

The Ystad Project   18
BJÖRN BERGLUND

The Luleälv Project   22
EVERT BAUDOU

The Barknåre Project   26
ULF SPORRONG

Prehistoric Fields in Southern Västergötland   28
CATHARINA MASCHER

An Abandoned Farm on Gotland   29
DAN CARLSSON

The Landscape and the Transformation of Society

The Old Agrarian Landscape before 1750   30
ULF SPORRONG

Land Reform and Industrialisation   36
KJELL HARALDSSON, GÖRAN HOPPE, JENS MÖLLER, OLOF NORDSTRÖM

The Urbanised Landscape   48
HANS YLANDER, STURE ÖBERG

Sweden's Cultural Landscape—a Regional Description   60
STAFFAN HELMFRID, ULF SPORRONG, CLAS TOLLIN, MATS WIDGREN

The Cultural Landscape: Selected Examples

The Skåne Plain   78
NILS LEWAN

Malmö   80
LENNART AMÉEN

Halland   82
BIRGITTA ROECK HANSEN

Blekinge   83
BIRGITTA ROECK HANSEN

"The Kingdom of Glass"   84
OLOF NORDSTRÖM

Öland and the Kalmar Coast   86
SÖLVE GÖRANSSON

Gotland   88
SVEN-OLOF LINDQUIST

South Vättern   90
REINHOLD CASTENSSON

The Östgöta Plain   92
REINHOLD CASTENSSON, STAFFAN HELMFRID

The Bohuslän Coast   94
RAGNAR OLSSON

Hönö—An Island Community   96
RAGNAR OLSSON

Göteborg and the Göta Älv Valley   97
RAGNAR OLSSON

The Västgöta Plain   100
BIRGITTA ROECK HANSEN

Viskadalen   101
BIRGITTA ROECK HANSEN

Håbol in Dalsland   102
BIRGITTA ROECK HANSEN

Flatåsen in Värmland's "Finnish" Forests   103
GABRIEL BLADH

The Plains around Lake Mälaren   104
BIRGITTA ROECK HANSEN

The Södermanland Lake Plateau   108
BIRGITTA ROECK HANSEN

Södertälje   109
GÖRAN GELOTTE

Stockholm   110
THOMAS LUNDÉN

Åkersberga   116
BIRGITTA ROECK HANSEN

Summer Stockholm   116
BIRGITTA ROECK HANSEN

Bergslagen   118
KERSTI MORGER

The Uppland Mining District   120
KERSTI MORGER

The Siljan District   122
BIRGITTA ROECK HANSEN

Voxnadalen   123
BIRGITTA ROECK HANSEN

Shealings and Crofts   124
BIRGITTA ROECK HANSEN

Round Alnösundet   126
IAN LAYTON

The Bothnian Coast   128
IAN LAYTON

Robertsfors   130
ERIK BYLUND

The Forest and Bog Landscape   132
IAN LAYTON

The Mountain Region   134
BIRGITTA ROECK HANSEN, STAFFAN HELMFRID

The Storsjön District   136
BIRGITTA ROECK HANSEN

Klövsjö   136
BIRGITTA ROECK HANSEN

Malmberget   138
BIRGITTA ROECK HANSEN

Planning for Future Landscapes   140
THOMAS HALL, MARIO PONZIO, LENNART TONELL

The Future of the Cultural Landscape— a Vision   152
GÖREL THURDIN

Mankind and the Landscape

Words change their meaning when there is a need for change. That is certainly true of the word landscape.

"Where does the boundary run between Södermanland and Uppland?" is a catch question that Stockholmers are sometimes asked by visitors from the country. The medieval provinces –"landskap"– no longer have any administrative function. Yet they live on in most Swedes' minds in a way that the "län" names have never done. The province names carry cultural heritage and identity.

Another kind of landscape is referred to when, at the beginning of his novel "The Red Room", Strindberg places his reader on Mosebacke in Stockholm and lets his gaze wander from detail to detail, sometimes to the far-off horizon, sometimes to places close at hand. These details are so cleverly chosen that, even if you have never stood on Mosebacke, you feel as if your senses are being filled with the sights, colours, sounds and smells of Stockholm.

Strindberg himself entitled this introduction "A Bird's Eye View of Stockholm". His landscape is not a province but a panorama. This meaning is synonymous with landscape painting, a change in meaning that came fairly late in history. The Dutch masters of the 17th century are usually reckoned to be the pioneers in this field, but the genre flourished above all in the 19th century. It is no coincidence that Strindberg was also a painter or that the Annual of the newly-founded Swedish Touring Club was decorated, both on the cover and at the beginning of each chapter, with stylised landscape pictures. These were steps towards the goal: "Know Your Country".

In "Nils Holgersson's Wonderful Journey through Sweden", Selma Lagerlöf blends the two concepts together. The panorama pictures that Nils sees from the goose's back introduce him step by step to the special characteristics of each Swedish province. The lines and coloured patches bear witness at one and the same time to mountains and valleys and lakes, to working life and culture, and to the way in which the blend of these features shifts from south to north in our oblong country.

What Selma Lagerlöf lets Nils read from these landscape pictures is a song of praise to hard work and progress, in places darkened by the heaths and moors of poverty. But black factory smoke and slag heaps are hardly cause for concern. Yet the reader has premonitions of future conflicts. Thanks to the sudden change of heart of a rich farmer, Lake Tåkern is preserved as a bird sanctuary just when the flock of geese are resting there. A little later, Nils is asked to free the bear country from human beings by setting fire to the thundering Colossus—the ironworks in Bergslagen "which runs non-stop at the same pace night and day". Prophetically, Björnmor the Bear Mother says she believes that human beings want to be "alone on earth".

A village in Linnaeus' home district, Brommeshult, in the parish of Virestad, Älmhult. This aerial photograph was taken in 1991, facing northeast. The village stands both below and above the highest shoreline. The central road runs along a flat, stony ridge surrounded by swampy forestland and bogs.

We often see only a short distance when standing in our forested countryside. These plots of land, cleared of stones, lie south of Brommeshult and have been abandoned.

Today the landscape is much more than a storehouse of useful resources. It has become the object of great administrative projects we are all responsible for. This gives our term an even wider meaning than it ever had before. The landscape is merely the visible surface of how our earthly resources have been utilised. What the economist calls land, the biologist the ecosystem, the chemist the environment, the forester timber capital, the civil engineer the infrastructure and the building contractor undeveloped property are examples of parts of a whole that have to be co-ordinated within limited amounts of land, water, air and sunlight. Nor is it merely a matter of static co-existence but rather of dynamic change. Nowadays human technology is a more powerful factor for bringing about rapid change than biological evolution.

A landscape that is to remain productive enough to meet human needs cannot be transformed without due care and consideration. It is the rapidly growing claims of humanity that force us to see the landscape as a total material reality and not merely as a province or a panorama picture to be depicted in words, water colours or film.

If the landscape is to be preserved, it must first and foremost be understood and respected as a whole, made up of a multitude of interwoven, interdependent parts, but it is not easy for us to see things in this way. This is not an attitude that is encouraged by our experiences and traditional ways of thinking. We do not see the landscape from a bird's eye point of view in our everyday life. That picture usually comes with the Sunday picnic or the tourist trip; and then it is the magnificence of the scenery or the mood of the place that strikes us. Normally we are down at ground level beneath the trees, at the same level as house doors and fences round fields. And then the poet Harry Martinsson's words in Cikada ring true: "Most of what lies in meadows and woods finds no place in our thoughts and minds. We ignore most of it."

At ground level our activities are governed mainly by physiological, economic and social interests. We not only live off what is in the landscape, we also use it as a means of expression through buildings and monuments. In all these contexts sins of omission are inevitable. We can only reach our immediate, practical goals by choosing to make use of what the surroundings offer on each particular occasion. Not even the landscape painter has any alternative but to select and summarize from the multitude of shapes and colours before his easel. Not even when we travel are we aware of everything that we pass by. The landscape as a totality remains obscure, even when our actions change it little by little.

Besides, this totality is out of reach of all the actors involved for other reasons. The land is divided into property and administrative units, mutually co-ordinated but separate squares on the playing fields of nature and society. That is how it has been for thousands of years and that is why the landscape we see today is not the result of some all-embracing plan. It is the result of countless people's and organisations' activities—and omissions—and of nature's reactions ever since Sweden was first colonised.

In the future, too, the total landscape will be changed by the gradual accumulation of many disconnected actions, each having an indirect effect and turning into something new. This is inevitable. The great problem is to get all those who influence the course of events to work together to ensure that mankind's demands are kept within reasonable limits.

Management of the landscape demands an understanding of what hap-

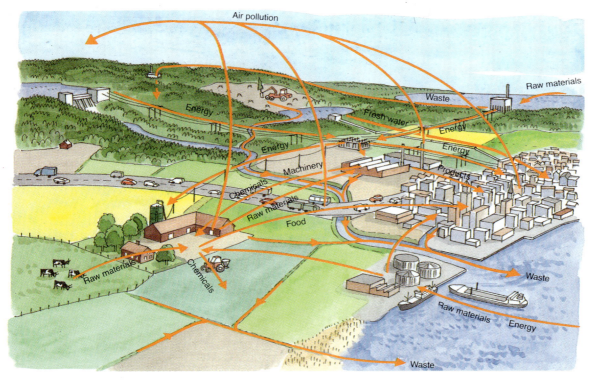

There is a constant renewal of material and energy in the landscape, in natural cycles and in one-way transformations and movement. Settlements and land use have to some extent been adapted to meet nature's conditions. But the increasing density of settlements, technological progress and changes in our life style greatly affect these processes, resulting in various environmental problems.

pens when changes take place. And this understanding must, as far as possible, try to make up for the omissions of the many actors on the scene. Among these shortcomings we must also count what many sciences do when they remove things from their landscapes and place them in the simpler world of the laboratory. This method wipes out the dependence on time and place that is crucial for everything in the landscape.

The only way to avoid these omissions is to look into every nook and cranny of life at one and the same time—and no one is capable of doing that. We have to take things in steps. Fortunately we have instruments that reveal and record much of what various "egocentric" points of view ignore. These instruments also reveal when people are talking about the same thing but in different terms. In addition they have space reserved for discoveries of phenomena that no one

Different land uses and types of trees appear as shifting colours in an aerial photograph taken vertically with IR film. This type of photograph is difficult for the uninitiated eye to evaluate, but it shows surface conditions and relative positions in an objective and measurable way.

A map is also a vertical picture, drawn with the aid of "sign language"—map symbols—after objects have been measured and selected. We can recognize in this map of land redivision in Brommeshult in 1851 the landscape shown in the aerial photograph, even though some of the buildings and clearings have disappeared and new roads have been built.

has noticed so far. Their ways of working possess these qualities because they provide cross-sections of the landscape without any gaps.

A map represents a horizontal section. It is a geometrical presentation of the view from a viewpoint or an aeroplane. The difference is that the observer is no longer restricted to one single viewpoint. On the contrary, one's eyes are directly above everything at one and the same time; in that sense they are everywhere.

A map shows the visible contents of the landscape at a certain point in time. Several sections taken over a period of time show changes in the landscape. They show how some things stay the same for a long time, while others appear or disappear from time to time. It becomes evident that at every point in time a landscape always consists largely of its past. This makes it a gigantic natural and cultural historical document with whose help one can reconstruct previous eras and forces which are never recorded in ordinary archives.

The other type of section without gaps is the vertical profile. It is less common than a map and has no special name, but it has a promising future.

While maps are most suitable for showing stable and relatively slow changes in the landscape, a profile provides better insight into its "everyday life". We can study points of contact and note channels of exchange between air, water, land and organisms, and we can determine the effects of our use of materials and technical equipment on the landscape. These vertical sections of the land, with its layers and relics, provide us with further evidence that the landscape is not merely on the surface but also in depth a historical document.

Maps and vertical profiles give us the primary instruments with whose help we can correlate information from the sciences with mankind's ambitions. This sort of survey is essential if the total landscape is to be respected in the future and held in trust as it should be.

Our contemporary cultural landscape consists of elements that have emerged in various eras—the geological ages, prehistoric times and modern times. It is like a jigsaw puzzle made of bits from different ages. Research into the history of the landscape tries to find connections between the bits of the puzzle and the contexts and lost worlds in which the puzzle was made.

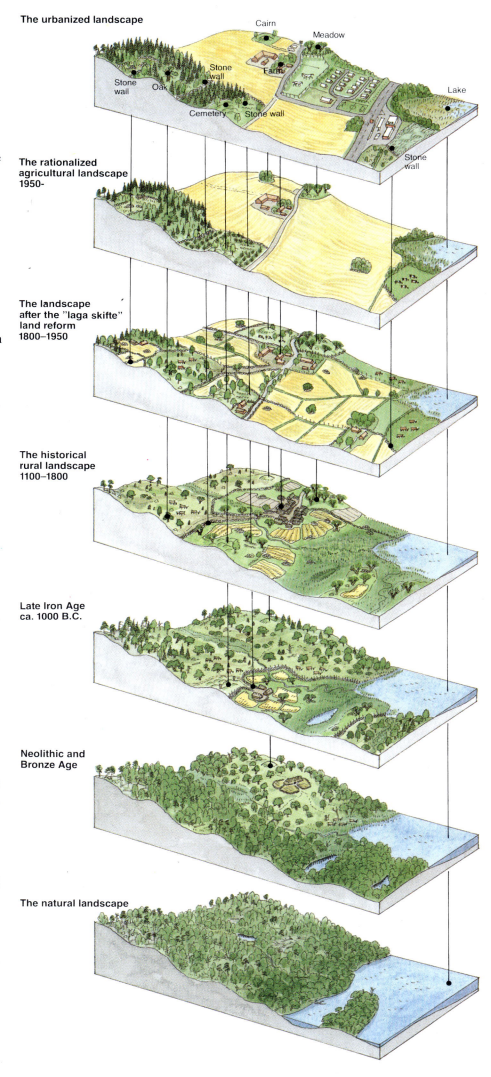

Patterns in the Cultural Landscape

TRADITIONAL SITES FOR SETTLEMENT

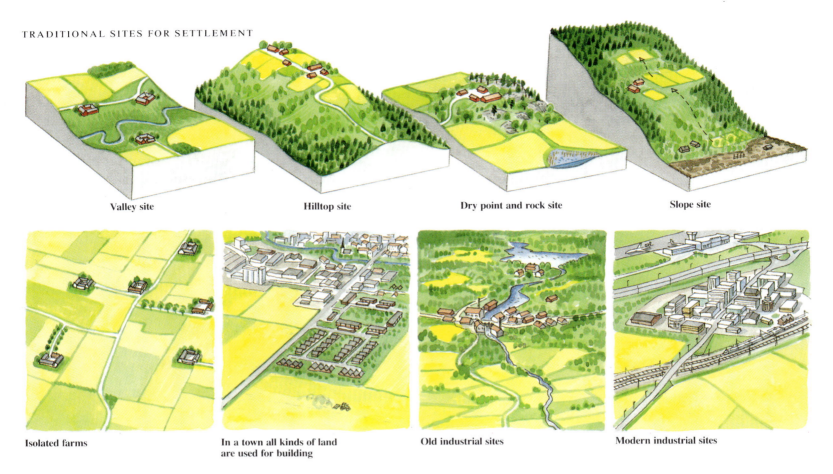

Valley site · Hilltop site · Dry point and rock site · Slope site

Isolated farms · In a town all kinds of land are used for building · Old industrial sites · Modern industrial sites

ESTATE BOUNDARIES AND TRANSPORTS

Rural estate boundaries still follow patterns established by the more or less radical redistributions of land in the 19th century.

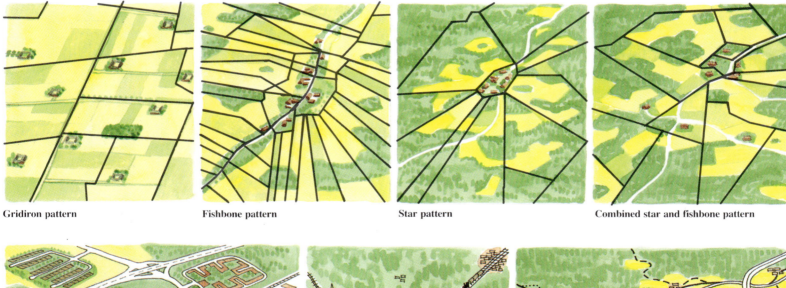

Gridiron pattern · Fishbone pattern · Star pattern · Combined star and fishbone pattern

The street network reveals the stages in a town's development.

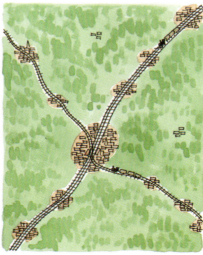

Railways affected settlement patterns. Railway towns became the new built-up areas of industrial society.

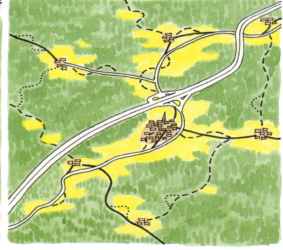

The road network has gradually been adapted to meet traffic needs and new types of vehicles.

DIFFERENTIATION WITHIN A TOWN

Competition for central location leads to differentiation within a town: the town centre various residential areas, industrial areas etc. The settlements reflect their functions.

Our knowledge of urban functions was used consciously after 1945 in the planning of new town areas.

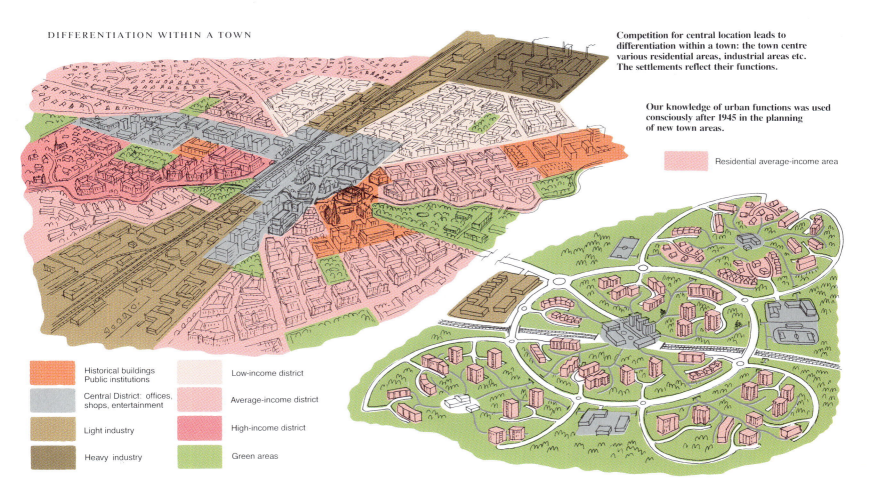

- Historical buildings / Public institutions
- Central District: offices, shops, entertainment
- Light industry
- Heavy industry
- Low-income district
- Average-income district
- High-income district
- Green areas
- Residential average-income area

THE LIFE CYCLE OF A SETTLEMENT

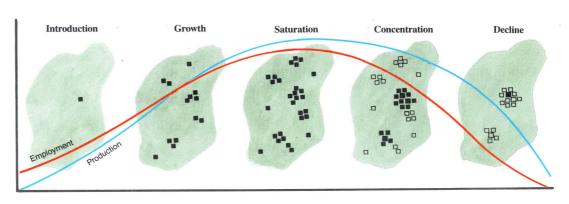

Introduction — Growth — Saturation — Concentration — Decline

Employment / Production

The patterns of settlement change constantly with changes in the economy and society. Today's patterns are the result of countless processes of this type in all areas of life.

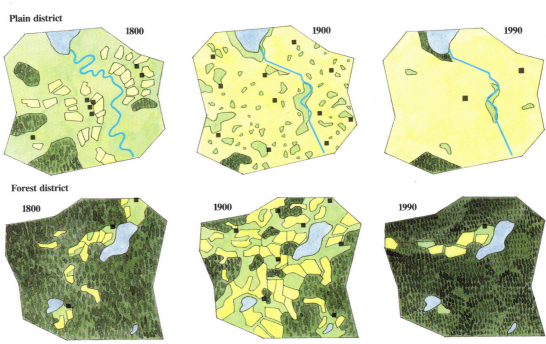

Plain district — 1800, 1900, 1990

Forest district — 1800, 1900, 1990

The amount of cultivated land grew over the centuries as new land was opened up. During the 19th century arable land expanded rapidly at the expense of meadowland. In the late 20th century agriculture became more intensive on the plains, where every obstacle to large-scale cultivation — ditches, knolls, boulders, marl pits — was removed. In contrast the scattered cultivated plots in forest districts were abandoned and returned to forest.

Ten Thousand Years in Sweden

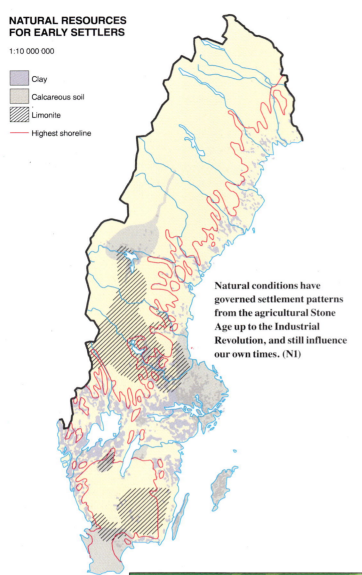

NATURAL RESOURCES FOR EARLY SETTLERS
1:10 000 000

- Clay
- Calcareous soil
- Limonite
- Highest shoreline

Natural conditions have governed settlement patterns from the agricultural Stone Age up to the Industrial Revolution, and still influence our own times. (N1)

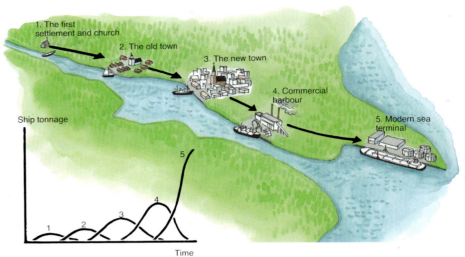

The rapid uplift of the land along the coast of Norrland, 80–90 cm in 100 years, made it necessary to move ports down to deeper water. The increasing draught of modern ships has speeded up this process.

The Land

The land that was freed from the inland ice sheet and rose from out of the sea gradually provided human immigrants with rich supplies of animal life for hunting. In some parts of the country the soil was suitable for agriculture and in many places there were readily accessible supplies of lake and bog iron to meet the needs of the Iron Age. The basic settlement patterns of Sweden were determined by nature.

The People

Let us look at a map of Scandinavia with the Baltic Sea to the east and the German-Polish coast to the south. Geographically, this is a large area, a large part of Europe. But it is not a central part of Europe, it is in fact on the periphery of the immense Euro-Asian continent. Peripheral areas have special qualities. Important historical events which originate in central areas spread like rings on the water out towards the edges. The traces they leave there, not least in

LAND UPLIFT IN UPPLAND

M a sl	Year
28.5	Ca. 2000 B.C.
18.5	Ca. 1000 B.C.
11.5	B.C.
5	Ca. 1000 A.D.
0	Ca. 1950 A.D.

Uppland was the last of the Swedish provinces to rise from the sea. It started as a seascape of skerries. As new islands rose up, the waves washed the earth from the tops down into the clay-filled fissures. As late as the Iron Age it was waterways that controlled the growth of settlements. The Bronze Age shoreline is 12–18 m above sea level today, the Viking Age's some 5–6 m. Lake Mälaren was still a sea loch that stretched all the way up to Gamla Uppsala. Land uplift in the low-lying landscape created new pastures and arable land all the time, providing space for an expanding population. In 98 A.D. the Roman writer Tacitus mentions the Sveas, the only people he has heard of in the Scandinavian peninsula, a people strong in manpower, weapons and fleets.

PERMANENT SETTLEMENT LATE IRON AGE – LATE MIDDLE AGES

1:10 000 000

- Late Iron Age
- Medieval expansion

The agrarian landscape is of very different age in different parts of Sweden. (N2)

As soon as the land began to free itself from the ice sheet 10,000 years ago, human beings came to Sweden. These people were remarkably skilful in the manufacture and use of flint and other stone implements. They must have been expert hunters. At first wild reindeer were their prey.

During the following few thousand years, in the Late Stone Age and the Bronze Age, agriculture became important and some settlements became permanent. People constructed graves, sometimes of monumental proportions. Broad-leafed forests with their pastures and wild life were an important source of food.

During the next millenium, in the Early Iron Age, agriculture began to be economically important, which meant that settlements became even more permanent in certain areas of easily cultivated clay and till. We can see this from the various enclosure systems that were built to protect the infields from grazing cattle. Certain groups of people produced and distributed iron, especially in southern Sweden. The plains became densely populated, but in the forest regions in the south the settlements were still sparse. Settlement and cultivation created villages separated by vast forests on the boulder-strewn and rugged till-covered bedrock which covers most of the land.

During the latter part of the Iron Age and in the early Middle Ages, 500–1200 A.D., a great increase in population led to more concentrated settlements on the plains, with settlements spreading into the forest districts. We can detect an administrative organisation of the country, at first in the form of small "kingdoms" and later as parishes, hundreds and provinces. Central places emerged connected with this administration; they had cult, judicial or administrative functions but were also trading places. A few of them became our oldest towns. Agriculture became increasingly important. The area of land under cultivation increased, which changed the organisation and structure of settlements. Now it was not only trading in iron and natural products that gave a financial surplus; agricultural yields on the plains also increased, so that produce could be sold.

The Middle Ages and early modern times saw the creation of many cultural environments which we proudly preserve today: towns, churches, villages, mines and ironworks. In some places estates using large-scale farming methods developed. Various forms of co-operation led in Sweden, as in the rest of Europe, to new settlement patterns. Villages or shared cultivation of the land appeared in most parts of the country. Settlement had found its permanent basic pattern of districts, places and roads determined by the distribution of important natural resources. The main features of this pattern still prevail, although close proximity to agricultural land, raw materials and energy sources is no longer necessary for survival thanks to advances in science and technology.

During the 18th and 19th centuries village society broke up and agricul-

the landscape, may be clearer than in the central areas.

This is exactly what has happened in Scandinavia. Sweden and the other Scandinavian countries have in their vast and shifting territories many well-preserved traces of long chains of processes and events. Relatively small populations and slow changes in the landscape over thousands of years have helped to preserve many of these traces. Long continuity is a characteristic feature of the landscape. Land uplift along the coasts of the Baltic and the Gulf of Bothnia makes it possible for us to see how the countryside gradually became populated and cultivated; but the history of colonisation is not, as some people imagine, a gradual "conquest" of land from south to north. In actual fact virtually the whole of the country, apart from the parts that were still under water, was being exploited by hunting man as early as the Early Stone Age. This first population phase took place fairly rapidly, during a period when the climate was extremely favourable.

The burial mounds of the Bronze Age are very evident signs of the great age of settlements on the southern Swedish plains. These barrows are in south-west Skåne.

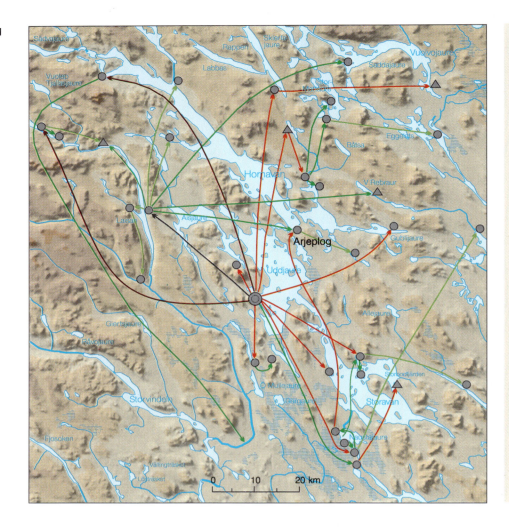

COLONISATION IN PITE LAPPMARK UP TO 1867

- ● Swedish farm
- ▲ Saami settlement
- → –1775
- → 1776–1800
- → 1801–1825
- → 1826–1850
- → 1851–1867

The example from Pite Lappmark shows how a district grew up by colonising previously unsettled land. The map shows a "family tree" of new settlements starting with a homestead established earlier than 1775 on the shore of Lake Uddjaure. Generation after generation it spread in new homesteads. Similar "family trees" have grown up round other early settlements in the district.

Colonisation proceeded in waves with an interval of about 30 years, a generation, between each wave. After the first generation settlers continued to colonise the district as sons moved away from the parent settlements. Colonisation in Pite Lappmark was dominated by just a few families. A considerable number of new settlers were Saami who gave up their nomadic life style.

The primary factors when choosing a site for a new settlement were suitable land and fishing waters at the shortest possible distance from the parent settlement. Settlers of about the same age often settled within close distance of each other.

ture was individualised and modernised, partly as a result of various land reforms which had a striking effect on the cultural landscape as well as on buildings and settlements. Draining and projects to lower the level of lakes also altered the landscape.

In the towns we can distinguish the first phases of industrialisation which often affected town centres. The iron industry entered an expansive phase.

Sweden became industrialised from the middle of the 19th century onwards. The Norrland forests were exploited for large-scale exports of timber and sawn wood; new industrial centres grew up round river estuaries. A rapid increase in the population and the mechanisation of agriculture resulted in a surplus of labour which was forced to emigrate or work in the fast-growing industries.

The population also experienced a social revolution, in which popular movements played a vital role. Their meeting places are yet another characteristic feature of Swedish architecture, particularly in country districts. Nor should we forget to mention the part played by sports associations.

Migration to towns increased dramatically as agriculture and forestry were mechanised. By 1930 as many people lived in urban areas as in the countryside. Less than half the population were farmers.

At this time our attitudes towards both nature and culture conservation changed. We also developed an interest in tourism which promoted natural and cultural values in Sweden.

Sweden became rapidly urbanised from the mid–20th century onwards. Today more than 80 per cent of the population live in towns. The depopulation of rural districts is a threat to marginal districts, and has also contributed to the debate on nature conservation.

Inner Norrland was still being colonised as late as the 20th century. Clearings for fields and meadows, like these in Västerbotten, create small glades in the forestland.

Memorial stones tell of the hard life families led when they had to make their living as colonisers in Lappland.

Sweden's Frontiers

National frontiers separate different judicial and military systems which create permanent differences in the cultural landscape and architecture. As late as the 13th century the Scandinavian frontiers were undetermined, but after that they remained stable for a long period south of Lappland. Certain stretches may have been marked out as early as 1000 A.D. The oldest frontier is that with Norway between Dals Ed and Sälen. Swedish settlements in the Viking Age penetrated as far north as Ångermanland. Åland was Swedish. In the 12th century Sweden began its conquest and settlement of Finland. In the 1290s Torgil Knutsson built Viborg as a fortress in the east. In the north colonisation of coastal districts reached Luleå and Oulu. In 1323 the Russian frontier was drawn straight across the Finnish peninsula.

In 1561 Reval (Tallinn) and Narva submitted to Sweden. The Baltic

During the Viking Age and the early Middle Ages Sweden expanded eastwards and Finland was conquered. Thereafter came the centuries dominated by the Hanseatic League and its cultural and political influences from the south. From 1560 and 100 years on, land was conquered again, rich provinces round the Baltic, which were then lost in 100 years of wars. Finland was lost 1809. Since 1814 Sweden has lived in peace within secure borders. (N4)

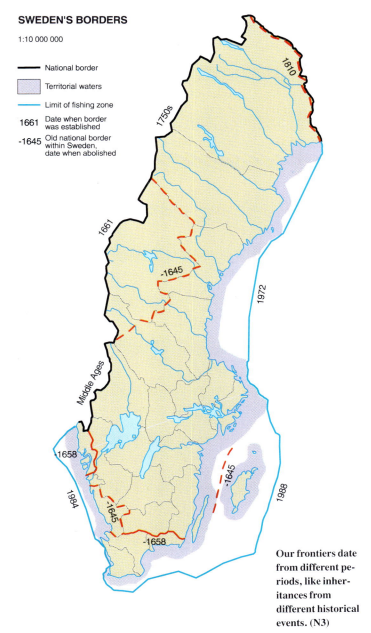

Our frontiers date from different periods, like inheritances from different historical events. (N3)

provinces were extended to include the whole of Livland, including Riga and the ports to the south. Ingermanland and the province of Kexholm were gained by the Peace of Stolbova in 1617. By 1645 Jämtland, Härjedalen, Gotland, Ösel and Halland had been wrested from Denmark. The Peace of Westphalia in 1648, when Sweden was recognised as a European power, brought part of Pomerania, Stettin, Wismar, Bremen and Verden. By another victorious treaty in 1658 Denmark was forced to surrender Skåne, Blekinge, Bohuslän, the county of Trondheim and Bornholm to Sweden. These last two territories were lost again in 1660. This was the climax of Swedish military expansion. But the country's resources were not strong enough to hold the Baltic Empire together when the neighbouring states joined forces to seek revenge.

The end came at Poltava in 1709. In the peace treaty after the Nordic War Sweden abandoned the Baltic provinces, Ingermanland, Kexholm, Bremen-Verden and parts of Pomerania. In the 18th century the Finnish frontier retreated and in 1809 Sweden was forced to surrender both the whole of Finland up to the Torneälven and Åland to Russia. The rest of Pomerania was handed over to Denmark in 1814 in exchange for Norway, which was ruled in a royal union with Sweden until 1905.

The Norwegian frontier had been marked out in the 1750s and the Finnish frontier in 1810. But not until our own time were the final limits of Swedish economic zone established. The last sea limits were agreed with Denmark in 1984 and with Russia in 1988.

Vegetation and Cultivation

RESEARCH METHODS

Growth and change in the cultural landscape, especially the effects of cultivation on the landscape, can be studied using environmental-historical/palaeo-ecological methods. In the sediment of lakes and the peat layers of bogs there are microscopic remains of plants and pollen which reveal the surrounding vegetation. The most important technique of all is pollen analysis, but in investigations into the history of cultivation it should be combined with several other methods which throw light on the cultivation of plants, the use of pastureland, erosion and nutrient balance. A combination of scientific and social-historical analyses provides a more complete picture of the relationship between society and the environment.

The areas to be studied are selected according to the source material available relating to the cultural landscape (maps, written sources, etc) or the prehistoric landscape (dwelling sites, graves). Besides having a rich supply of social-historical source material it is also vital that the natural-historical material to hand is of good quality, that is to say, that there are sediment basins, lakes and bogs close to old settlements and land used for cultivation. Pollen analysis is best used if central districts can be compared with peripheral districts. It is also important that pollen diagrams illustrate local changes, for example within a village or in a peripheral, extensively exploited forest area. For this reason it is advantageous if lakes/bogs are relatively small (<200 m in diameter). Soil profiles can also be used to interpret the local development of vegetation, for example in burial mounds, under stone walls, etc. According to the size of the areas involved we use the terms regional and local pollen diagrams.

For our own times we have aerial photographs and maps that describe the landscape. For the past we are obliged to use the fragments which various source materials provide about the dwelling sites and landscape of those times. In the Ystad project in Skåne, for example, a series of landscape maps were prepared that were based on the following material:

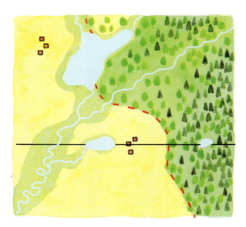

This schematic drawing presents a cultivated landscape with what here are called a central district and a peripheral district, providing good field conditions for environmental-historical research. The map shows two small lakes (local information) and one large one (regional information).

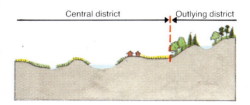

The pollen diagram shows along the vertical axis how the percentage of pollen for each species compared with all pollen counted has changed through the ages. Generally speaking these curves reflect the development of vegetation as a result of both changes in the climate and man's use of the land. We can see from the columns tree and bush pollen on the one hand and grass and herb pollen on the other how the open landscape round Lake Krageholmssjön has grown at the expense of the forests.

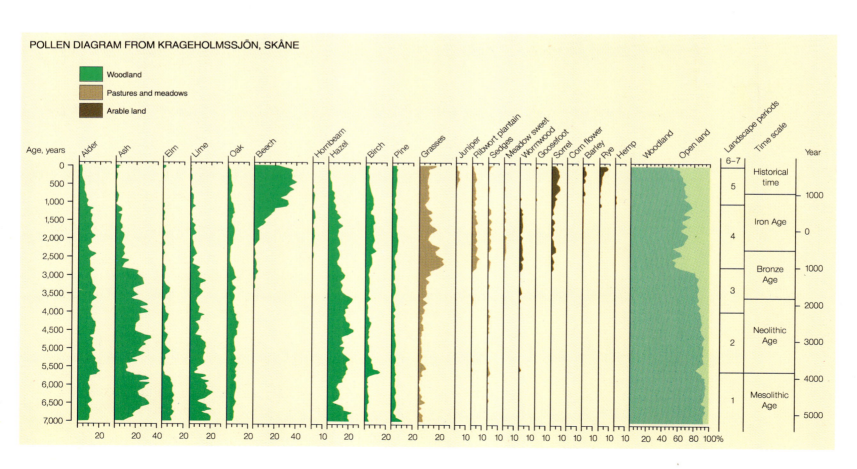

Natural forest

4000 B.C.
Coppiced woodland
pollarding, grazing, cultivation

1000 B.C.
Meadow
mowing, grazing, cultivation

1800 A.D.
Arable and water meadow
cultivation, mowing, grazing

1900
Arable land

This drawing illustrates the development of forestland into various types of open cultural landscape in southern Sweden. At times the landscape has been in a state of change. The upper part shows the development on rich, productive soils while the lower part shows poor, often stony soils.

The present landscape: soil maps, hydrological maps (natural hydrology based on the Skåne Reconnaissance Map of 1812–20), vegetation maps and the Economic Map.

Historical/prehistoric environments: sequences of layers in lakes/bogs, changes in the shorelines of lakes and the Baltic, charcoal analysis, pollen analysis, survey maps, land registers.

Settlements: archaeological surveys and excavations, place names, land registers, population statistics, economic maps and travel accounts.

THE EMERGENCE AND EXPANSION OF THE CULTURAL LANDSCAPE

The introduction of agriculture to the south of Sweden about 6,000 years ago led to a gradual transformation of the forests into open land—to produce crops in fields and fodder for cattle in pastures and meadows. Our knowledge of traditional land use combined with interpretations of pollen diagrams allows us to sketch the development of the landscape from Stone Age forests to the monotonous fields and plantations of modern industrial farming. Right up to the 19th century, throughout the country, the dominant need was to expand cultivation for fodder.

The development of cultivation can be mapped with the aid of pollen diagrams showing what type of grain was grown. During the Early Neolithic Period the northern limit passed through Central Sweden, but a thousand years later, at the end of the Middle Neolithic Period, grain was being grown at several places along the Norrland coast, perhaps even in Härjedalen. At this time there was also some expansion in northern Norway and southwest Finland. During the early Iron Age, especially in the Roman Iron Age, cultivation became more firmly established along the Norrland coast, but still mainly on the coast. A third wave of expansion took place in the Viking Age and the early Middle Ages, when cultivation increased in early central districts at the same time as new areas were cleared and colonised in marginal districts—in the highlands of central and southern Sweden, in the valleys of Norrland and in the coastal archipelagos.

In each region with pollen diagrams we can see that the cultivated landscape expanded in waves. At certain times the area of open land increased noticeably, and these expansion phases correspond in general to the extension of the limit of cultivation northwards. Even though these phases were regional, the following expansion periods appear to be general in many parts of the country: in the Late Neolithic Period, the late Bronze Age, the Roman Iron Age (0–400 A.D.), the Viking Age, the early Middle Ages (800–1200 A.D.) and the period between 1750 and 1930. This also allows us to divide the history of the cultivated landscape into regular periods. The reasons for this development have been the subject of lively debate. It is likely that a growth in population together with new agricultural techniques and ideas spreading from the continent played a more important role than environmental factors. The interaction between man and his environment was important, however, for mobilising the nutritional resources of the land by, for example, working and manuring it.

Natural forest

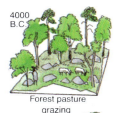
4000 B.C.
Forest pasture grazing

1000 B.C.
Grassland grazing

700 A.D.
Heath grazing

1950
Forest

Early Neolithic Age

Late Neolithic Age

Roman Iron Age

Viking Age

CULTIVATION OF CEREALS
- Definite evidence
- Rare or uncertain
- No cultivation
- Not described

Thanks to comparative pollen analysis it is possible to describe the cultivation of cereals in Scandinavia in four eras. (N5)

Landscape Research — An Interdisciplinary Science

The academic disciplines involved in the project each had their special responsibilities but collaborated in interdisciplinary seminars and symposiums.

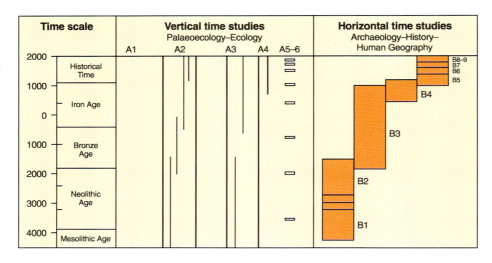

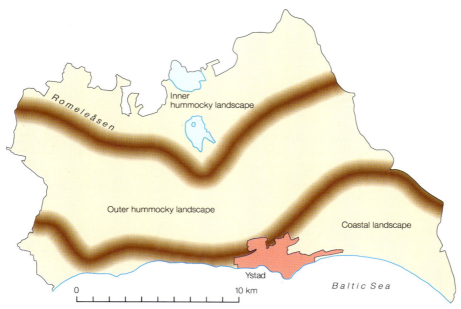

The map covers the area investigated by the Ystad Project, showing landscape zones and areas of special interest.

The Ystad Project

The Ystad Project—or more officially "The Cultural Landscape over 6,000 Years"—was an interdisciplinary research project conducted at Lund University between 1982 and 1990. Some 25 scientists were involved, supported by grants from Riksbankens Jubileumsfond. The aim of the project was to describe changes in the landscape over a long period within a representative area of the southern Swedish plains and to analyse the causes of these changes, in particular with regard to the interplay between social developments and the natural environment. Apart from providing increased knowledge of the dynamics of the landscape, the project aimed at being useful for environmental and cultural conservation work.

The area of the project comprises broadly the municipality of Ystad in southern Skåne. Three landscape zones may be distinguished there.

The Coastal Landscape, less than 25 m above sea level, is a low-lying plain with easily cultivated soils. At present this coastal district is totally covered by agriculture, industry and buildings. This area used to have many different types of biotopes, including sea beaches, shallow lakes or coast lagoons, river mouths and varied broad-leafed woods.

The Outer Hummocky Landscape, less than 70 m above sea level, is an undulating plain with great variation in soil types, but with a predominance of clay. At present the outer hilly landscape is almost completely devoted to agriculture. This area is somewhat less rich in biotopes than the coastal district owing to its inland location.

The Inner Hummocky Landscape is an undulating inland area with varying types of soils, from heavy clay to stony till. The eastern part is between 40 and 90 m above sea level, the western part (Romeleåsen) 70 to 170 m above sea level. At present the inner landscape is cultivated less than the areas in the south; both pastureland and productive woodland are extensive. This area has the same kind of variation in biotopes as the outer

ORGANISATION

The Ystad Project covers the period from the final phase of the hunting Stone Age 6,000 years ago up to today's industrial landscape. This project has been divided into the following sub-projects:

A1-A2 Changes in regional and local vegetation
A3 Palaeohydrological and palaeoclimatic changes
A4 Land erosion
A5 Reconstruction of vegetation and land use in various eras
A6 Production bases in various eras
B1 Introduction of agriculture
B2 Expansion of settlements during the Mesolithic Period
B3 Changes in settlements during the Bronze and Iron Ages
B4 Village settlements in the Late Iron Age
B5 Developments in settlements, production and social organisation during the Middle Ages
B6 Large estates and expansion of settlements in the 16th and 17th centuries
B7 The agrarian landscape from the late 17th century up to Land Reform in the 19th century
B8 Agrarian expansion in the 19th century
B9 From the production society to the service society in the 20th century

Scientists representing quaternary geology and plant ecology, archaeology, history and human geography have presented various theories and methods based on different kinds of source material. Students at various stages of their education have participated. Information has been exchanged at seminars and on field trips, as well as in project reports and other publications. Research results have been presented in three major monographs, in more than 200 articles and in exhibitions and lectures, some of them in the Ystad district.

DEVELOPMENT OF SETTLEMENTS

Late mesolithic ca. 3500 B.P.

Early neolithic ca. 2700 B.P.

Late Bronze Age ca. 800–500 B.P.

Roman Iron Age ca. 200 A.D.

Late Viking Age ca. 1000

Early 14th century

18th century

Ca. 1815

Ca. 1915

Ca. 1985

Six thousand years of settlement, as revealed by the investigation, are summarised here in general maps covering ten eras.

landscape and has today the most varied range of natural environments.

The project began by drawing up inventories for the whole area, but the later analysis dealt with four areas in depth: Köpinge, Bjäresjö, Krageholm and Romele. The village of Bjäresjö in particular was a key district for the period from 800 A.D. up to modern times.

DEVELOPMENT OF POPULATION AND SETTLEMENTS

The development of the population was calculated for the whole period from 4000 B.C. up to the present, using unreliable estimates for the period before 1750. In absolute figures this means about 100 persons 6,000 years ago and some 25,000 people in the 20th century. It is possible to distinguish expansive periods between 1200 and 1350 and from the 16th century onwards. The town of Ystad was founded about the year 1200.

Maps were drawn showing the distribution of buildings in ten different periods of time. The coast was the first district to be settled, together with parts of the inland, but during Mesolithic and late Neolithic times up to the middle of the Bronze Age the settlements grew and spread from the coast inland. In the early Iron Age, 200 B.C.–200 A.D., settlements were concentrated along the coast; in the late Iron Age settlements began to expand and were now concentrated in villages within the whole area except for the hills inland (Romeleåsen). Churches were built in some villages, where estates grew up. At the end of the Middle Ages there was a new wave of expansion inland, now in the form of isolated farms, especially on Romeleåsen. The land reforms of the 19th century resulted in the settlements being split up, so that only a few villages were left in the 20th century. Instead the town of Ystad and other minor service centres expanded during this century.

RECONSTRUCTIONS OF THE LANDSCAPE

Maps were drawn reconstructing the whole landscape for the same periods as for the settlements. This development is illustrated over three periods of time: the Bronze Age (ca. 700 B.C.), the Viking Age (ca. 1050 A.D.) and the present day.

By analysing the development of vegetation we are able to distinguish seven periods in the history of the landscape round Ystad.

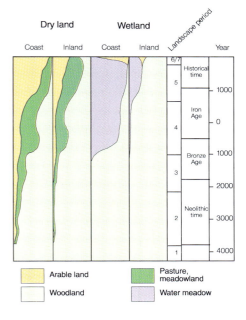

The upper curve shows the main trends in the population of the Ystad area over 6,000 years. Below, the last thousand years have been "stretched" and divided up into town and country. Developments are shown in even greater detail in the lower diagram for the last three centuries.

PERIODS OF LANDSCAPE HISTORY

When the information from the investigations is correlated we can distinguish seven periods:
1. Untouched forest landscape before 3800 B.C.; only slight, local influence round settlements
2. Culturally-influenced forest landscape, 3800–2200 B.C.; nomadic agriculture together with pasture farming in woodland
3. Forest pasture landscape, 2200–1000 B.C.; gradual deforestation, expansion of settlements, nomadic agriculture combined with pasture farming
4. Open pasture landscape, 1000 B.C.–700 A.D.; permanent settlements and agriculture in a pasture landscape
5. Infield-outfield landscape, 700–1800; consolidation of the village landscape with expanding estates from the 14th century onwards
6. Agricultural landscape, 1800–1950; increased cultivation after the redistribution of land and the splitting up of farms
7. Industrialised agriculture after 1950 creates a large-scale, more or less monotonous, urbanised landscape.

The same changes probably took place in large parts of southern Scandinavia. Social changes probably play a dominant role, including influences from Central Europe ever since the agricultural Stone Age. In the long term natural factors such as the climate and hydrology also play a major role. Availability of soil nutrients was probably of great significance for technological innovations such as fertilising techniques, cultivation systems and methods of working the land.

The Late Bronze Age. The coastal district and the outer landscape was a mosaic of half-open countryside dominated by pastureland. The Bronze Age barrows marked the villages with their elevated location above the pastures. Winter fodder was taken from both dry and wet meadows, in the form of hay and leaf fodder. Settlements were now firmly established, usually on high land in the landscape, probably isolated farms with long houses. Small fields were cultivated within enclosed areas close to the farms. The forest areas inland were without settlements, but we may suppose that shepherds drove flocks of sheep, goats and young cattle here. Fishing in rivers, lakes and the Baltic was also important, of course.

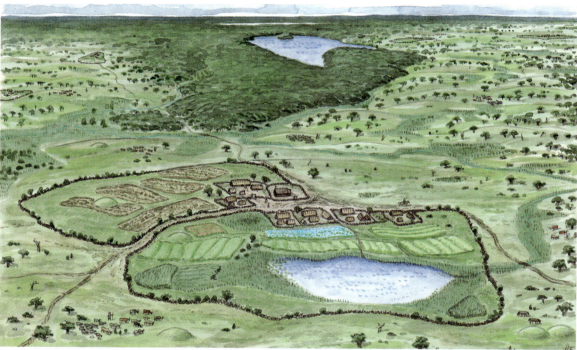

The Viking Age. Villages with infields and outfields left their mark on the landscape. The villages, located on high hillsides, were surrounded by enclosed fields and meadows. The wetlands of the river valleys and marshes were now all unwooded hay meadows. A cattle track led from the village to heavily grazed pastureland. The farms were half-timbered buildings; in large villages there was often a main farm which developed during the Middle Ages into an estate. The first churches were built in the 9th century, in the form of stave churches. Inland there was an unsettled pasture landscape of meadows and grass heaths scattered with juniper bushes and heather.

Modern Times. The industrialised agricultural landscape means maximal exploitation of the land. Vast areas of arable land have been created by draining wetland, channeling streams into culverts, cultivating natural pastures and other such measures. The Ystad area is dominated by large estates, but Bjäresjö remains a farming village with its roots in the Late Iron Age. The medieval church stands on the same spot as in the Viking Age. Each farm has large farm sheds. In Bjäresjö and other villages there are also smaller houses belonging to town commuters. The fragmentation of villages that took place in the 19th century is illustrated by scattered, isolated farmsteads. Inland there are small patches of forestland, the relics of old grazing forests.

Late Bronze Age, ca. 700 B.C.

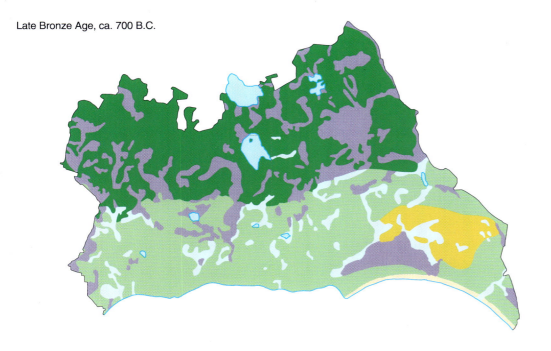

Ca. 700 B.C.

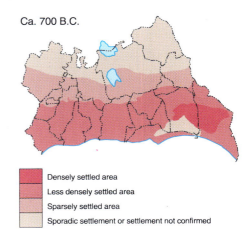

- Densely settled area
- Less densely settled area
- Sparsely settled area
- Sporadic settlement or settlement not confirmed

YSTAD AND THE SURROUNDING DISTRICT, LAND USE AND SETTLEMENT

- Arable land
- Open pasture, grassland with meadows and arable fields
- Semi-open coppice-pasture with meadows
- Open wetland: meadows and natural fens
- Wetland with coppices, pasture and meadows
- Fen wood-pasture with coppices and meadows
- Wood-pasture with some undergrowth
- Open natural fens, fen wildwood
- Fen woodland
- Deciduous woodland
- Conifer plantation
- Open sand heath with dunes, occasionally with oak/pine
- Dry grassland with scattered trees and shrubs
- Wet grassland with scattered trees and shrubs
- Lake, pond/river
- ■ Isolated farm
- ● Village, hamlet
- ○ Settlement abandoned during the eighth century
- Town (Ystad), other built-up area
- + Church
- ⌐ Manor, castle/park
- ---- Hundred boundary
- --- Parish boundary

Late Viking Age, ca. 1000 A.D.

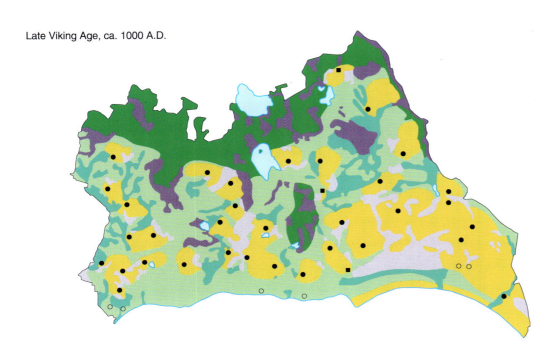

Late 20th Century, ca. 1985

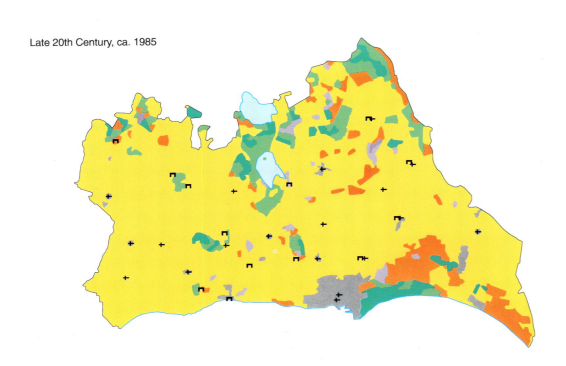

Ca. 1985

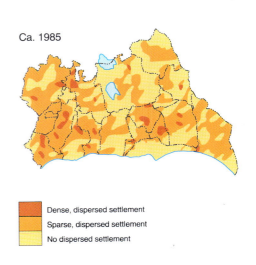

- Dense, dispersed settlement
- Sparse, dispersed settlement
- No dispersed settlement

21

Cultivated land on the river terraces in the lower Luleälv valley

Sitojaure in the upper reaches of the Lilla Luleälven stands 630 m above sea level in the birch-forest region. The system of reindeer trapping pits which cuts across the valley was probably created in the Middle Ages. The high-lying areas round the sources of the Luleälven have been used for hunting and fishing since the Iron Age and during historical times for an increasing amount of reindeer husbandry.

The Luleälv Project

In few places in Sweden are the contrasts between nature, industry, culture and ethnicity in two neighbouring areas as great as they are between the cultivated landscape of the lower Luleälv valley and the forest and lake landscape of the upper Lule älv with the high mountains to the west. Upper Norrland lies on the northern edge of Europe, in the outermost part of the vast Eurasian continent. Cultural influences, ideas, trade and people from far and wide have met in the river valleys for thousands of years. The rules were changed when national frontiers cut off several of the old, natural links, and independence diminished with the growth of central state power. In the early self-subsistent economy local factors determined life, but economic, cultural and political changes in the outside world increased the significance of outside factors more and more. Finally, world economy took over and nowadays it is international decisions that determine what happens in the Luleälv valley.

In 1980 the Luleälv project at Umeå University began to study this long and complex process. The aim was to determine how the use of resources and the development of society had interacted in Upper Norrland, and to study the causes of changes over a period of 2,000 years. Processing the prehistoric source material that had multiplied enormously during the 1980s together with previously unused historical sources made it possible to follow this interplay. The aims focussed on a number of areas: ecological, economic, cultural-historical and linguistic. The studies were to be geographically and chronologically so representative that they would result in an overall picture of changes in the river valley, and generalised so that they could be applied to other areas as well, mainly in northern Scandinavia. This project has resulted in some dozen doctorial theses and major works and almost two hundred monographs.

The division into periods that follows is based on characteristic features of the use of resources and the development of society. The names of the prehistoric periods relate to the terminology used in Finland and northern Norway.

EARLY METAL AGE: 800 B.C.–200 A.D.

Two thousand years ago the hunting and trapping culture was predominant throughout the Luleälv valley, from the coast to the mountains. Cultural forms and settlement patterns varied according to the resources available. Down by the coast seal-hunting and sea-fishing were the dominant means of livelihood; in the inner coastal area, which is an ecological border zone, hunting and fishing were possible both at sea and inland. The most important game animals in the forests were moose, beaver, forest birds and fish. The other rich ecological border zone comprises the large forest lakes to the west and the foothills of the mountains with forest fauna and reindeer pastureland.

Large finds of seal-oil production have been made along the shoreline of that period, indicating production that far exceeded local needs and for which there is no previous evidence. Finds from the same period of bronze objects and moulds for such objects from Russia have also been made. This constitutes the earliest evidence of trade between Upper Norrland and a foreign area. When surplus production and trade were established, the previously simple hunting society began to change.

LATE METAL AGE: 200–1323

At the beginning of this period a new means of livelihood, reindeer husbandry, was developed by the Saami population of the Upper Norrland forests. Pollen analyses at dwelling sites have shown changes in the vegetation of the same kind as are found at reindeer enclosures from modern times. The reindeer herds were small but managing them meant that many settlements were established at different topographical sites. There were still settlements by lakes and rivers, but many were located in the forests

All the projects together cover 2,000 years but each one concentrates on a different period of time.

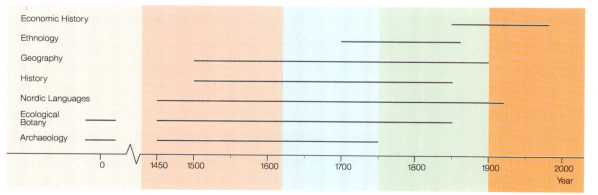

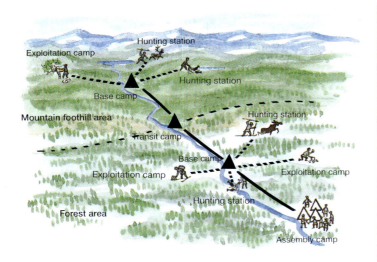

Using anthropological theories a model has been constructed for the settlement patterns along the Upper Norrland mountain rivers during the millennia before Christ. There was a base camp in the forest, with moose hunting and fishing as the primary means of livelihood during the winter, spring and early summer, and one in the foothills of the mountains which was used for reindeer hunting during the late summer and the autumn. Raw materials for stone implements, for example, could be collected and worked at fixed places. Several groups would meet at an assembly settlement at fixed times to discuss matters of mutual interest such as marriages and the exchange of goods.

A remarkble Stone Age dwelling site was found in 1983 during the project's field survey at Älvnäset, where the Stora and Lille Luleälv meet at Vuollerim. It is a fishing site from about 4000 B.C., which in fact places it outside the project's brief. But with 20,000 visitors a year and through the information centre built on the site the research project was linked to the present in a way which had not been planned. When this photograph was taken, the large 11×5 m floor had just been uncovered within the low embankment.

DEVELOPMENT OF SETTLEMENTS IN THE PARISHES OF KALIX–PITEÅ

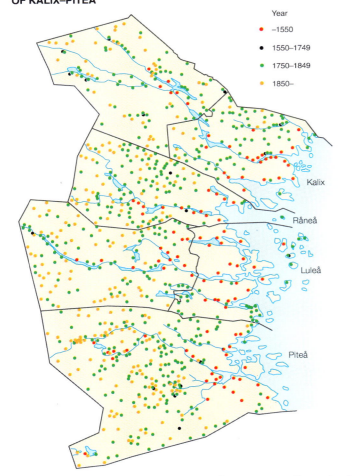

The very oldest settlements were on the coast and along rivers. There was no extensive colonisation between 1550 and 1749, but thereafter the areas between the river valleys began to be settled.

on dry ground rich in lichen and near mires with good pasturing. Reindeer bones and fish bones have been found in hearths, but mainly moose bones in early hearths. From the later part of the period many traces of settlements are now found in mountain districts. It is possible that there were already the beginnings of reindeer husbandry in the mountains.

Changes in the use of resources ought to have created new relationships within the community. Changes also took place along the coast. On the stony shores of the coast of Upper Norrland and further south there are thousands of small hut foundations, mainly from the latter half of the period. These huts were connected with seal-hunting, and people lived there in the season. The question is whether these huts belonged to the forest people or to those in the first cultivated districts. Cereals and cattle were being farmed at the mouth of the Ume älv as early as about 500 A.D. and in the Luleälv valley from the 11th century according to pollen analysis.

The well-known finds of metal objects at Saami places of sacrifice inland in Upper Norrland date mainly from 1000–1300. They consist largely of various kinds of silver, pewter and bronze objects from Finland, the Baltic countries and Russia, with a few from Norway, Central Sweden and Germany. These finds bear witness to the Saami's distant trading and cultural contacts. A new external influence along the coast of Norrland was the ports which began to grow up from the 13th century for trading to the south.

The Late Metal Age saw the establishment of the pattern for the Luleälv valley's later industries, settlements, contact networks and ethnic groups. Cultivation, trade and changes in fish catches were governed by external factors, whereas reindeer husbandry formed part of the internal development, even though changes in the outside world may have played a certain role.

THE LULEÄLV VALLEY BETWEEN TWO PEACE TREATIES, 1323–1617

The peace treaty between Sweden and Novgorod at Nöteborg in 1323 was signed during a period of rapid expansion. The northward expansion of Swedish farming along the coast led to a break in the ancient links with the east and the south-east. There were already the beginnings of cultivation there, but the stronger state found it economically and politically important to assert Swedish interests. One evident sign of this Swedish expansion is the early 15th-century church at Gammelstad, the largest church north of Uppsala. It was maintained by an extensive farming community in the lower Luleälv valley, a community which was socially and economically organised to effectively exploit the many resources of the district. The distribution of place names ending in -*mark* and -*byn* indicates that this farming district also expanded a little inland during the Middle Ages. This is also confirmed by several pollen analyses which show traces of sporadic cultivation and cattle farming during the Middle Ages as far inland as Edefors, about 70 km from Gammelstad. The Birkarls, who were probably peasant merchants from the coast, brought the inland riches of furs and fish to the trading stations on the coast. The trading interests of Central Sweden were safeguarded in Magnus Eriksson's laws of the 1350s, which regulated the right to trade.

The state extended its power into the country in the 1550s by taxing

Fishing settlement at Brändö-Uddskär with jetties, huts, cottages and a chapel. This settlement dates at least from the 17th century, if not earlier.

Changes in the use of resources in Lule Lappmark in the early 17th century are also evident in increased fishing, which to some extent was to make up for the reduction in tax revenue from furs. The diagram shows the Crown's tax revenue from dried fish in Lule Lappmark, 1555–1620.

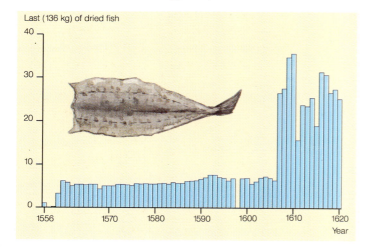

The State's tax revenue from and purchases of squirrel and marten furs in Lule Lappmark

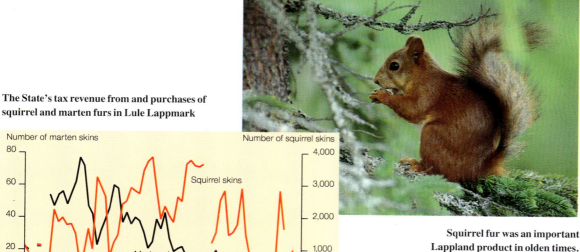

Squirrel fur was an important Lappland product in olden times.

Saami households individually, reducing the Birkarls' privileges and demanding that tax that was primarily paid in skins and dried fish should be paid direct to the state Saami tax collectors. Reindeer husbandry by the forest Saami was not yet very widespread and the same is probably true of the mountain Saami.

By the 16th century there had been a change in the catches of sea fish. The fishing huts were no longer in use because the increasingly important herring fishing required harbours, where buildings grew up. Seal-hunting developed in the 17th century when fire-arms came into general use. But the main supply of oil, blubber and herring came from Österbotten.

By 1600 the Swedish state had successfully extended and consolidated its sphere of influence to the north, to begin with along the coast and then inland. The Peace of Stolbova with Russia in 1617 put a stop in practice to any expansion towards the White Sea, even though some attempts were made later. For the Luleälv valley this meant that by this time the whole valley was definitely under the control of the same state authorities and institutions.

STAGNATION AND PROSPERITY, 1617–1750

From the time when the first land registers were drawn up in 1543 up to 1750 the number of houses in the coast parishes grew very slowly, but between 1750 and 1810 the number trebled. The size of the population is uncertain but ought to have been related to the number of houses, which indicates stagnation in the farming districts after the expansion of the late Middle Ages and consolidation in the 16th century. Two of the causes are the continual conscription of soldiers and a poorer climate at times. There was little cultivated land and grain was imported. Cattle breeding played a more important role, providing butter for sale. In the long term the founding of the town of Luleå in 1621 was important for trade and capital.

The Saami area developed quite differently. About 1660 the tax on skins was cut sharply at the same time as more reindeer, reindeer calves and dried fish were taken in payment. Even if reindeer husbandry had been of some importance previously, this change must have encouraged nomadic reindeer husbandry greatly. In the mountain Saami villages of Sirkas and Tuorpon in the Lule Saami district the number of taxpayers rose by about 250 per cent during the period 1680–1780. During the same period, however, the forest Saami village of Jokkmokk had an unchanged population. This boom for the mountain Saami is confirmed by the fact that a large number of silver objects were bought in Bergen and Trondheim when the Saami sold skins along the northern Norwegian coast. In the 18th century Saami also bought silverware from goldsmiths in Stockholm and Norrland.

The efforts made by the Swedish state to extract the riches of Upper Norrland led to a number of unsuccessful attempts in the 17th century to open mines for silver, copper and iron. Not more than about 13 kg of silver per year was produced in the Lule Saami district between 1662 and 1702. During the later part of this period tar production was started as well as ship-building, a more profitable enterprise.

This period may be seen as a time of experimentation. Nomadic reindeer husbandry was an ecologically successful innovation; the new methods for exploiting forest production on a large scale were promising, but iron production had not yet found its form. These changes in the use of resources were the result of the demands of the government in Stockholm.

INDUSTRIALISM AND THE WORLD ECONOMY, 1750–1900

The growth of the population com-

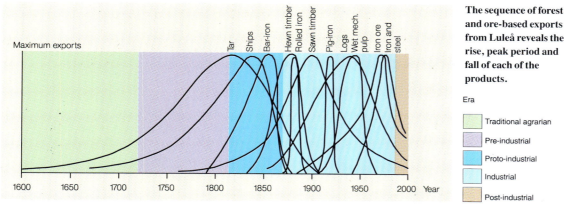

The sequence of forest and ore-based exports from Luleå reveals the rise, peak period and fall of each of the products.

Floating timber down the as yet unexploited Porsi rapids downstream from the confluence of the Stora and Lilla Luleälv at Vuollerim in 1932

The population of Lule Lappmark (parish of Jokkmokk) increased notably after about 1880 and decreased after 1950.

Reindeer husbandry with its two-thousand year history still flourishes, though in new forms. A reindeer enclosure at Karats, Jokkmokk, in the Lilla Luleälv district.

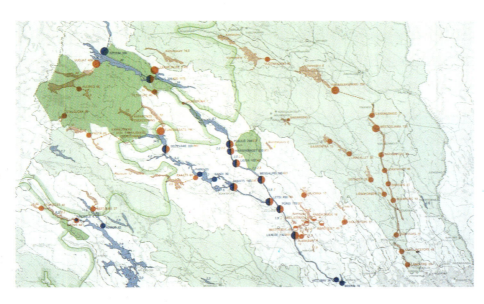

Existing water power (blue) and commercially viable projects (red) on the Lule älv. Half-filled symbols indicate an alternative that excludes the opposite symbol. Red areas are reservoirs to regulate the flow of water. Light green areas are river areas protected from exploitation. Dark green areas are national parks.

ploiting the resources of the landscape. Fishing lost ground during the 19th century in favour of timber-floating, which later in its turn had to make way for the expansion of hydroelectric power. But it was not until after the Second World War that high-tension technology had developed sufficiently to make it possible to transmit power over long distances. The changes in settlements and population inland that resulted from the building of power stations were rapid and revolutionary. On the coast the town of Luleå increased in importance as a gateway to the valley, resulting in increasing urbanisation.

The lower Luleälv valley and the coastland was industrialised during the 20th century. Sawmills expanded—and disappeared. This industry was followed by the pulp industry and in 1940 Norrbotten Ironworks at the Luleå ore terminal, which was greatly expanded in the 1950s and onwards but now, like many old industries, finds itself in a precarious situation as a result of competition. The planned investment in "Steelworks 80" was abandoned in the face of the international steel crisis but left a large building site created by infilling in the harbour at Luleå.

Ethnological interpretations of estate inventories from the late 18th century onwards give a detailed picture of how individual families utilised the resources and how occupations were distributed among the ethnic groups. To the west there were the Saami, practising reindeer husbandry, in a central area in the forests there were Saami, Finnish and Swedish settlements with mixed forms of livelihood and in the lower river valley there were the Swedish farmers.

Agriculture in the whole of the Luleälv valley changed during this period from being self-subsistent to specialised farming, more and more often combined with paid employment. A few of the farmers produced special products for sale, but most of them increased their amount of paid employment in some other sector. By about 1900 almost all agriculture in the Saami territories had ceased, but reindeer husbandry continues.

Since the Second World War changes in international economy have determined most of what happens in the Luleälv valley. The valley was integrated with the Swedish state in the 16th century but is now integrated with a world economy.

bined with an increase in the area of cultivated land provided a surplus of labour that could be used to exploit the resources of the forests and the mineral rock. The production of tar, sawn timber and iron led around 1900 to large-scale exports from the Luleälv valley of timber and iron ore for the expanding international economy, thus altering the conditions for ex-

The rune stone at Lingnåre gives us the names of some Viking people: "Huskarl and Djure, father and son, raised this stone for Djurger, the brother of Huskarl and the son of Djure. And Fastegn carved these runes."

The Barknåre Project

Barknåre and Lingnåre are in the Hållnäs peninsula in northern Uppland, where the land has been rising about 70 cm per century. Originally they were two coastal settlements. Lingnåre was abandoned in the Middle Ages, leaving a fossilised cultural landscape for posterity. Barknåre still exists today.

The villages of Barknåre and Lingnåre were studied in the 1980s within the framework of a research project in which various university departments at Stockholm and Uppsala collaborated, supported by grants from the Research Council for Humanities and Social Sciences.

RESEARCH METHODS

Field surveys. Both settlements provide field remains that can be mapped and analysed. The Lingnåre site in particular is rich in fossil traces: fields, meadows, graves, house foundations, rubbish pits, a rune stone, blacksmiths' hearths, wells and so on. These remains provide information about the landscape about 1,000 years ago.

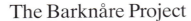

Archaeological excavations. A few graves have been excavated in both Lingnåre and Barknåre. Most of them are cinerary graves, but during the final prehistoric period burials were made at farms under Christian influence, that is to say, the bodies were buried uncremated. This means that we are able to collect information about the people of Lingnåre, how tall they were, how healthy they were and so on. Archaeological investigations also tell us something about their houses, and by investigating rubbish pits we can find out something about their food and eating habits and sometimes about their indoor activities, including craftwork.

Osteological analysis. A study of bones tells us something about the animals that were hunted and those that were domesticated. Most of them in the earliest period were sheep, but there were also pigs and cattle as well as horses. Fish was the most important food as long as the coast was not too far away, but later, when the shoreline had receded, it was game.

Palaeo-ecological investigations. Pollen analysis and studies of seeds and plants in cultivated land give us information about crops and the consumption of vegetables. To begin with barley was grown throughout the area, but later rye was introduced.

The picture of Lingnåre shows an archaic cultivated landscape of irregular field plots surrounded by cairns of cleared stones. The Viking Age farm stood on the rise in the middle of the picture.

The results of investigations provide the basis for this picture of what the Lingnåre dwelling site may have looked like in Viking times.

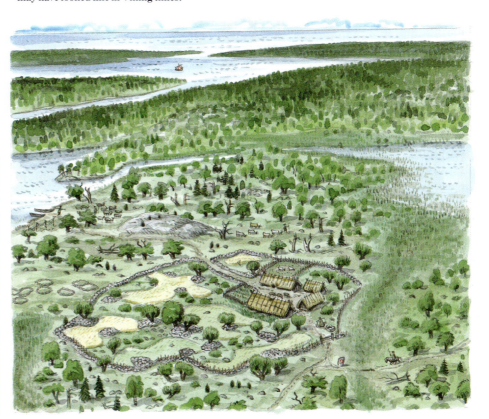

Johan Rhezelius, a professor at Uppsala, drew and described the ruins of medieval Lingnåre in "Monumenta Uplandica", 1635–38. He identified house foundations, wells and a cellar.

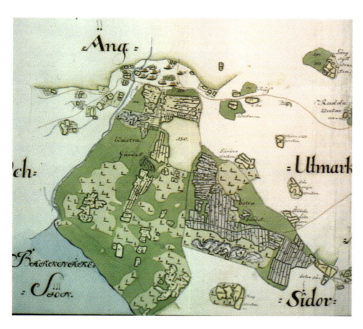

The oldest map of Barknåre, dated 1752, shows the medieval strips of land in the village. Each small strip belongs to one of the farms in the village. The pattern of strips in the eastern field has been preserved in the ground up to our own time.

Pollen samples can be taken in the ponds which abound in this boggy landscape.

Place names. If one is to understand the meaning of place names, one often has to find out how the names were first spelt, but even then it is often difficult to interpret their meaning.

Lingnåre was written *Linganori*, which has been interpreted to mean "the place by Ljung (E. heather) Bay" or more correctly "Ljungnoret", and Barknåre was written *Bierkanori* or "Björknoret" (björk=birch, nor=creek or stream that connects two lakes).

Early surveyors' maps. The earliest map of Barknåre is dated 1752 and was commissioned by Lövsta Mill, which wanted to redistribute land so as to have better access to the raw material for charcoal. Just before the map was made the mill had acquired a large number of farms at Barknåre because the farmers there had fallen into debt.

This purchase is also the reason why the fields have been preserved in their old forms. With the 1752 map in your hand it is actually possible to orientate yourself and interpret all the details of the cultivated landscape such as ditches, cairns and enclosures.

The map shows two enclosed fields divided into strips. Each field was left fallow every other year (two-field rotation). The strips we can see on the map belonged to farmers whose land was distributed according to a principle reminiscent of the medieval solar pattern. Thanks to these well-preserved forms we are able to interpret their age and function.

Written sources. Lingnåre and Barknåre are also mentioned in documents kept in the national archives, the county archives and the municipal archives. These consist of papers drawn up by tax officials, courts, churchmen and not least in this case Lövsta Mill. Among a vast number of documents in the mill's library there are lists of the farmers at Barknåre and their deliveries of charcoal. We can also see what was taken from the mill's stores for its own use. This material gives us a picture of a poverty-stricken district.

SETTLEMENT HISTORY

Lingnåre Farm was probably established in the 9th century at the head of a sea loch. The people there lived by fishing, hunting, cattle breeding and to some extent agriculture. This environment close to the coast was utilised in an optimal way and we know that the inhabitants lived fairly well. For example, osteological studies give us an idea of their health. By studying the farm's rubbish pits we can discover what animal food they enjoyed. We also know from palaeoecological studies what vegetable food they ate.

The site flourished and expanded. There was a busy forge and more and more farmsteads grew up. Suddenly, however, the inhabitants' state of health deteriorated in this area and about 1350 the site was abandoned. A fossilised cultural landscape has been preserved to this very day.

Barknåre, also dating from the 9th century, was not abandoned, but lived on. Originally the hamlet consisted of two farmsteads, each with its own cemetery. In the course of time these farmsteads were divided up more and more and some of the inhabitants moved out to surrounding land and sites that have medieval names. This probably took place as a result of the division of estates and inheritance.

The sea shore receded more and more from the village, so gradually agriculture became the main source of livelihood. Land was cleared and cultivation organised with regular crop rotation and the use of fallow. The two original farms collaborated in this work and the strips of land in the fields were distributed between them. Gradually the farms were divided into more and more units and the strips were redistributed among them. A cultivated landscape developed that is characteristic of much of medieval Sweden.

In the 17th century Lövsta Mill was founded just south of Barknåre and the village became involved in charcoal production for the mill. This is the reason why the cultivated landscape was preserved in an ancient form, since the forest became more important than the fields. In the course of time the farms fell into debt and were then sold to the mill. Only two of them remained in the possession of farmers, and these two still exist as farms. The mill closed down in 1926 and the new owners sold off the smallholdings in Barknåre in 1930, keeping only the forestland. In 1920 the district was flourishing and well populated; today the traditional industries have disappeared and the population is more than halved. Most of the cottages today are second homes.

Barknåre's old eastern field and its medieval strips show as fossilised traces of cultivation in the right foreground of the picture.

Prehistoric Fields in Southern Västergötland

The existence of countless traces of old cultivation in the forest districts of southern and central Sweden has long been known. If one reads old topographical and historical descriptions, one often comes across informative examples of this. Even early historians like Olaus Magnus and 18th-century travellers like Carl von Linné (Linnaeus) and Per Kalm were amazed at the number of abandoned fields hidden in the southern forest districts. They all write about the deserted villages and the depopulation that must have struck these districts at an early date. One of the more detailed descriptions of the trials and tribulations of prehistoric cultivation is given by Gunnar Olof Hyltén-Cavallius in his well-known book *Wärend och Wirdarna*, first published in 1863. Here he presents, along with many tales and legends, his own views and those of other historians on the widespread occurrence of abandoned fields in the forests.

The southern parts of Västergötland are a typical forest district with many lakes and bogs. The area lies above the highest shoreline and the soil consists mainly of sandy till. Since the 17th century the landscape has been dominated by small-scale cultivation, with a large number of isolated farms and few hamlets or villages. At a first glance at old survey maps the settlements appear to be comparatively recent. The small, stony fields seem rather primitive. On the basis of appearance and place names, many of them ending in *-torp* and *-red,* it has long been thought that Västergötland's forest district was typical marginal land, not used for permanent settlement until the Middle Ages. Newly-discovered prehistoric fields have, however, altered this picture dramatically.

Cultural-geographical investigations have revealed a picture of an extensive prehistoric cultivated landscape in the forest. Two different main phases in this prehistoric cultivation may be distinguished: the first came in the late Bronze Age, about 800–600 B.C., when large areas were cleared by burning and prepared for cultivation. Gradually large clearing cairns were built up on the sandy hilltops. The next important cultivation phase occurred in the centuries following the birth of Christ. The land was divided into long strips separated by stone walls, banks and terraces. It has been proved that large strip systems were planned according to set measurements and laid out along long base lines. This suggests large-scale landscape planning in these districts even in prehistoric times.

Environmental-historical analyses provide a picture of a varied pattern of cultivated fields during the Bronze and Iron Ages. Within this area small fields cultivated each year were carved out of a pasture landscape rich in herbs and bushes. Large parts of the arable land were left fallow for long periods. Agriculture was based on a combination of grain crops and cattle farming. Traces of settlements have also been found in trial excavations and by means of phosphate analyses. The traces of dwelling sites consist mainly of post holes, hearths and cooking pits, as well as piles of rubbish containing sherds, bones and iron slag.

Graves from the Bronze and Iron Ages and carved stones are often found near prehistoric cultivated land. The late Iron Age cemeteries and notable numbers of long, narrow strips of land even in historical times suggest that the best land on the hilltops has supported settlements ever since the late Bronze Age right up to the present day. However, this does not exclude the possibility that parts of the forest district may have been abandoned at certain times.

A prehistoric field division close to the village of Läggared in the parish of Hillared was discovered and surveyed in 1988–89. This regularly divided land is connected with the infields on the map dated 1700, which indicates that the strips may be from premedieval times.

This photograph of Läggared was taken from the south-west. Traces of old strips can still be seen in the fields today. The long, narrow strips divide the moraine ridge into a regular pattern. When the redivision of land took place in 1873–76, several of the farms were moved from their original sites along the edge of the high land.

The excavated remains of prehistoric and medieval farm buildings at Fjäle in the parish of Ala on Gotland

An Abandoned Farm on Gotland

In an attempt to solve the question of Gotland's early settlements, an interdisciplinary investigation was carried out at the abandoned farm of Fjäle in the parish of Ala. The farm was established during the early Iron Age and abandoned in the 14th century. The central parts of the farm area were then used as meadow and pastureland, which has preserved the forms of the abandoned cultivated landscape. It has been possible to identify in the fields arable land, buildings, roads, wells, enclosures and graves for this farm, which was in continual use for about 1,200 years.

The presence or absence of specific types of prehistoric remains at various periods has come to govern our interpretations of prehistoric communities. A classic example is the presence of a very large number (some 1,500) of well-preserved and clearly identifiable house foundations dating from the early Iron Age on Gotland and Öland. It is believed that the large number of abandoned houses proves that some form of disaster struck this area. The continuity of settlement between prehistoric and historical times has therefore been questioned.

Later investigations, however, have shown that these farms usually survived during the late Iron Age, the Middle Ages and into historical times, even though old buildings were abandoned.

On Gotland buildings and walls were constructed mostly of stone during the early Iron Age and many of these mighty stone constructions have survived to the present day. It has therefore been relatively easy to study them, and our knowledge of the use of land and its management in those times is comparatively good.

The situation for the late Iron Age is quite different. Buildings and fences at that time were mostly constructed of wood, which leaves few traces. From this period there is some material, including hoards of silver, which is richer than in the rest of Sweden, as well as a large number of medieval stone buildings and churches, but the ordinary farmhouse is practically unknown. We do not have detailed knowledge of buildings and the cultivated landscape before the late 17th century, when land registers and maps provide us with reliable information.

A DESERTED FARM ON GOTLAND

- ■ House
- R Single grave
- ● Cemetery
- ○ Well
- Stone wall
- Wooden fence
- Road
- Cultivated field
- Other field
- Forestland
- Wetland
- Bog

This farm was established some time between 100 and 200 A.D. The buildings were placed on a natural outcrop of rock. Fields were cultivated close to the farmhouses. A stone wall protects an enclosure which probably contained meadowland as well as arable land.

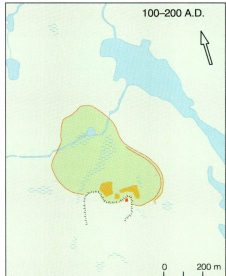

As time passed the farm's acreage increased, initially within the infield area but later outside the enclosure as well. In the course of the early Iron Age the area increased from about 2 ha to 4 ha.

Gradual changes took place in the location and construction of the buildings, as well as in the burial of the dead. During the Viking Age the area of cultivated land was probably as much as 7–8 ha.

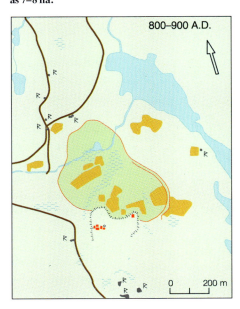

About 1200 a new farm was established on the northern edge of the farm's infields. Up to the 14th century the area of cultivated land grew to a maximum of about 12 ha. Much of the increase in arable land was on land that had probably been meadowland before.

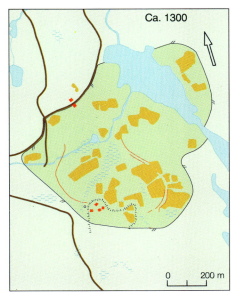

Fjäle

The Landscape and the Transformation of Society

The Old Agrarian Landscape before 1750

A village (or hamlet) consists of two or more registered and permanently inhabited agricultural units with a restricted area of ownership (territory) within which all parties own their property separately, jointly or in mixed forms. Within the framework of the village territory decisions were made jointly concerning, for example, enclosures, walls, fences and roads. The houses were usually grouped in one or more clusters, either according to the topography or arranged in a strict geometric pattern, but they could also be scattered. The opposite of a village (or hamlet) is an isolated farmstead. From the 16th century onwards more and more holdings were divided up, which made it difficult in many places to distinguish between an isolated farmstead and a hamlet. A compact cluster of small, separate farmsteads may physically resemble a hamlet. Functionally all villages have certain features in common, but as regards age and ways of operating they may differ greatly in different parts of the country.

System of cultivation comprised in olden times two components of land use: crop rotation and field enclosure (to protect sown fields). The system of regularly leaving fields fallow was reflected in the division of fields and their enclosure.

With regard to the fallow system, the terms normally used are one-field (annual sowing), two-field (fallow every other year), three-field (fallow every third year), four-field or even more complicated crop-rotation or fallow systems. A sown field was protected from grazing cattle by an enclosure between sowing and harvesting.

One-field was the most common form in terms of area in Sweden around 1750, occurring generally in the South Swedish highlands and in western Sweden, as well as in many places in Norrland. This method required either good manuring or space for new arable land to move to, letting the forest take over. Two-field rotation occurred mainly in the eastern central parts of Sweden, but was also found in Norrland and in a few places in western Götaland. Three-field rotation was predominant in Skåne and in a transitional zone between one-field and two-field in north-east Småland. Quite a few villages in Falbygden also used three-field rotation.

Village forms. When speaking of types of villages, the starting point is usually the way in which the farms are built in relationship to each other and the terrain. We usually distinguish between green-villages (farms grouped round an open common), cluster villages (the farms are built irregularly in one or more groups according to the terrain, often with kin-relationship within the clusters), linear villages (the farms in a row along roads, terraces, river banks and the like) and geometric villages (usually in linear villages with single or double rows of farms). In some places, including parts of Småland and Halland, there were also villages where the farms were quite scattered but where there was still a functional link within the loose-knit village.

Division of arable land. Where a more or less exact land survey existed (in the form of a land register, for example) land was usually divided according to a regular pattern. We find examples of this in Skåne, which has used two forms of division since the Middle Ages—*bolskifte* and *solskifte* (approx. farm division and solar division). *Bolskifte* was the dominant form in this province. In eastern Central Sweden including Öland *solskifte* was the dominant form, though it was called *laga läge* in Östergötland. *Solskifte* (*laga läge*) referred to the se-

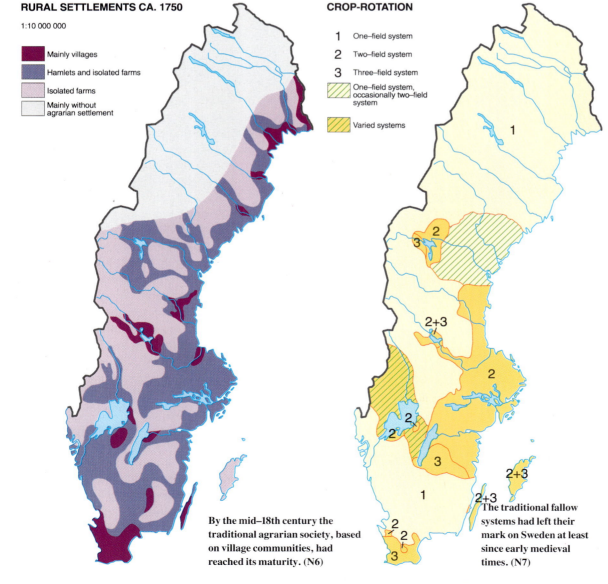

By the mid–18th century the traditional agrarian society, based on village communities, had reached its maturity. (N6)

The traditional fallow systems had left their mark on Sweden at least since early medieval times. (N7)

Skåne

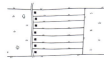
Öland

Västergötland

Dalarna

Storsjön

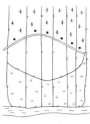
River valley

In the old agrarian landscape there were regional differences in the system of land division into strips. (N8)

quence of the land parcels and their breadth based on the relative sizes of the farms as shown in the tax register. When this system was fully applied, it would also affect the plots in the village.

In other parts of the country completely irregular or at any rate unsystematic forms of land division were used. Some examples of this are found in Västergötland (*stångskifte*), probably applied by drawing lots and/or with reference to laws of inheritance, and in Dalarna (*tegskifte*), which was connected with the principle of real inheritance and which led in time to a very flexible land-ownership system. Less complicated mixed systems are found in the form of long, narrow parcels in the Norrland valleys and the big-lake districts, or the division of fields through inheritance, for example in Hälsingland.

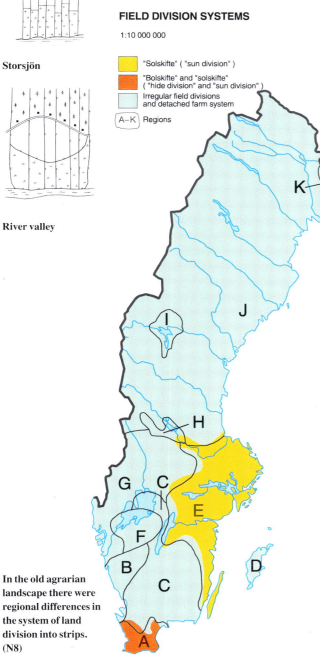

FIELD DIVISION SYSTEMS
1:10 000 000

- "Solskifte" ("sun division")
- "Bolskifte" and "solskifte" ("hide division" and "sun division")
- Irregular field divisions and detached farm system
- A–K Regions

REGIONAL VARIATIONS IN SETTLEMENTS 1750

Isolated farms are found in all regions away from village settlements.

A = Large villages, often grouped round a village common, the village green, and the village pond, which was fenced off from the village buildings but open to the pasture land. When the population grew in the 18th century the village green was filled with "gate houses", homes for those without land such as village craftsmen, and later often a school house and other village institutions.

The arable land was organised in fields which have been divided up, at least since the Middle Ages, into more or less regular strips. The number of fields might vary, but it was usual to have three, often with an additional meadow.

B = Clustered villages or loose-knit settlements

C = Clustered or kin villages, often on high slopes

D = Isolated farms, or partially divided farms

E = Geometrically planned (large) villages or (smaller) irregular cluster hamlets on high slopes. Along cliffs in the west or on the uplifted land along the east coast of Öland linear villages grew up which often became geometric in plan during the Middle Ages.

F = Nucleated villages (in Falbygden) or large clustered villages (on the plains) have greatly varied village forms but as in Skåne the villages were commonly grouped round an open place. The way in which the land was divided was irregular with respect to the shape of the strips, while the division into fields is like that in Skåne.

G = Clustered hamlets or loose-knit settlements.

H = Arable land was divided among all the children in a family according to the law of inheritance. Those who had enough land were allowed to build on it. The result was large, irregular clustered villages—more than 50 farms was not unusual—with little arable land for each farm.

I = This previously Norwegian area was originally full of isolated farms. As a result of successive divisions, mainly in the 19th century, we now have long linear villages. The fields were not much divided into strips and used a two-field system.

J = Clustered or linear villages with few field strips along rivers or on scarps.

K = A common form of settlements consists of long lines of farms on embankments or terraces along rivers. Every farm was surrounded by its own fields, so varied types of strip farming were less common.

THREE PIONEERS

Sigurd Erixon, 1888–1968, Professor of Nordic and Comparative Ethnology at the University of Stockholm, 1934–55. Extensive research on ancient buildings, working life, village forms and village organisations, regional variants and ways in which folk culture spread.

David Hannerberg, 1900–81, Professor of Human Geography at the Universities of Lund and Stockholm, 1950–69. Research on population development, harvest yields and the rearing of cattle. Well-known for his brilliant metrological analyses of villages and fields on old maps, which reflected the history of their cultivation and settlement.

Eli F Heckscher, 1879–1952, Professor of Economic History at the Stockholm School of Economics, 1929–45. His great works on economic history have long formed the basis of our understanding of the ways in which developments in Swedish politics and economics affected settlements and landscapes.

CULTURAL LANDSCAPES CA. 1750

1:10 000 000

1 = **Skåne plains.** Settlements in dales. Nucleated villages with half-timbered farmhouses built round a yard. Meadows in low locations and broad-leafed woodland. Three-field rotation system, large fields. Various forms of field strips, including solar distribution (*solskifte*). Large estates with castles or palaces and parks.

2 = **Blekinge.** Valleys and coastal districts. Settlements, ranging from isolated farms to relatively extensive villages, lack organisation in the transitional zone. Villages not regulated until the 18th century land reform. One-field district devoted mainly to cattle breeding. Extensive meadows and pastures along the coast.

3 = **West Sweden.** Isolated farms or scattered village unpatterned settlements, often connected with high land. Cattle rearing predominant; the district has extensive grasslands. Fields usually one-field system. In places land division has occurred as a result of inheritance.

4 = **Southern Swedish Highlands.** Settlements often on high land, close to fine till. Isolated farms and kin-related village clusters common. Geometric building patterns from the *storskifte* reform. One-field districts with small, irregular fields, extensive grasslands and broad-leafed forests. Fields divided into parcel forms.

5 = **Öland and the Kalmar district** has solar land distribution (*solskifte*) with patterned settlements. Villages on Öland follow a uniform pattern along cliffs or on high shorelines in the east. Inland in southern Öland the land was used for grazing, timber and firewood, which led to the creation of Öland's Stora Alvaret (a limestone heath). Two or three-field systems. Closer to the coast there are meadows and pastures.

6 = **Falbygden** is one of Sweden's oldest cultural landscapes with an ancient system of fields and settlements. One-field system in the west and irregular settlements associated with dales and rivers; in the east large villages with three-field systems close to rivers. The villages in Falbygden have a well-developed but irregular field strip system whose origin is unknown.

7 = **Lake Vänern plains.** Settlements are often on hilltops, with a great variety of types from small hamlets to large, irregular, scattered villages. Extensive grasslands with varying systems of cultivation. Two-field systems south of Vänern and on the Vadsbo plain, otherwise various types of multi-crop systems.

8 = **Gotland** has been dominated for a thousand years by extensive wetlands and isolated farms with connected fields, meadows and pastures. Fields use a two or three-field system.

9 = **Eastern Central Sweden.** Settlements on moraine ridges facing south and west. Arable land on slopes running down to water meadows. Eastern Central Sweden is characterised by geometrically organised villages in central, open districts and small irregular villages elsewhere. The fields have the solar strip system (*solskifte*) with two-field rotation. The lake plateau in Södermanland and the shores of Lake Mälaren have many large estates.

10 = **Western Svealand Forest district.** Above the highest shoreline there are settlements beside lakes and rivers and above them, on hilltops. When the population increased in the 17th and 18th centuries the settlement pattern became one of isolated farms. Three-field systems were common, with little fallow. One-field systems were common in the north. Scattered Finnish settlements using slash and burn farming.

11 = **Bergslagen.** Below the highest shoreline settlements are located along rivers and lakes; above the highest shoreline they are on hilltops. This district is dominated by iron and charcoal production. Agriculture is a complementary industry with large areas of meadowland for the many horses. Finnish settlements in the north.

12 = **Dalarna's cultivated districts** are associated with the sediment of the river Dalälven. Regular settlements and the solar strip system (*solskifte*). High land was colonised in the Middle Ages. In the settlements along the Västerdalälven and Österdalälven a direct inheritance system led to a unique type of settlement and field pattern, with small-scale strips and unstable ownership. The settlements consist of large kin or clustered villages of up to 50 farms. Three or even four-field systems.

13 = **Southern Norrland coastal and valley district.** It is primarily the sedimentary soils of the Ljusnan and Voxnan valleys and the areas round the Dellen lakes which were extensively cultivated, with unsystematically formed settlements. There are also settlements on high land above the highest shoreline. The strip system of the central districts arose as a result of the successive division of property. A two-field system. Another characteristic feature is summer farms and shealings in the hills.

14 = **Inner Southern Norrland** lies mainly above the highest shoreline. Settlements and cultivation are found either along the river valleys or on ridges. The lack of arable land has led to a concentration of agrarian settlements in a few places in the form of large groups of smallholdings with some mixed ownership. One-field fields are uncommon, while there are extensive hayfields.

15 = **Central Norrland's coastal and valley district.** Cultivation is possible in the valleys of the Ljungan, the Indalsälven and the Ångermanälven mainly up to the highest shoreline and in the Nordingrå district. Both cultivation and settlements lack fixed forms. Simple division of property is common and the fields are left fallow without any clear farm boundaries. Flax cultivation is common.

16 = **The Lake Storsjön district.** Calciferous clay till on Cambro-Silurian bedrock makes it possible to cultivate large parts of this district. Settlements stand mainly high in the landscape or on terraces running down to lakes and rivers. Before 1645 this district was part of Norway and was dominated by isolated, separately owned farms, though some division of farms occurred. Mainly a two-field system.

17 = **Northern Norrland's coast and valley district.** The cultivated landscape is dominated by the big rivers and their sediment below the highest shoreline. Colonisation took place upstream, and here and there large, irregular agglomerated settlements have grown up. Usually, however, the farms lie in a row along the rivers with little mixed ownership. One-field system. The fields are block-shaped and the large villages have unsystematic mixed land ownership.

18–19 = **Inner Northern Norrland and Lappmarken** had no real cultivated district prior to 1700, and some scattered colonisation up to 1750.

20 = **The Mountain Region**

21 = **Tornedalen.** Cultivation is associated with fluvial sediments below the highest shoreline. Settlements are on embankments and terraces along the river banks, so the farms are in long rows with a very special ownership system. Extensive hayfields.

The map of Norrby in the parish of Björnlunda, dated 1787, is fairly unusual for Södermanland. It shows a geometrically patterned village with solar strip division (*solskifte*) in the fields.

The land belonging to Norrby is today crossed by Highway 57 and the main western railway line. The buildings stand on the old village site.

THE VILLAGE LANDSCAPE

A great many villages in Sweden before 1750 looked like Norrby in the parish of Björnlunda in the heart of Södermanland. The principles governing the use of land—fields, meadows and pastures—were the same over much of Sweden and village activities were strictly regulated by village laws. In contrast, their physical form might vary from district to district according to the terrain, the ways of organising the use of resources and the proportions of the various types of land.

Norrby stands on a small hill to the north of Lake Ålsken. At the top stand the farm houses, dry and sunlight, on special house plots with a splendid view across the cultivated landscape. On the slope running down to the lake we see the parcels of arable land and round the fields, meadows, pastures and forestland.

The arable land, which belonged to individual farms, was controlled by rules concerning rights and obligations in the peasant society; it was, after all, possible to measure and value arable land, thus providing an instrument by which various duties could be allocated among the farmers. This meant that the one who had a great deal of land carried the heaviest burdens but also enjoyed the greatest privileges. This was often reflected in the farmhouse plots: a large plot meant that one owned plenty of land and vice versa.

Norrby is an example of a village divided according to *laga läge*. It was planned according to medieval ideals. The central point of the pattern of ownership is the arable land along the shore of Lake Ålsken. This is typically divided into strips and groups of strips. In the northern part of the arable land we find the farmhouse plots grouped to form a village plot, which is divided up in the same way as the arable land. We note that the village plot has a very regular pattern. In this case it was probably the result of a division of plots in 1759 which followed the regulations of the law of 1734, which in turn was based on medieval principles.

The seven farms in the village each received part of the village plot as its farm plot. Note that the width of the plots varies: the larger the farm, the broader the plot. In this system, the plot functioned as a measure of ownership. What is interesting is that the division of arable land followed the same pattern. Here, too, there was the same sequence as between the farms. The law expressed this principle in the statement: "The plot is mother of the strip." This system of land division in a village was widespread in eastern Sweden from the Middle Ages onwards, being called *solskifte* in the provincial lawbook and *laga läge* in the Östgöta lawbook. Note that the south farm always gets the south or east end parcel in each strip, "following the sun".

Meadowland was not always divided among the farms, but the hay harvest was divided in proportion to the share each farm had in the village. The principle of division within the village was followed. Nor was the pastureland or the grazing ground closest to the village divided, although individual holdings might occur. Forestland or outfields were used for summer grazing. In general the landscape was well grazed, and we find it difficult today to imagine how open the landscape was before the days of modern agriculture. The outfields were also used to provide timber and firewood.

A great deal of the information we can collect about the ways villages functioned is to be found in our old, large-scale surveyors' maps. These are often accompanied by a detailed description of conditions in the village. In the present case, the surveyor tells us: "Fishing in this village is pursued in Lake Ålsken, whereby the use of seine nets occasionally provides small catches of pike, perch and bream, but not enough for household requirements. In Lake Syltsjön there are small carp but the landowners do not make use of this fish since they do not think it is worth their while."

This photograph of Tärnö was taken facing north-east and may be compared with the map from 1730. The remains of a medieval stone building stand close to the north shore on the forest-clad height in the middle of the photograph.

THE ESTATE LANDSCAPE

The Tärnö estate lies in the parish of Husby-Oppunda in Södermanland, adjacent to Lake Långhalsen. No other province in Sweden is so distinguished by its estates and manor houses as Södermanland. Admittedly the estates in Skåne are larger and have more impressive architecture and parks, but at least in parts of Södermanland the manors lie closer together and have set a more definite mark on the cultural landscape with their parks and great open arable landscapes. In the story of Nils Holgersson, Selma Lagerlöf called this province "the beautiful garden of Eden" and at least its inner and coastal districts certainly live up to this description.

If we look at things in a historical perspective, the estates of Södermanland are small compared with those we find in the rest of Mälardalen, in Östergötland and Västergötland and in Skåne. Perhaps the explanation lies in the nature of the landscape.

The Södermanland lake plateau comprises a fissured landscape rich in lakes and rivers which shows a great variety of land forms. In her geography book Selma Lagerlöf writes: "Nothing was really allowed enough elbow room." Today the manor house at Tärnö stands right alongside the road running from Husby-Oppunda to Vrena in a really beautiful landscape. However, closer investigations reveal that the romantic nature of the manor countryside was preceded by a more harsh landscape in the Middle Ages.

Most of the estates on the Södermanland lake plateau do not date back to prehistoric times. A survey of the terrain shows that there are a large number of small cemeteries with no special prehistoric remains within the present Tärnö estate. In the north-west, on the Hästnäset peninsula, there used to be a Viking farmstead where there are the remains of buildings and cultivation. The soil has a high phosphate content, which indicates a long period of settlement, and several layers of household rubbish. The farm seems to have been abandoned during the Viking Age or the early Middle Ages. It is not mentioned in any written documents.

About 200 m north of Tärnö lies a small cemetery related to a farmstead which stood on a magnificent height north of the lake. There are

Soldier's croft

Non-commissioned officer's house

Officer's house

Colonel's residence

OFFICIAL RESIDENCES

Virtually the only way in which the State or the Church could maintain their officials in the agrarian society (officially up to 1870) was to provide official residences. These were civil residences (for judges, pilots and post carriers, for example), military residences and ecclesiastical residences (for vicars, for example). The income from the arable land and forests was the salary for the employee.

Official residences from the time prior to 1870 whose names are still in common use are vicarages (often on Church land since Catholic times), curates' residences (quite often Crown property or estates taken over by the Crown) and soldiers' crofts (the obligation for local farmers to provide soldiers—usually two to four in a system of military units—with two acres of arable land, meadowland for two loads of hay, a cottage and an outhouse).

The scope and maintenance of the armed forces according to the allotment system include the following categories:
Noblemen's military service: Manor farms
Cavalry: Crown farms to maintain the cavalry.
Armed forces: All military crofts, for example boatswain's crofts, hussar crofts, cavalry crofts and soldier's crofts.
Officer's residences: Military residences generally established on Crown land or on estates taken over by the Crown during the reign of Karl XI. Their names are often connected with the serviceman's rank or position: colonel's residence, captain's residence, sergeant's residence, drummer's residence, trumpeter's residence and so on. Standard plans were usually used for these houses, which were built all over the country and are still a striking feature of Swedish architecture.

The map of the Tärnö estate dated 1730 makes it possible to estimate the estate's geographical development and size up to the mid–18th century.

also two cemeteries close to each other north-east of the farm. None of these places have a name, which might suggest that they were abandoned before written documentation could be made. The explanation might be connected with the establishment of Tärnö as a manor.

The first time we come across Tärnö in documents is in 1303 (in *Ternum*), but it is not until 1436 that the place can be related to a well-known family, the Örnfots, who lived at Tärnö at that time. From about the same period are the remains of a medieval stone building standing on a cliff close to Lake Långhalsen. Excavations have shown that this house was probably built about 1500. This is confirmed by both coins and dating by ^{14}C-method.

Just west of the house on the cliff lies Gammelgårdsudden, with remains of buildings and cultivation. There are no prehistoric remains here, but no documented evidence of later modern buildings either.

During the early 17th century Ebba Grip built a manor house at about the same place as the present house. The medieval house was probably abandoned at this time. By now Tärnö looked more or less as the farm does today. We have a series of documents showing what the manor house itself looked like through the ages.

These include a surveyor's map of Tärnö from 1730 drawn by Mårten Rivell, a surveyor in Södermanland. This is an interesting map because it partly documents the development of the estate as described above. It also illustrates how the estate landscape was organised. As late as 1730 it is possible to see the components of the landscape round which the Tärnö estate was built up.

Round the manor farm itself is all that is needed for a large-scale household: farm buildings, gardens and vegetable and herb gardens. Tracks and paths are also marked. By studying the way in which the fields are divided we can identify the farms which quite possibly existed even in prehistoric times.

Each arable field in the farming community, and of course in the organisation plan of an estate, has its own name. The east field was called Wistagärdet, but we know of no place that this name can be related to. Wista may very well have been an old place name—perhaps where the two cemeteries lie. It is quite possible that a farm of that name can have stood on this hill at some time in the distant past.

The other information the map gives us is that the landscape round Tärnö manor is very similar to that surrounding other farm villages. There are fields based on the two-field system, and meadows that mostly lie close to lake shores and wet land or are leafy meadows on sandy slopes and heights. There are also fairly small outfields.

The only signs today that some noble family lived here at this time are the large manor house, the gardens and the avenues of trees.

Land Reform and Industrialisation

LAND DIVISION REFORMS

Agriculture has had many different forms and developed in many different ways in Sweden. This means that modernisation plans have developed from different starting points, often using different methods and achieving different results. Thus it is extremely difficult to present a true picture of the background and effects of land division on the cultural landscape of the whole of Sweden.

Agriculture has always needed laws that clearly state who has the right to a certain piece of land and how that piece of land may be used. From the Middle Ages up to the late 18th century these laws presumed some form of open fields of arable land and meadows with intermingled strips of different owners, while pasture and forestland (*utmark*) were usually owned jointly, that is to say, the landowners/farmers in a village had joint use of them. This common land (*utmark*) was used by everybody but cared for by none. There were very limited opportunities for developing individual ideas in a village. The system of divided arable land was adapted to cultivation based on regular fallow periods. This system presupposed access to natural meadowland.

During the 18th century agricultural innovators argued in favour of abolishing the existing open field-system demanding that each farm's strips should be amalgamated. The first land reform (*storskifte*), which began in the 1750s, did not, however, change the system of common fields.

Later the *enskifte* reform became more radical when it introduced the division of common land and the right to move to new farm sites where the land was not divided. The real dissolution of villages came in the first decades of the 19th century. Countless farms were moved out to village land that was divided up into relatively separate units.

Those who took the initiative were often ordinary farmers, even though noblemen who owned farms were perhaps better informed about the new methods of agriculture. When *laga skifte* was introduced, which could affect farms both negatively and positively to a much greater degree than the *storskifte* reform, it seems as if the owners of large farms were often more interested in reform than the small farmers. On the plains small farms were usually forced to move out to poorer land, which meant more work and lower unit yields. In the long term this meant that many farms had to close down, their land being taken over by the units that survived.

Many farms changed their forms of production when they were reformed; this is particularly true of the farms on the plains. On the more marginal village land there used previously to be many crofts and cots whose occupants did day work on the farms in the village. After *laga skifte* had come into force, these contracts were cancelled and the crofters found themselves living on land belonging to other farms. Many crofts and cots disappeared or had to be moved. At the same time cultivation on the village farms expanded and intensified, so

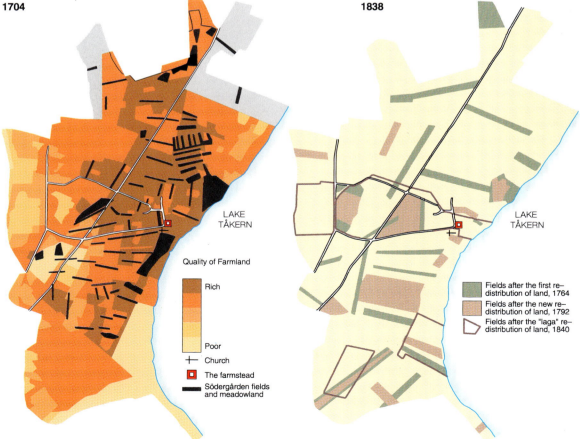

The first major redivision of land at Väversunda near Lake Tåkern, 1765, resulted only in a slight reduction in the fragmentation of land. In the new ownership pattern the medieval strips are still visible, thanks to the ditches.

The maps show all the land belonging to Väversunda Södergård, called Berzeliusgården after the famous chemist who was born there in 1779. The map on the left shows the medieval division of the land according to a map dated 1704 and the tax register for that time. The map to the right shows the changes in the farm's land between 1765 and 1838 as a result of two major land reforms and a final *laga skifte* redivision, when the farm's fields were all gathered together close to the farm. Most of the farms which were moved out to poorer soil on the farm estate are no longer under cultivation today.

The pattern of the *laga skifte* reform still leaves its mark on the plain. The old church village stands near Lake Tåkern, which was partly drained in the 1840s. The village had its outfields on the slopes of Omberg in the background.

that more people found themselves working as labourers paid in kind or by the day. These changes affected the landscape as larger areas became cultivated, mainly at the cost of meadowland, and as the pattern of buildings changed. Small crofts and cots disappeared or were moved to places set aside for them, and farmhouses were moved out from the villages. It is true to say that today's plains landscapes reflect to a high degree the land reforms carried out in the 18th and 19th centuries.

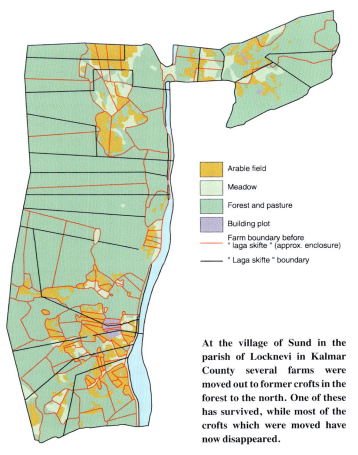

At the village of Sund in the parish of Locknevi in Kalmar County several farms were moved out to former crofts in the forest to the north. One of these has survived, while most of the crofts which were moved have now disappeared.

But it cannot be said that land reform everywhere led to the same sorts of changes as on the plains. In forest districts agriculture was only one of several means of livelihood for the population; woodcraft, charcoal burning or transporting goods by horse were just as important in the struggle for survival. When farms were moved out as a result of *laga skifte*, they were not necessarily in a worse position; they could, for example, benefit from access to better or more forestland. In general the forest districts were reformed later than farms on the plains. The farmers on the plains were probably keen to develop their farms individually, whereas the farmers in forest districts, where agriculture was less important and many farms already had much of their land in separate units, were more interested in having common land privatised to an even greater extent. This phase in land reform was not introduced until the 1780s, when the forest districts became more and more affected by land reform.

The number of possible alternative farm sites was also limited in the forest districts. Many crofts had to move or disappeared when farms moved out to their sites. Nowadays, however, most of these crofts have disappeared. It is not possible to claim, however, as it is concerning villages on the plains, that farms that were moved were at a disadvantage and disappeared, while farms that stayed in the village survived. Yet it is reasonable to argue that the landscape in forest districts is also the result of land reform. The farms are usually scattered, and more marginal land has been cultivated in recent years. The crofts suffered because they had to move to less favourable sites. The forest districts may also be said to be the landscape of land reform because the large privately-owned areas of forestland that were created have survived, providing a basis for today's relatively large-scale forestry.

The situation was quite different in northern Sweden. Here in the 19th century there was room for new farms, but land ownership and boundaries were not regulated. Colonisation in northern Sweden was encouraged by what was called *avvittring*, that is, land was split off from state-owned land and allocated to pioneers. The state, however, retained most of the forestland.

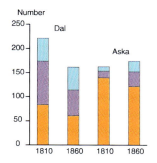
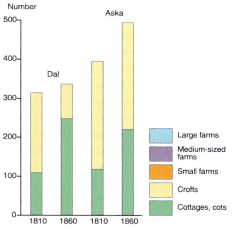

The number of crofts, cots and farms of various sizes in Dals and Aska Hundreds in Östergötland during the last period of land redivision, 1810–60.

Land redivision swept over South and Central Sweden in two waves lasting 100 years. The plains were affected first. In the forest areas land reform began when the forests could be divided. (N10)

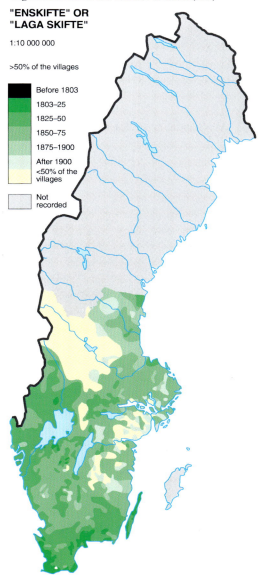

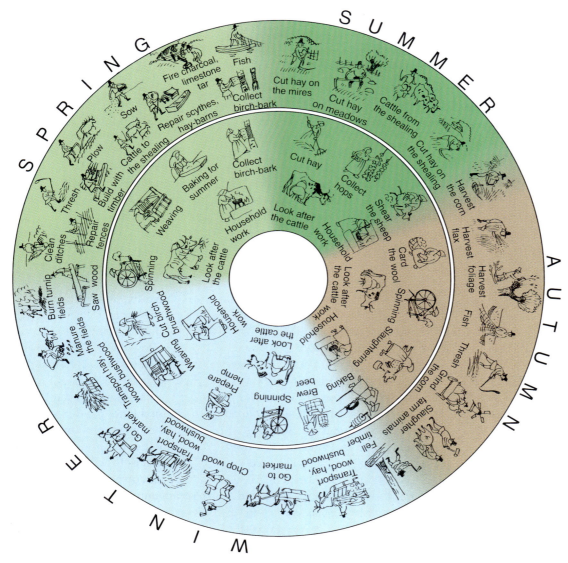

The variety of work on self-subsistent farms provided jobs for all the members of the family in an annual cycle. This example is from the north of Sweden. Production and the use of time were different further south, but the annual cycle and the variety of work were similar.

THE TRANSFORMATION OF PEASANT FARMING

During the 18th and 19th centuries Swedish farmers strengthened their positions in the Swedish economy. The number of freeholders increased greatly when farmers were allowed to buy Crown land and many estates owned by noble families sold off part of their land. The meaning of land ownership changed for farmers, too. Previously the rights that yeomen farmers had to work arable land and forest were extremely limited, not only for those who were tenant farmers but even for freeholders in village communities. Now that they were allowed to a greater extent to choose their methods of cultivation and to specialise, to redivide their farms, establish crofts and employ the number of workers they needed, farmers were able to improve their chances of gaining personally from the resources offered by the arable land and forest they owned. In addition greatly decreased taxation meant that farmers could sell a larger share of their produce.

By acting more energetically in the Riksdag and in their dealings with the authorities yeomen farmers were able to influence legislation concerning forest laws, the distillation of spirits and the obligation to provide services for ironworks.

The work of a farmer was not only on the land. As a mainly self-sufficient householder with regard to both consumer goods and investment goods (seed and machinery), he was a jack of all trades. Admittedly the amount of work through the year varied according to what needed to be done, but his work changed with the seasons. Many farmers also made money by selling other goods and services apart from foodstuffs. In Bergslagen and other iron-producing districts farmers produced charcoal as a complement to their farm work. Other important forest products were sawn wood, tar, potash and firewood. In many regions homecrafts played an important role in the economy; many households produced various kinds of handcraft. Yeomen farmers who were able to exploit many different sources of income were not as vulnerable to crop failures as, for example, the farmers on the plains, who lived mainly by selling corn. Doing all kinds of different jobs was a kind of insurance, which also introduced greater variety into the landscape.

Greater variety in industrial life created opportunities for an increasing number of yeomen farmers. The division of farms that took place in the 18th and 19th centuries can partly be explained by the fact that many farmers involved themselves more deeply in work outside arable farming and cattle breeding. It is true that much new land was brought under cultivation, particularly in the 19th century, when most meadowland was converted to arable land, a large number of drainage projects were launched to create farmland out of old lake beds and many mires were turned into fields. However, the expansion of arable farming could not alone explain the rapid growth of both the population and the number of farms. In connection with the Emigrant Commission in the early 20th century large amounts of information were collected concerning the division of farms. This information seemed to indicate that farm division was very frequent in Sweden, especially after the ban on dividing farms of less than a certain size was lifted in 1747. Today we know that this picture of farm division was partly incorrect. While there was extensive farm division in some parishes and hundreds, in others it hardly occurred at all. In certain districts the number of farming units even decreased when small farms were combined to make large-scale farming possible.

The commonest form of farming in Sweden in the early 18th century was the yeoman farm. This meant that the farm was usually small enough to be worked by the family alone. During the following centuries, however, there was growing interest in farming on a large scale. These discussions were mainly among the owners of large estates, who were in the best position to establish large-scale farms thanks to the large amounts of land they owned and their good access to capital. The idea was that large-scale

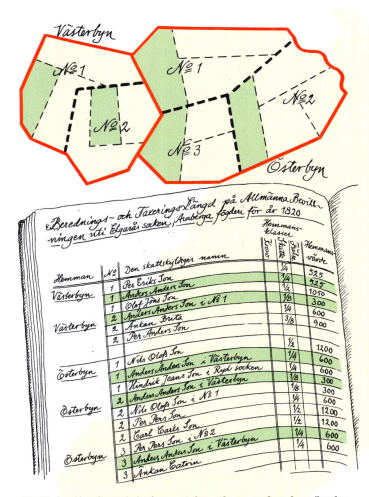

A farming unit might consist of several taxable units. If farming units are counted according to the tax register, the result is an over-assessment of the number of small farms. This is what happened in the Emigration Commission's report, 1910.

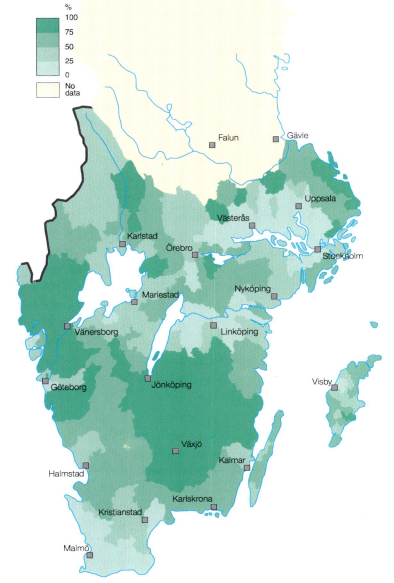

The Emigration Commission's report shows the parts of southern Sweden where "peasant farms" (2–20 ha) were most common in 1902. The actual number was overestimated, but the regional similarities are correct. (N11)

PERCENTAGE OF "FAMILY FARMS" IN SOUTHERN SWEDEN, 1902

farms could be run more economically, using labourers who could be exploited to a greater degree than the relatively independent yeomen farmers. However, it was not only owners of estates and other wealthy persons who were interested in developing large farms.

On the plains of Västergötland and Östergötland yeomen farmers had also built up large land holdings by inheritance, marriage and purchase. There are quite a few examples, especially in west Östergötland, of farmers who ran farms on market principles, which meant that most of the produce was sold, often in a processed form (schnapps) and that the labour force consisted mainly of farmhands, servant girls and labourers paid in kind. Rich farmers also leased land in order to increase their holdings and land reforms led to a better organisation of the land.

Developments during the 19th century resulted in many farms no longer functioning primarily as family farms. Land division in many parts of Sweden meant that farms were too small to wholly support the farmer and his family, so they were forced to work outside the farm. When farms were amalgamated to make large-scale units, the work could no longer be done mainly by the members of the family; large numbers of paid workers had to be employed. In spite of this, yeoman farms continued to form the majority of farms. With the exception of the plains of Västergötland and Östergötland, Skåne and the Lake Mälaren district, a very large percentage of farms at the beginning of the 19th century were still yeoman farms.

Why was it that yeoman farms were so resilient? Large farms were not able to utilise to their full extent the advantages of large-scale farming and thus drive the yeomen farmers off the market. Nor is it certain that the wide range of activities that characterised yeoman farming was a disadvantage when it was necessary to adapt farming to suit the market. The relative advantages of large-scale farming (access to land and capital) were compensated for by the fact that yeomen farmers had access to cheap labour—their own family. Their wide range of activities lengthened the working year and utilised labour in a rational way; in fact it was differentiation rather than specialisation that increased profitability. This factor was of great importance during the latter half of the 19th century when cheap grain poured into Europe from Argentina and Australia, lowering the price of grain, at the same time as the production of animal produce was stimulated, which favoured the relatively more labour-intensive organisation of yeoman farming.

Another explanation of the survival of so many yeoman farms is that as long as these farmers were not weighed down with debt they could always depend on self-sufficiency when there was an agricultural crisis. Many yeomen farmers wanted above all to remain independent. To attain this goal they were willing at times to lower their consumption considerably, as well as to work far more than a large landowner could demand of his paid employees.

The number of smallholdings varied in different areas.

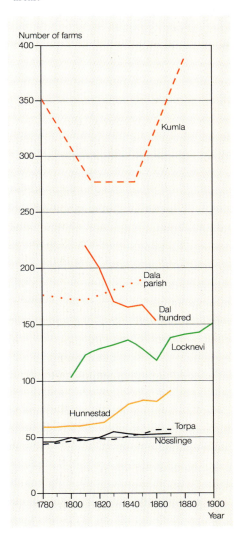

LARGE-SCALE FARMING, 1862

1:10 000 000

Percentage of market value of farmland per county
- 50
- 25
- 10
- 0

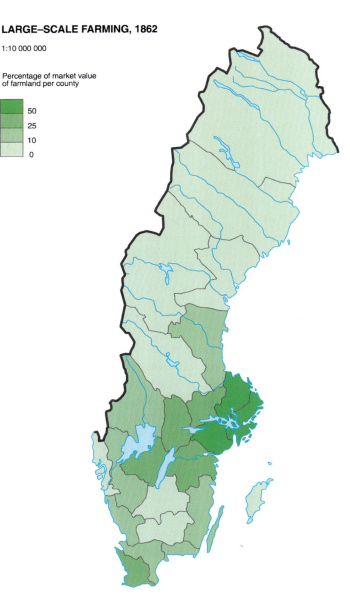

The counties of Uppsala and Södermanland proved to be regions with large-scale farming in 1862. This map is based on the large-scale farms' share of the total market value of all farmland. (N12)

THE TRANSFORMATION OF FARM ESTATES

Farm estates are a dominant feature of many districts on the plains. Many of them have a history that stretches far back into the Middle Ages. The estate landscapes that we see today, however, are mainly the outcome of 19th-century processes: farm buildings for cattle, machinery and fodder, and labourers' barrack-like homes built largely in the 19th century. This is true of many of the manor-house buildings, too, which were renovated or rebuilt after the old buildings had been demolished. This period of extensive building is evidence of an economic boom; the changes were most noticeable in the regions round Lake Mälaren and in Skåne.

Large farm estates are not evenly distributed throughout Sweden: there are no manors, for example, in Norrland. Large-scale farming is common in the counties of Södermanland, Stockholm and Uppsala; other counties with large estates are Malmöhus, Västmanland, Örebro and Östergötland.

AGRARIAN CAPITALISM

The development of farm estates in the 19th century into rationally run units producing goods for sale took place rapidly. They were now worked by farmhands, servant girls and labourers paid in kind instead of peasants and crofters who were obliged to do day work. Production was now centred on sales in a quite different way from previously, and the surplus was largely used for investment. Estates were run like any other market-oriented company.

"LOW" FARMS

This transition was most evident in the many new buildings that were erected, in Skåne often in brick. The majority of Skåne's present agrarian buildings were probably constructed in the closing decades of the 19th century. On many estates owners simply closed down whole villages or parts of them; instead "Low" farms, as they were called, were created: large tenant farms run by a powerful tenant, many of whom came from Denmark or Germany. These Low farms were built like small palaces surrounded by a park. The inhabitants of the villages who had previously done day work on the estate had in principle two options: to move or to be a labourer paid in kind on the new farm. Although they were not unknown in other parts of Sweden, Low farms were mainly built in Skåne.

THE LABOURER SYSTEM

The old system of yeomen farmers and crofters who were liable for day work was gradually replaced during the 19th century by the labourer system, which was based on employed labour. A farm labourer (*statare*) was a married man employed for the year whose wages were paid mainly in kind

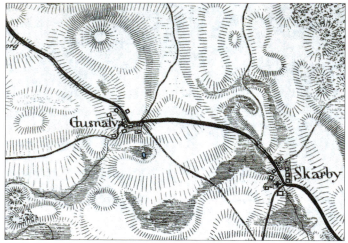

The villages of Gussnava and Skårby in southern Skåne both belonged to the Marsvinsholm estate. A comparison of the Economic map dated 1914 and the Skåne survey map dated 1812 reveals how the owner of the estate, Eric Piper, did away with the whole of Gussnava, replacing it with the "low" farms of Erikslund and Gussnavagården.

and only partly in cash. He received meat, flour, milk, firewood and clothes and his employment included living quarters. A common condition for being employed was that his wife should look after the milking. The introduction of this system of payment in kind to Skåne took place at the same time as the Low farms were established. Farm labourers paid in kind became common in many parts of Sweden in the 19th century. The increase in the number of labourers in Skåne was at the expense of the yeomen farmers on the estates; in Mälardalen, however, it was mostly crofters who were replaced.

Marsvinsholm

Marsvinsholm in southern Skåne stands in the midst of the agricultural landscape. The castle is surrounded by barns and farm workers' cottages. The Malmö-Ystad railway runs across the bottom of the picture, where the remains of Marsvinsholm station can be seen. The two groups of buildings are linked by an avenue which was constructed when the railway was opened in 1874. The line was principally financed by some dozen estates –"the Counts' line"– which were able to transport corn and butter rapidly to the international harbour at Malmö. The large fields on either side of the avenue bear witness to the rationalisation of agriculture which began as early as the mid–19th century and has continued in our own times. Almost all obstacles to cultivation including have been uprooted.

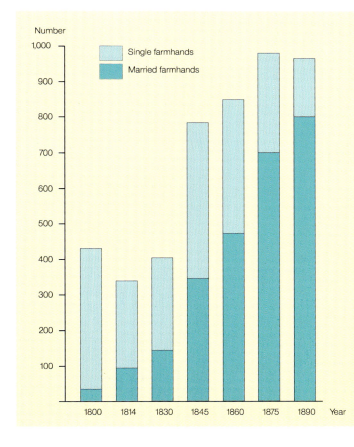

When no other statistical information is given, "married farmhand" may be the same as agricultural labourer paid in kind (Sw. statare). The diagram shows how the number of such labourers on estates in Malmöhus county more than doubled in the 19th century. At the beginning of the century only a few percent of them were married, but by the end of the century most of the labourers were married.

The development of Low farms and the increasing number of labourers paid in kind are signs of the emergence of capitalistic agriculture, in which the estates in Skåne played an important role as producers and exporters, both to Sweden and to foreign markets, principally England. The effects of this development on the landscape are still evident.

MEMORIAL TO A CROFTER

"Seldom is one's heart so close to being broken by melancholy as when one stands by the overgrown foundations of an old croft. We often find them in the forests in Sweden. A hump in the ground sometimes still reveals the site of a modest old cottage. A little way off lie a few stones—once the barn and the stable... The square patches down in the forest glades are a clue to the former fields, cleared from the forest by sweat and toil. A stretch of road can still be seen, too. During the first year or two after the croft was abandoned, perhaps the cat, now wild, had prowled round here, looking for the sardine tin full of milk on the mouldering doorstep. But in the end the fox would get the cat. Then, thoughtlessly, one touches the dry grass round the stones, wishing one could blow fresh life into the dead, telling them that one loves them, telling them to come back, if only for one day, free from aches and pains.

One wishes, with feelings deep in one's heart, that these people lived a happy life."

From *Statarnoveller*
by Ivar Lo-Johansson

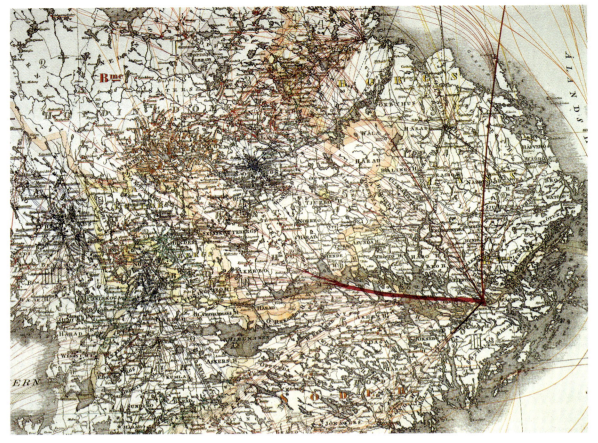

When Karl XV was the Crown Prince, he drew a map of the Swedish iron industry in 1855, before the "death of the mills", showing mines, forges, hammers and export ports. Lines connect mines, mills and ports. The close ties between Bergslagen and Stockholm are very evident. Information was collected from the mill owners.

The ironmills were not merely locally concentrated units of production. All those who dealt with the production and transport of raw materials within the surrounding district also played a decisive part in iron production. The mills were integrated with the surrounding agrarian community.

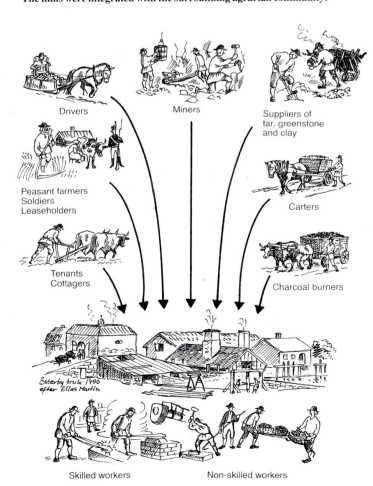

THE TRANSFORMATION OF IRONWORKS

The earliest manufacturing in Sweden took place within the framework of peasant society, using small furnaces to produce iron from local raw materials: ore from mines, lakes and bogs. This production was part of the annual cycle of the farm year and was the responsibility of people within the complex system of the local community. With the exception of furnaces and forges it required hardly any separate buildings.

While iron production only built up a simple organisation within the farm framework, the production of silver and copper required a completely separate system. As early as the Middle Ages this led to special buildings and an extensive organisation.

In the 16th century blast furnaces and modern forges replaced the old smelting houses and unhealthy smithies. Mining and manufacturing became more independent occupations in peasant society.

Behind this development lay the immigration of mainly German craftsmen, and an initial flow of capital into Sweden through its ports. No real mill towns were built in the 16th century. Most of the people involved lived in agricultural dwellings at a short distance from the ironworks. Other factories also arose, mainly in the towns but also in the countryside, especially in Mälardalen. Many of them survived for only a short time, however.

It was not until the 17th century that it was possible to speak of a breakthrough for Swedish manufacturing. In Central Sweden, which had many blast furnaces and forges, a shortage of wood forced a division of processes; the blast furnaces remained in Bergslagen, while the forges moved away. In southern Sweden, where there were fewer ironworks, the blast furnaces and the forges usually remained together.

The ironworks communities were generally speaking small, with their production located alongside a waterfall in the river which provided the necessary power. At larger ironworks manor houses and palaces with well-designed gardens began to be built for the owners to live in. The workers' homes usually stood close to the workshops, in an irregular fashion. The ironworks communities were also the centre of a good deal of farming work. Even the foundry craftsmen used to farm a little. This integration of manufacturing and farming set its mark on the landscape.

The emergence of ironworks and other factories led to an increasing demand for forest products, charcoal in particular, which improved the economic position of the farms that supplied these products. In many cases this resulted in more farms being divided, without any evident lowering of living standards.

During the great Nordic war of the first decades of the 18th century, Sweden's industrial life stagnated seriously, but when the country had recovered after peace was declared, there was an explosion of investments in new factories: ironworks, paper mills, textile companies, glassworks, sawmills and so on. These factories were spread throughout the country.

The organisation of ironworks developed during this period, not least through the establishment of a number of crofts whose owners formed the flexible labour reserve which was necessary in a community with an irregular work rhythm and many unspecified jobs. In the 18th century factories played an important role, more important than in previous eras, in strengthening the economic position of farmers and in shaping archi-

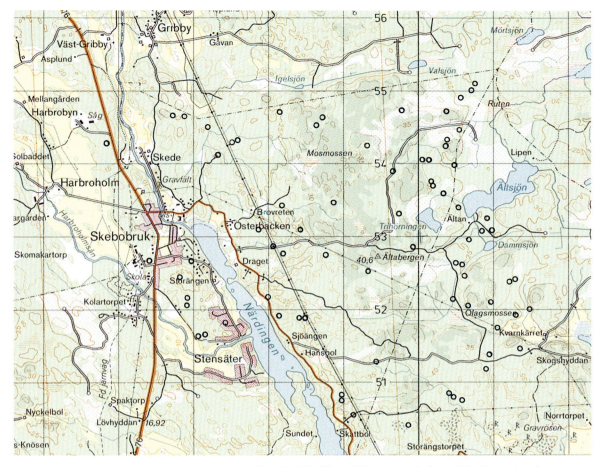

Out in the forests of Central Sweden it is still possible to see, in the form of old charcoal stack foundations, traces of the unbelievable extent of charcoal production needed to process iron. The charcoal stack foundations in the forests belonging to Skebo Mill were surveyed in 1978.

Iron production required the extensive and troublesome transportation of ore, charcoal and iron in particular. This example is from Skebo Mill around 1870. Iron ore was transported to Edsbro, pig iron to Skebo and bar iron to the wharf at Skärsta. Iron ore was carried by horse and cart to Grönö, by boat to Skärsta and by horse and cart to the blast furnace at Edsbro.

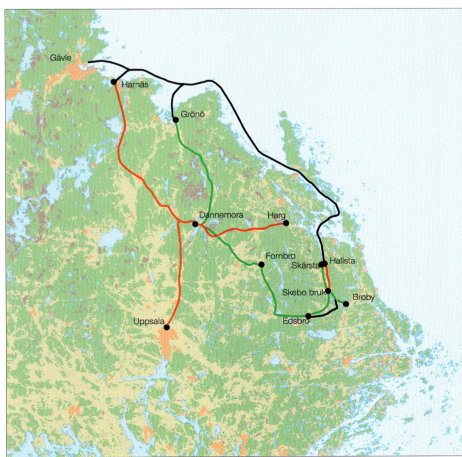

tectural patterns in the surrounding districts.

The buildings of the ironwork communities in pre-industrial society clearly reflected its work and organisation. Any land that was not built on or used for storing material was used both by the company and the craftsmen to grow food. The patriarchical system was evident in the dominant manor-house buildings, in the streets of the skilled craftsmen which ran up to the manor house and in the more diversified dwellings of the unskilled workers. A very great deal of the overall system lay outside the ironworks community itself, and was connected with the surrounding farmland.

Pre-industrial society reached its peak in the mid–19th century. The industrial revolution brought great changes, of course. Factories were no longer so dependent on water power, so they could be located much more freely. Full-time specialists replaced many unskilled workers. The growing number of employees demanded new homes. Some of them had to live in converted industrial premises, at the same time as large workers' barracks were built, consisting of one-room flats and a kitchen, often of a very low standard. While the managers tried to preserve the classical architecture in the centre, new buildings were erected outside the centre without any evident plan. The integration of industry and farming was no longer so apparent, even though the new apartment buildings were provided with allotments, mainly for growing potatoes.

A large number of employees still lived in crofts and other cottages in the surrounding countryside, from which they travelled in and out to work. Many of the ironworks did not operate very reliably. There were often both long and short breakdowns, and the plots of land round the houses in the countryside were seen as a kind of insurance. Many cottages stood at the roadside or at crossroads, which made it easier to get to work at the factories or to work in agriculture, road-building, ditching and river clearance.

At the turn of the 19th century small private houses began to be built. By then conditions in industrial towns had stabilised enough for employees to dare to invest in a house of their own close to the works. The management often encouraged those

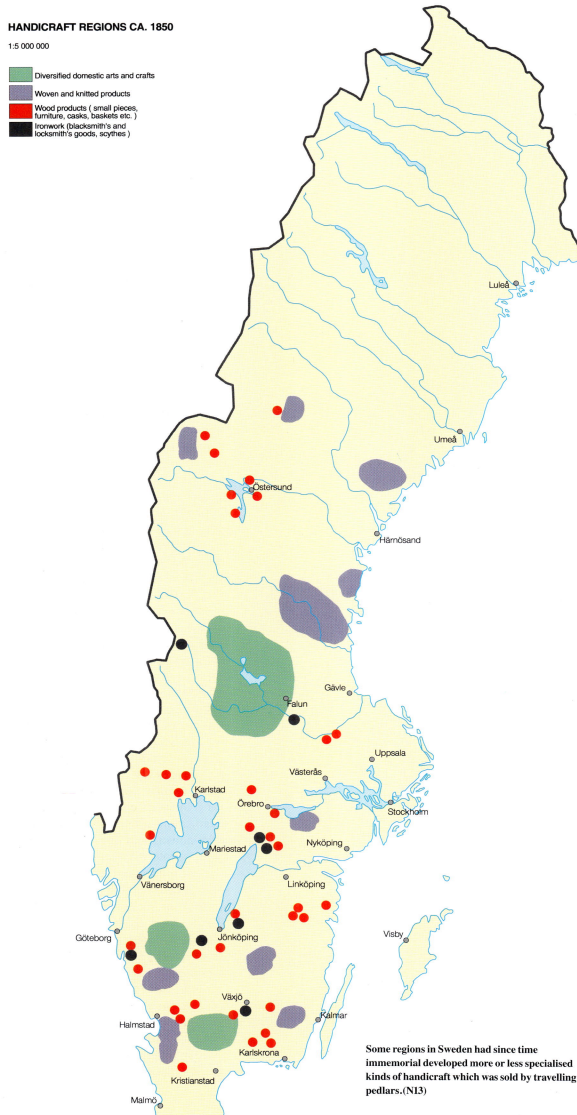

HANDICRAFT REGIONS CA. 1850

1:5 000 000

- Diversified domestic arts and crafts
- Woven and knitted products
- Wood products (small pieces, furniture, casks, baskets etc.)
- Ironwork (blacksmith's and locksmith's goods, scythes)

Some regions in Sweden had since time immemorial developed more or less specialised kinds of handicraft which was sold by travelling pedlars. (N13)

who wanted to build a house, because that would tie them down to the town. Usually these houses had large gardens which continued to produce food until the middle of the century.

CRAFTWORK FOR SALE AND PROTO-INDUSTRY

The term "proto-industry" has come to be applied to the extensive "industrial" production that arose, particularly in country districts, in Western and Central Europe in the 18th and early 19th centuries. Many regions during this period were famous for their production of textiles and other goods for sale which were of great economic importance. Production in country districts was decentralised and used simple methods, and it was mostly initiated by merchants in the towns. They placed their contracts out in the country, in the first place to avoid the oppressive regulations of the guilds, but also because of the higher wages in towns.

Certain criteria are usually given for the term "proto-industry". The goods must be sold on an anonymous and distant market. The workforce must consist of farmworkers, crofters or farmers who work alternately with agriculture and craftwork for sale/proto-industry. The emergence of a proto-industry in a region also presupposed surplus production of foodstuffs in another relatively close region.

What characterises Western Europe, in contrast to much of the rest of the world, is the existence of an early, flourishing proto-industrial sector before the industrial revolution. This was a necessary condition for the early industrial revolution and partly explains the relative superiority of Western Europe in the long term. The industrial revolution is no longer seen as a break in the economic history of Europe; rather it is its continuity that is emphasised. The French historian Fernand Braudel sums up the argument in the following words: "The arrival of steampower accelerated everything in the West as if by magic. But this magic can be explained, for it had been prepared and made feasible in advance."

Swedish craftwork which was offered for sale developed rapidly in the second part of the 18th century and expanded in the early 19th century, reaching its peak in the 1840s. After factory-made goods in large quantities poured into the country, production

The sawmill at Askesta on Lake Marman in Hälsingland, shown here in a picture from about 1870, was one of the largest in Gävleborg County in 1900. At this time over 116,000 m³ of sawn timber, 18,500 m³ of planed wood and over 392,000 hectolitres of charcoal were produced at the mill, which had 280 employees. In 1923, when it was closed down, it was owned by Bergvik & Ala AB.

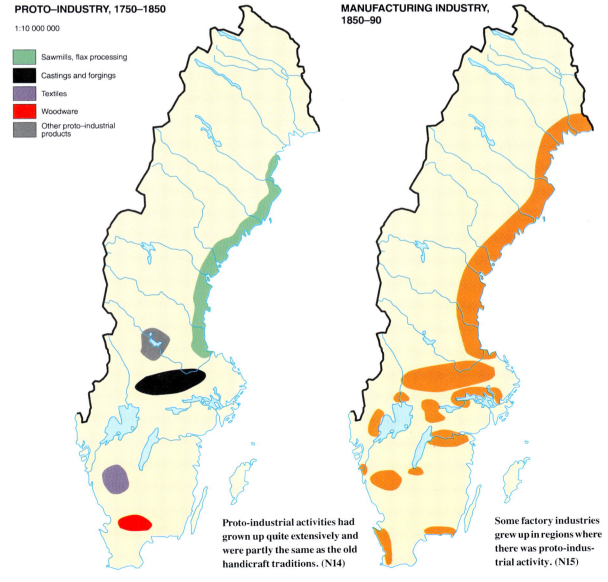

PROTO–INDUSTRY, 1750–1850

1:10 000 000

- Sawmills, flax processing
- Castings and forgings
- Textiles
- Woodware
- Other proto–industrial products

Proto-industrial activities had grown up quite extensively and were partly the same as the old handicraft traditions. (N14)

MANUFACTURING INDUSTRY, 1850–90

Some factory industries grew up in regions where there was proto-industrial activity. (N15)

stagnated and died out in some regions. By the end of the 19th century the production of craftwork for sale had virtually ceased.

There were, however, considerable regional variations. In places such craftwork survived into the 20th century. In Sweden textile work was the most important craft, but woodwork and metalwork were also famous. Other materials such as leather, horn, bone and clay were also used. Craftwork was characterised by regional specialisation. It was at its weakest in areas where arable land and forestland belonged to large estates, whose owners kept their crofters and paid employees under strict control.

Three areas in Sweden are famous for their extensive production of craftwork for sale: southern Västergötland (textiles), the border country between Småland and Skåne (carved wood, wrought iron etc) and Dalarna (all kinds of craftwork).

But even outside these districts every kind of craftwork was produced. Admittedly sawmill production, boat-building and similar activities are not exactly handcrafts; nevertheless, they were organised in the same way. They were combination occupations that were of decisive importance in regions where the land could not support the local population.

Did the industrial revolution have its starting point in proto-industry, and were the proto-industrial regions the first to be industrialised? The answer depends on the kind of connection we expect—a connection through the workforce and capital or regional homogeneity. We find in Sweden and the other Scandinavian countries factories whose production is based on a proto-industrial phase, even though there are countless cases where no such connection can be proved. Many investigations show that there were proto-industries in most industrialised regions. Proto-industry is perhaps therefore a necessary condition for the later development of factory production, but not in itself a sufficient reason.

Industrialisation also reinforced any regional specialisation that had become more evident in the centuries before the industrial revolution, thanks to the growth of proto-industry and the production of craftwork for sale. To this very day we live with a pattern of localisation that has its roots deep down in agrarian society.

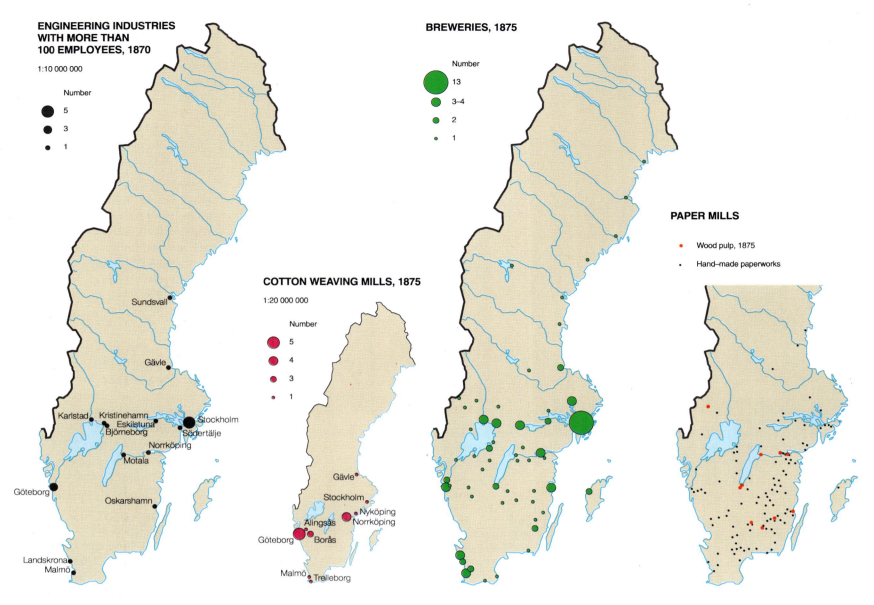

The series of maps above shows the location of some of the more important early industries around 1870. The large towns and coastal settlements in the south of Sweden dominate the picture. The map showing papermills also comprises places where manual paperworks were in operation at some time between 1650 and 1850. (N16, N17, N18, N19)

EARLY INDUSTRIES

Industry in the modern meaning of the word began to develop in Sweden in the early 19th century. Its roots lay in the mills and factories which were established with state support in the 18th century and in the proto-industry that was already firmly established in various parts of the country.

The conditions necessary for industrial companies (raw materials, capital, power, labour, transport and new technology or knowledge) were not usually met in the locations of their predecessors. The various mills and simple mechanical installations such as waterwheels or stamping mills required comparatively little power and had therefore been placed where there were good supplies of charcoal (ironworks) or rags (papermills), which were just as important as a power supply, which was usually provided by a dammed stream. Now the need for power was much greater. Many early industries such as textiles, paper and iron that required large amounts of power were therefore located by large rivers like the Göta Älv or the Motala Ström. Gradually steam replaced water as the main source of power. This meant that access to power was no longer a decisive factor for localisation.

The need for raw materials grew larger and it was no longer feasible to deliver the necessary quantities by horse and cart. This is one of the principal reasons for the development of a new transport network with a greater capacity. The Göta Canal is probably one of the best known of the new transport routes, but it was both preceded and followed by many other canals. Sweden's topography is, however, not favourable for canals. Instead, in the 1860s, the railways offered cheap mass transportation, which facilitated industrial localisation.

The other conditions for industrial production, capital, technology and labour, were more mobile. The fact that an area had had pre-industrial mass production did not necessarily mean that formal industries were located there, even if a trained workforce and capital were available. The Småland iron and paper districts are examples of this type of area; the other, more permanent localisation factors were more decisive. Labour and capital, like ideas and knowledge, had to move to places suitable for large-scale production; these places were often suitable for several types of industry, so complete industrial com-

Motala Engineering Works, one of the oldest and largest in Sweden, was built on an island in Motala Ström. Sweden's first steamship and its first locomotive were built here.

BIRTH–PLACES OF EMPLOYEES, 1855

- Hävla bruk (orange)
- Motala Mekaniska Verkstad (red)

Number of employees
- 125–173
- 75–124
- 30–74
- 13–29
- 3–12
- 1–2

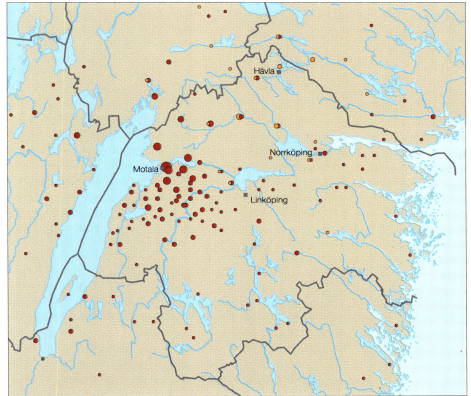

Hävla Mill dates from the late 17th century and was one of the ironworks that were transformed into a modern industrial centre that has survived to this day. During the 19th century various iron products were manufactured apart from the traditional bar iron. The capital generated by pre-industrial production was invested in modernisation and development at the mill, where there were good power supplies and a skilled labour force. When Hävla became a true industrial centre in the 1850s, more labour was needed. This was recruited in the same way as for the mill—from existing or recently closed ironworks. Thus relatively few agricultural workers entered industrial society via Hävla.

Motala Verkstad was established in 1822 to facilitate the construction of the Göta Canal. It quickly became one of Sweden's largest industries with a workforce of more than 1,000 in 1860. Many different products were manufactured here, from puddle iron to boilers, locomotives, bridges and ships. The works was located on a site well provided with waterpower—where Lake Vättern ran out into Motala Ström, a stretch of river where mills, smithies and other industries had grown up since the Middle Ages. As for the workforce, one might have expected that it would have been recruited from the traditional iron industry. In fact quite a large number of the employees came from purely agricultural districts on the Östgöta plain. The skilled workers, however, were usually recruited from previous industries or works. Surprisingly, many workers had work experience which, apart from farm labouring, included some period of "industrial training" at, for example, a cornmill.

munities grew up, not least round railway stations. Such communities, which were typical of the development of 19th-century Sweden, had a great effect on the appearance of the cultural landscape, partly because of their mere existence and size, but also because they attracted labour and capital from other places, where both mills and settlements diminished in size and the forest began to return.

These industries first functioned like large mill communities. Thus the early 19th-century engineering companies often had their own farms to provide their employees with food, and for many years it was also customary to provide them with accommodation. In principle, however, industrialisation meant that the workforce moved away from the agrarian society in which ironworks, factories and other mass production had their roots.

The increasing population, more accessible labour, new technology in both agriculture and proto-industry and a growing demand for various products both at home and, thanks to the Free Trade laws of 1846, abroad, all helped to create the right conditions for industry in Sweden. The transformation of yeoman farming and estate farming was one of the factors that contributed to this development in several ways.

The Urbanised Landscape

The transformation of the cultural landscape in the 20th century is the result of several interacting and mutually dependent processes. Radical rationalisation of the industries that require large areas of land goes hand in hand with rapid industrialisation. More and more people are employed at all levels of trade and commerce. A self-subsistent economy is replaced gradually by a market economy. Public services including research, education, medical care and defence expand. Incomes rise and a welfare state grows up. Living conditions and life styles change radically.

The industrial society is replaced by a service society. The size of families decreases. Household work, above all cooking and washing, is rationalised. Women go out onto the labour market and their financial and social position is strengthened. People are healthier and live longer. Cars become everyman's property and geographical mobility breaks all records. Cultural impulses from abroad increase and become part of everyday life. Immigration increases and Sweden enters a multicultural era.

The physical expression of this structural transformation is in the first place urbanisation and the expansion of communication systems. The number of people living in towns and urban districts in Sweden more than doubled in the fifty years between 1920 and 1970. The old transport routes, coastal shipping and the railways were complemented or replaced by a widespread road network for the steadily increasing number of motor vehicles.

Functionally, places in Sweden grew together into a system. In an initial phase towns were connected for the rapid transport of goods and long-distance business trips. In a second phase a dense network of roads round towns created large local labour and service markets.

Mechanisation, specialisation and large-scale operations had not yet begun to affect farms and agriculture in the 1920s. At Lilla Skattegården in the parish of Borgunda, Västergötland, photographed in 1931, the old times are still evident in the farmhouse built in 1860, and the barn built in 1879.

A PICTURE FROM 1920

A Swedish family in 1920, Margareta (35) and Folke (38) and their children Johan (9), Lisa (7), Rolf (5) and Stina (2) are an ordinary family living in the Swedish countryside. Margareta is a housewife and has a long working day, since meals are largely produced within the home. Margareta looks after the pig and the hens as well as the vegetable garden. Folke is a farm worker on a large farm nearby. The family's income is mainly Folke's wages, 37 kronor a week for a 48-hour working week, but Margareta gets about five kronor a week for piece work she does for a clothes factory in the nearby town. So far the family does not have a radio, a telephone or electricity.

In the early 1920s refrigerators had not yet been invented. Both in town and in the country ice was used for cooling. It could be kept in large blocks covered with sawdust through the whole summer. This photograph shows ice being cut from Lake Ulvsunda for the Stockholm Ice Company in February, 1921.

Buses were a new form of transport. The SJ No 1 bus with its trailer was built in 1921 and put into service on the first SJ bus route between Dingle and Gravarne in Bohuslän on 20 June 1921. The engine developed 40 hp and the bus could carry 14 passengers and a load of 2,000 kg.

The first hydro-electric power station was built at Trollhättan in 1910. The waterfalls at Trollhättan could now be transformed into electric power by means of turbines and generators.

Railways were the most important means of transport for both passengers and freight from the latter part of the 19th century up to the 1930s. The size and architecture of railway stations reflected the importance of the railway towns, as here at Nässjö in 1922.

Elementary schools, compulsory in 1842, had a six-year course from 1878 onwards and were run by the local municipality with State aid. School gymnastics at Norra Finnskoga in the far north of Värmland in the 1920s.

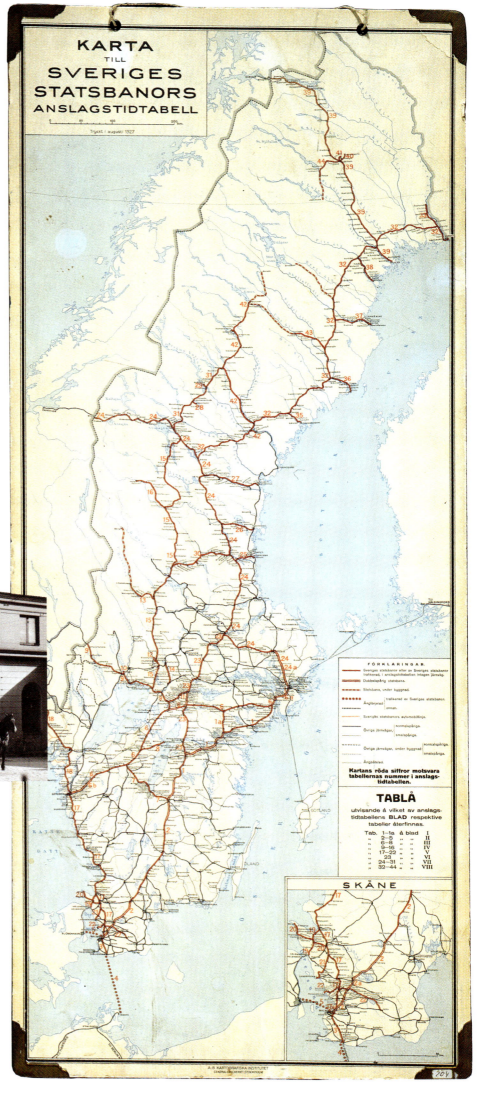

Domestic heating uses a great deal of energy in Sweden. The supply of fuel in the 1920s is illustrated here by Åland schooners unloading firewood at Strandvägen in Stockholm; in the 1990s oil is delivered to the terminal at Sundsvall.

THE TRANSFORMATION OF INDUSTRY

The technical advances in industry and the home between 1920 and 1990 meant radical improvements for both everyday life and working life. The roads were opened up by the removal of countless gates and surfaced with asphalt or oil gravel. Concrete bridges of increasingly large dimensions crossed rivers large and small. Roads and railways were straightened to allow higher speeds. New, broader roads were built, often running parallel with old ones. More and more towns were bypassed. Building technology changed: new materials were introduced. Walls of glass or plaster were used more and more instead of the classical wooden facade.

Hydro-electric power stations dammed the rivers and we got used to having cheap energy. Coal and oil-fired power stations and later nuclear power stations contributed to our energy supplies. The electric power stations in the landscape are surrounded by transmission lines ranging from 400,000 volt high-tension cables to a few remaining wooden poles carrying 12,000 volt cables.

The size of buildings in the landscape became more and more impressive. High-rise blocks began to compete with church spires in the towns. Goods distribution required larger and larger warehouses, terminals and storage centres. Large companies boasted of their international successes by building impressive office blocks. The banks signalled their power in the community by commissioning palace-like headquarters in the big cities.

Out in the country farmers built larger and larger farm buildings equipped with the latest technology. Countless old unwanted buildings were demolished. Second homes became a feature of the landscape, often in special holiday estates. Radio and later television masts transmitted their messages to aerials on chimneys and roofs. Recently satellite dishes have become a common sight on houses.

The most audible element in the landscape is the car. Without cars our modern society would not function. Almost four million cars and lorries are seen, heard and smelt in our environment today.

While a Swede in the 1920s would hear the church bells ring on a Sunday, he is more likely to hear a motor mower in the 1990s.

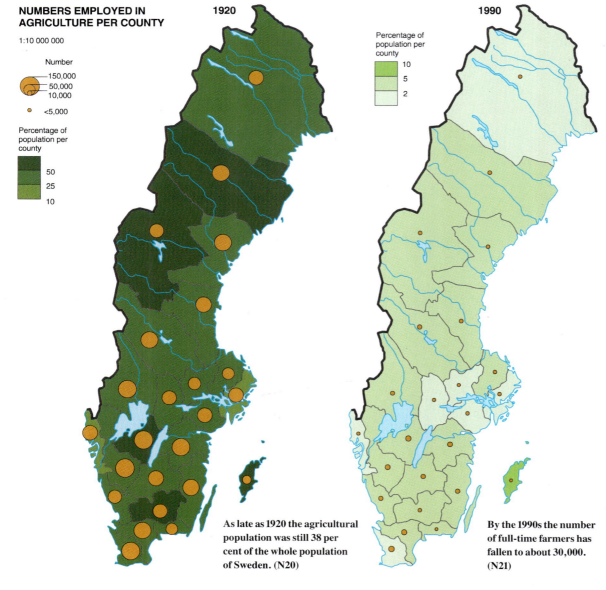

NUMBERS EMPLOYED IN AGRICULTURE PER COUNTY
1:10 000 000

Number
- 150,000
- 50,000
- 10,000
- <5,000

Percentage of population per county
- 50
- 25
- 10

1920 — As late as 1920 the agricultural population was still 38 per cent of the whole population of Sweden. (N20)

1990 — Percentage of population per county: 10, 5, 2. By the 1990s the number of full-time farmers has fallen to about 30,000. (N21)

The transformation of industry does not leave immediate traces in the landscape in a unambiguous fashion. In fact the difference between what is shown by statistics and what we see around us is so large that we can speak of a visual misunderstanding (VM).

The concept of visual misunderstanding was coined in a study of industry in Uppsala. Roughly speaking we can say that most people believed that Uppsala was dominated by undergraduate life in 1920. The students' white caps and the university's impressive buildings were the most evident features of street life. In reality, however, the town was dominated by commerce, craft industries and small, cramped factory premises. When statistics showed a major growth in the number of students and a decrease in the number of industrial employees in the 1950s and 1960s, many people believed the reverse to be true. The students had stopped wearing their white caps, so they were no longer evident in the streets. Big, new, rational factories and warehouses grew up round the town centre, giving a false impression of a great increase in industrial employment, although the opposite was the case.

New technical advances used to be inseparable from economic growth. We are both able to and can afford to do what we like with the landscape with our new machines. It has been said that we Swedes move more earth in our country than the combined forces of erosion.

The main country roads, the oldest of which dated back to the 17th century, had not yet been rebuilt for motor traffic in 1920, but the gates were removed at this time. Speeds were low and journeys bumpy. The few cars on the roads attracted great attention. Today's streams of traffic roar down smooth, broad asphalted roads. Exhaust fumes and noise have become environmental problems.

Vast amounts of labour were required to link the country toghether with heavy copper telephone cables. Today's fibre-optical cable network was laid at express speed for our computer socciety. In 1990 two men with machines could do the work it took 20 men to do in 1920.

Changes in retailing between 1920 and 1990 can be summed up as: from village store to supermarket. The former type of shop is represented here by The Cooperative Shop *Framtid* at Immeln, Östra Göinge in Skåne in 1931, the latter type by a supermarket and carpark which could be almost anywhere in Sweden—or the world.

FEATURES OF THE LANDSCAPE

The features of the landscape made by man generally speaking looked the same in 1990 as they did in 1920. They are also connected by the same topographical logic.

If we study the details more closely, we note that the dwelling houses have become larger. Features like airports have increased in number, while others have disappeared, like the barges that carried firewood and their quays.

The road network has become more dense, but the railway network has diminished and industries have moved away from high-rise blocks in towns to space-demanding single-storey buildings outside towns. Factory chimneys have become less common. The mountains of coal and coke one used to see in ports have been replaced by oil storage tanks. Natural forests have been replaced by uniform plantations.

A REVOLUTION IN MOBILITY

Our geographical mobility has changed dramatically during the 20th century. On average a Swede travelled at the most a couple of kilometres a day in 1920. The corresponding figure for 1990 was about 40 kilometres. Commuter journeys now account for a quarter of all travelling. The greatest change came with the breakthrough of motorism. Today almost one Swede in two has a car and each car covers more than 13,000 km a year. Every third kilometre driven by a car is either a journey to or from work or a business trip. Domestic airlines, which are principally financed by business travel, have expanded to become some sort of everyman's means of travel, thanks to heavy subsidies for students and pensioners.

This increased mobility demands good communication routes. Sweden has 50 metres of road and 1.3 metres of railway track for every Swede; in addition there have to be car parks and other areas for traffic systems, both indoors and outdoors.

Roads occupy more space than any other constructions in the landscape, both in and outside towns. The difference between roads in 1920 and today is not only that there are more of them and that they are wider. The enormously increased intensity of traffic, creating noise and pollution

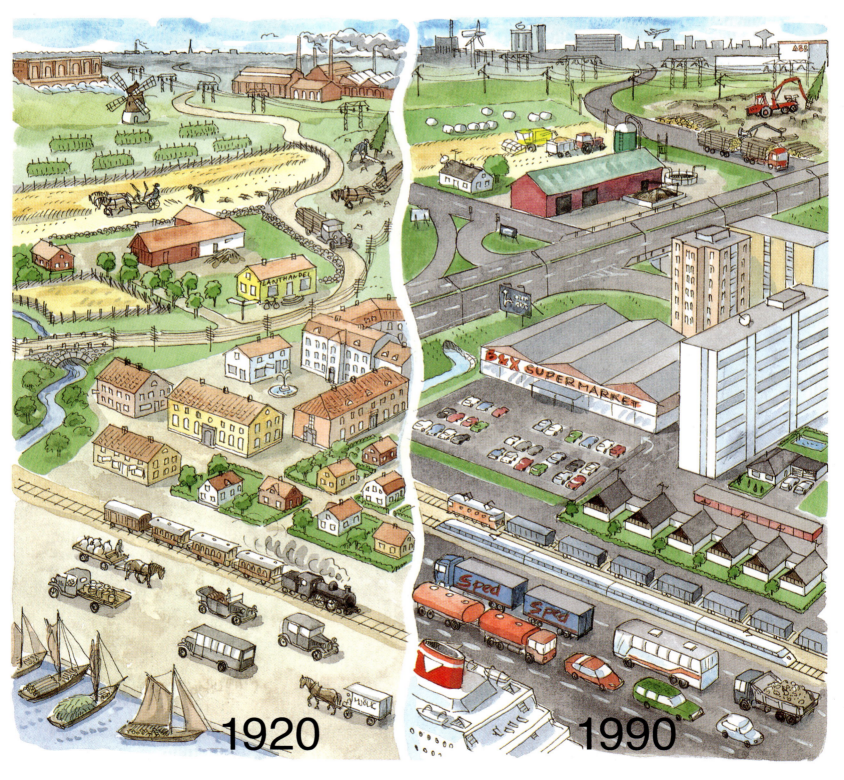

1920   1990

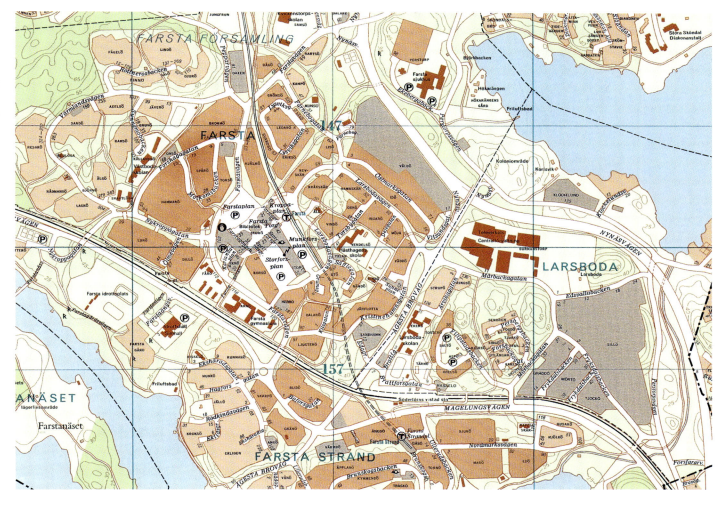

Traffic demands more and more space in and round towns. Farsta, a southern suburb of Stockholm built in the 1960s, is well served by a motorway and an underground line. The white areas and lines on the map are car-parks, roads and paths, the broader ones for cars, the narrower ones for pedestrians.

The photograph of the yard outside the München Brewery in Stockholm in 1931 gives some idea of the short-distance transport system which had not changed much over the centuries. A container terminal in 1990 illustrates today's wholly mechanised and standardised transport system.

problems, has changed the landscape qualitatively.

In 1920 there were just over ten metres of road per inhabitant, three metres of which were classified as country highways. As for road width, it was stated that it "should be about 2.5 metres for every lane of traffic, so that vehicles can safely use the road, which means about 5 metres for two lanes of traffic. If two ordinary vehicles are to be able to meet, the width should not be less than four metres." The width of a country highway was traditionally 6 metres, plus ditches, if any. The road surface consisted of a 10–20 cm thick layer of gravel or broken stone on a 20–40 cm thick base of stone. The gradient of a country highway was not to exceed 1:20.

In 1990 each inhabitant had about 50 metres of road, of which 1.5 m was trunk road, 10 m country highway, 4 m county road and 32 m private road. Half the road network was open for public traffic. Road width varied normally from about three metres for small private roads up to 16 m for major roads with two lanes in each direction. A motorway could be as much as 50 m broad and a roundabout could occupy 4 ha of land. It has been calculated that between 15 and 20 per cent of the area of a Swedish town was taken up by traffic.

A suburb is a built-up area outside the centre of a town. The distinction between the centre and its suburbs may sometimes be difficult to see. Old suburbs built before the car was common property are close to the centre or round railway stations. Trams and to an even greater extent buses allowed later suburbs to spread out over large areas.

CONCENTRATED LIVING PATTERNS

Urbanisation is manifested principally in the growth of towns and the depopulation of the countryside. It has been in progress for about 100 years and is now more or less completed. We have to go back to the time of the Great Migrations to find an equally radical change in the whole settlement pattern of both Sweden and Europe. Geographers describe urbanisation as the increasing concentration of work places and dwellings. Functionally this is connected with the growth of the large-scale production of goods and services.

Originally governed by the demands of working life, urbanisation has now become more and more evidently governed by young people's desire to enjoy town life. It is usual for young Swedes to move to places that are larger than their home towns. This phenomenon is sometimes called the city lights effect. The throb of city life is magnetic.

The physical growth of towns and urban districts was usually preceded by general and detailed planning, but these plans were adapted to meet reality as regards the terrain and land ownership. For example, privately-owned undeveloped land could more easily be expropriated for expansion than state-owned land belonging to the church or the Ministry of Defence.

Within these urban districts and towns the functions of buildings became more specialised. Large, continuous residential estates without work places, and business and industrial estates without houses became more and more common. The dream of having a house of one's own continued to be realised, and large districts of private houses grew up outside town centres.

While the characteristic feature of old towns was a concentrated, small-scale environment of courtyards, streets and enclosed squares, the ideology of the new 1920s town architecture was openness, with buildings far apart from each other and large open spaces of grass or small bushes between them. Especially during the building boom of the 1960s and 1970s, the big-is-beautiful philosophy dominated the residential estates, which were placed far from the old town centres. Sparsely built-up areas and decentralisation were clearly the guidelines for town planning, from the national level down to the placing of individual high-rise apartment blocks.

In between these two levels, it became popular to build suburbs.

A suburb is an urban area outside a town centre. The boundary line between the centre and a suburb may be difficult to distinguish; old suburbs were built before cars were everyman's property and are therefore situated near the town centre or along a railway line. New suburbs, connected to a town only by car or bus, have been built for the last thirty or forty years.

In 1920 there were 110 towns according to the legal Swedish definition. With only a few exceptions, however, these towns were also the largest agglomerations of urban areas in the country. Of Sweden's 5.9 million inhabitants at that time, 30 per cent lived in towns.

Today there are about 110 urban areas with more than 10,000 inhabitants; they may be looked upon as today's towns, as defined by their size. Today 55 per cent of the present population of 8.5 million live in these towns.

If instead we use the same definition by size for urban districts in 1920 and 1990 and choose the usual international definition, which is places with more than 2,000 inhabitants, the percentage of the urban population in Sweden has doubled since the 1920 figure of 36 per cent. Today more

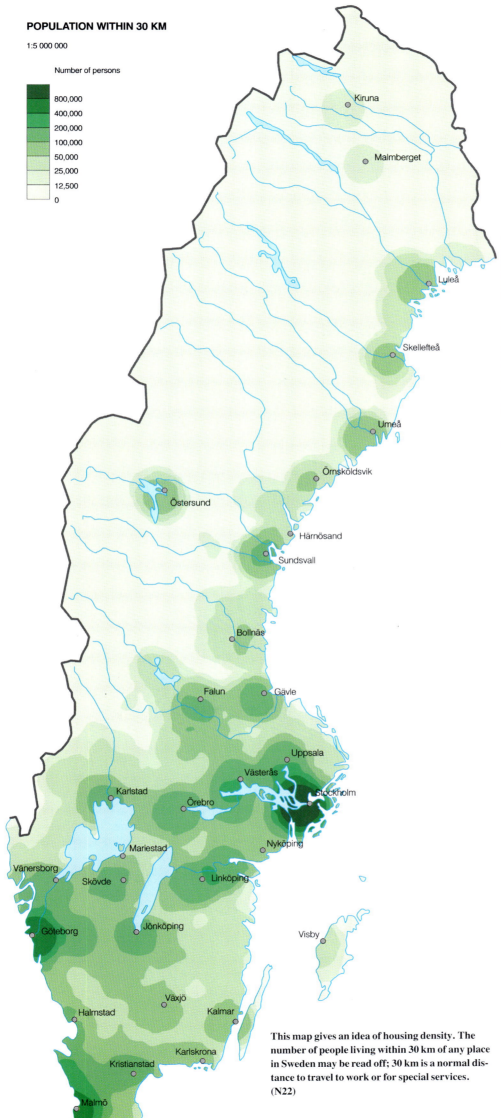

POPULATION WITHIN 30 KM

1:5 000 000

Number of persons
- 800,000
- 400,000
- 200,000
- 100,000
- 50,000
- 25,000
- 12,500
- 0

This map gives an idea of housing density. The number of people living within 30 km of any place in Sweden may be read off; 30 km is a normal distance to travel to work or for special services. (N22)

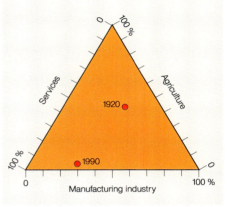

This triangular diagram sums up the transformation of society during the 20th century, from an agricultural and rural society to an urbanised industrial and service society.

than three out of four Swedes live in such urban agglomerations.

In 1920 slightly more than every other Swede (55%) lived in rural districts. The urbanisation phase which had been in progress for a century was almost half completed. The concentration of settlements in urban districts and towns can be explained by both push effects like unemployment and pull effects like a surplus of vacant jobs, but a freer life style and better services are also thought to attract migrants to towns.

By 1990 urbanisation was a more or less completed process, but migration is still taking place between urban districts, mainly from small places to larger ones. Only every seventh Swede lives outside an urban area. The industries which demand large areas of land employ less than four per cent of the work force. Nowadays Swedes live and work in urban areas. Every fifth inhabitant lives in one of the three big cities, Stockholm, Göteborg and Malmö. One in three lives in a large town, that is, in one of the other urban areas with more than 50,000 inhabitants. Another 20 per cent live in other towns, that is, urban areas with between 10,000 and 50,000 inhabitants.

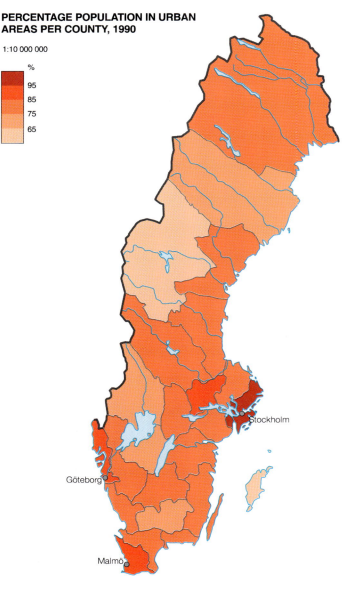

PERCENTAGE POPULATION IN URBAN AREAS PER COUNTY, 1990

1:10 000 000

%
- 95
- 85
- 75
- 65

Urbanisation has reached such a stage in the whole of Sweden that the differences between counties in percentage of people living in urban areas are now (1990) very small. If the definition of an urban area was higher, there would be greater differences. (N23)

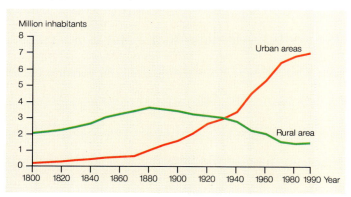

With the low definition of an urban area (200 persons in a built-up area) the rising curve for the urban population in Sweden crossed the falling curve for the rural population as early as 1930.

GROWTH OF URBAN AREAS

The official population statistics make it possible to follow the development of towns and rural districts over five-year periods from 1800 onwards. It is also possible to study the development of individual towns from this date.

Throughout the 19th century the towns' formal boundaries actually coincided fairly well with their administrative areas. But with the arrival of industrialism and the railways a number of new places had grown up outside towns in the form of suburbs, railway settlements and industrial settlements. Towards the turn of the century it became increasingly necessary to include these new urban developments in the statistics.

The 1900 census included figures not only for administrative districts in the form of *towns, urban districts* and *municipal districts* but also for "urban-like communities", later called "urban communities in rural districts". From 1920 onwards the term *agglomerations* is used more or less as it is today. The term *built-up area* (*tätort*) was first used in 1930.

In the course of the 20th century another reason emerged for recording *urban districts/rural districts*. Many towns were now incorporating large rural areas, with the result that a town could include both rural populations and several small places apart from the central town. The two reforms of the municipalities which took place after the Second World War meant that almost all municipalities had one or more built-up areas. In the end the administrative term *town* was abolished altogether in 1971.

Up until the 1950 census it was the parish civil registration offices that decided what was to be counted as a built-up area, based on instructions from Statistics Sweden (SCB). Nevertheless, there were different interpretations in different places, which made comparisons difficult. The 1960 census contained two innovations: boundaries were marked on large-scale maps so that built-up areas were clearly defined in size; and all boundaries were determined by one person in order to get comparable results. This system was still in use in 1990, which meant that it was also possible to report the size of built-up areas at that time.

In 1960 a common Scandinavian definition of a built-up area was agreed. In brief this said that a built-up area is any collection of buildings with a population of at least 200, provided the distance between buildings does not normally exceed 200 metres. On top of this there is a not unimportant criterion concerning urban land use. Such land is counted as part of a built-up area and can sometimes connect various belts of urban development. When urban area boundaries are drawn, no attention is paid to existing municipal boundaries.

It is also important to remember that towns and urban districts include by definition both land and people. In SCB's reports on built-up areas there are therefore demographic statistics as well as area statistics.

During the expansive 1960s there were many people who feared that large parts of Sweden's farmland would be covered with asphalt. Built-up areas at that time comprised only 0.80% of Sweden's total land area. Since then the urbanised area has grown fairly slowly, to 0.98% when the boundaries were first drawn in 1970, 1.17% in 1980 and 1.23% at the latest census in 1990. Even after the population stopped growing in towns and other urban areas, their built-up area continued to increase as a result of the increasing demand for land for housing estates. A decreasing amount of this expansion of built-up areas has occurred on farmland. But urbanisation also leads to demands for large areas of land for industries, warehouses, roads, airports and so on, all close to built-up areas and often on flat farmland. Altogether this, plus built-up areas, amounts to about 2.5 per cent of the area of Sweden, compared with 7.8 per cent for arable land.

The maps of built-up areas have also been used to find out how much "public-access land" (according to the law of free access to private land) is available for outdoor recreation close to towns. As one might expect, this resource varies greatly with different types of landscape. Umeå, for example, had 160 ha of such land per 1,000 inhabitants within a zone of 3 km^2, Uppsala had 50 ha while Lund had only 5 ha per 1,000 inhabitants.

The areas that lie outside built-up areas in the report are classified generally as rural areas although they may contain private houses, countryside, forestland and uninhabited land. A great many rural areas are connected through employment and industry with built-up areas by commuting. All

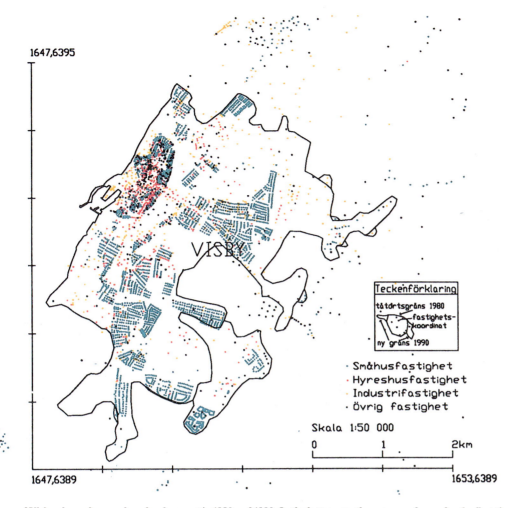

areas within 30 km from a built-up area with at least 2,000 inhabitants (urbanised rural area) are included here. Only 100,000 people live in the remaining genuine rural areas.

The above figures may explain why the rural population in the 1900 census increased for the first time in the 20th century by 21,000. This increase is in the big-city counties and Kopparberg, where it is largely the result of second homes becoming permanent dwellings. Especially round Stockholm and Göteborg this trend has also led to the establishment of a number of new built-up areas that are reported in the 1990 statistics. In those cases where the population of a built-up area has fallen below 200, the "built-up area population" is reported statistically as having decreased and the "rural-district populations" as having increased!

The map of Visby above shows urban development in 1980 and 1990. In the latter year the map was drawn for the first time with the aid of the computerised coordinate system of the central real estate data. The aerial photograph taken in 1986 emphasises the differences in land use and vegetation.

In as short a time as ten years changes in population and buildings lead to considerable changes in the statistical status of small places. (N24)

CHANGES IN PLACES DEFINED AS URBAN AREAS (>200 INHABITANTS), 1980–90

1:10 000 000

- Added
- Removed

EMPLOYMENT BY INDUSTRY, PER COUNTY, 1990

1:5 000 000

Number of employees
- 1,000,000
- 500,000
- 100,000

- 🟢 Agriculture, forestry etc.
- ⬛ Manufacturing industries etc.
- 🟦 Private services sector
- 🟥 Public sector

Percentage employees of all population
%
50
45

In our modern society most working people are employed in some part of the service sector, which in 1990 was mainly in the public sector. (N25)

A PICTURE FROM THE 1990s

A typical Swedish family in 1990 lives in a town of about 50,000 inhabitants. Most households do not have any children at home, but in our example the husband is 40, the wife 38 and the two children 9 and 11. The family earns 120,000 kronor net (disposable income after tax) a year, which is enough to own a house in the suburbs and run a car. They share a small country cottage with the wife's parents. The family's home was built in 1950 and has been renovated. It has 110 m² of floor space, with a toilet, bathroom, electric central heating and a well-equipped kitchen.

Parts of the family's consumption have limited effects on the urban landscape, such as watching television (90 minutes per person per day), reading newspapers and magazines or listening to the radio (about 140 minutes per person per day).

Other parts, such as the family's geographical mobility, have major effects. They travel a great deal during the week, at the weekends and on holidays—altogether 60,000 km a year. The reasons for travelling are in order of importance: leisure activities, commuting to work (mostly the husband), visits to relatives and shopping. The family consumes 0.7 tonnes of food and almost four tonnes of beverages a year. The family sends 1.3 tonnes of rubbish to the town dump every year, half of which is used to produce heating and the rest as landfill. The consumption of energy (electricity, 23,000 kWh/year, petrol 1.5 tonnes/year) also requires physical facilities in the landscape.

In the 1980s attempts were made at Skarpnäcksfältet in the south of Stockholm to recreate the "town atmosphere" of old times with enclosed spaces and variation in architecture, a clear internal organisation and an urban character in streets, squares and parks.

There are hundreds of large antennae in Sweden that radiate or receive electromagnetic waves such as radio waves. Most of them are owned by Telia (formerly Swedish Telecom).

The new producers of energy include the nuclear power stations at Forsmark, Oskarshamn and Barsebäck. There are also experimental stations based on renewable forms of energy, solar energy and wind power. In 1988 there were only eight large wind-power stations producing a total of 11 GWh on average.

Sweden has about 200 airports, 25 of which are major public airports with one or more tarmac runways up to three kilometres long. Taxiways, aprons and hard standings, hangars, control towers, terminal buildings, fuel depots, radio beacons and runway lighting systems are physical elements which together create an airport's morphology.

Uppsala University, founded in 1477 and the oldest in Sweden, is in one of the country's six university towns. In 1920 a total of just over 5,000 undergraduates studied at these universities. The corresponding figure in 1990 was just over 170,000. In spite of this large increase Sweden has only half as many people with university degrees per 1,000 inhabitants as the USA, for example.

Cultural Landscape Regions

Regional Variations and Regional Divisions

Regional divisions are useful for various purposes; they can be infinite in number. Sometimes they are made for official purposes and are of legal or economic significance, for example administrative divisions or companies' operational or sales areas. Divisions may be made for purely scientific purposes as well, for reports of regional analyses, or for educational purposes, to give information about Sweden. Divisions can be based on one single phenomenon or on a mix of many factors, which can be distributed rather differently. The choice of boundaries is therefore often subjective and would differ according to the writer of the report. Here we give some examples of divisions, only two of which are more or less officially recognised.

AN ANTHROPOLOGICAL DIVISION

Gustaf Sundbärg, a statistician, found clear demographical differences in Sweden. A dividing line between east and west Sweden was called the Flodström line after a scientist who thought it represented a dividing line between different ethnical groups. Many cultural phenomena differ on either side of this line; it may also be explained as the meeting zone of the cultural impulses that spread on the one hand from Mälardalen and on the other hand from Skåne-Denmark.

STEN DE GEER, 1920

In 1920 Sten de Geer developed a system for the geographical description of Sweden that divided the country into "district types", whereby both natural features and human settlements were assessed. His system is still of interest for geographers.

NATURAL GEOGRAPHICAL REGIONS

The Nordic Council commissioned a system for dividing Scandinavia into natural geographical regions for the purpose of conserving the countryside and natural resources. These regions mainly reflect differences in natural vegetation.

NATURAL AGRICULTURAL REGIONS

The natural agricultural regions (production districts) were set up for statistical purposes. They were based on local conditions affecting agriculture such as soil quality, topography and local climate. For practical reasons their boundaries were adapted to suit administrative districts to facilitate statistics.

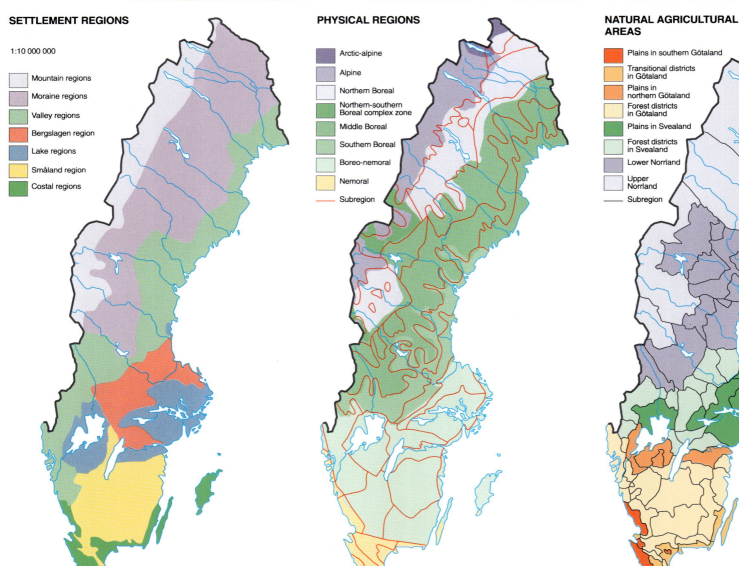

DEMOGRAPHIC REGIONS ACCORDING TO G SUNDBÄRG, 1910

INDUSTRIAL REGIONS ACCORDING TO WILLIAM-OLSSON

During Sweden's long industrial history different parts of the country have at times been characterised by some form of specialisation which is still apparent in the landscape but which from an economic-geographical point of view largely belongs to the past. Some of the specific industrial regions that William William-Olsson was able to identify in his survey during the 1940s and 1950s have in fact totally disappeared, while others have declined or been transformed. The shoe industry, the textile industry, the steel industry and mining are examples of these changes. Many new modern industries in the landscape hardly differ from office buildings or blocks of flats. One example is the high-tech industrial suburb of Kista to the north of Stockholm. As a result of changes in the latter half of the 20th century many districts in Sweden have lost much of their special character; iniformity is growing.

STANDARD SPOKEN SWEDISH

1. South Swedish diphthongisation, back r and the sje sound; rising intonation followed by a slow fall at the end of the sentence; tense throat sound in many parts of Småland.
2. Diphthongisation in Mälardalen (e/ä after long vowels), merging of short e and ä, open ä and ö before r, and slightly falling intonation at the end of the sentence.
3. Open long and short ä and ö, back sje sound, in stronger dialectal variants an open å sound (in korv, for example), burred r (back r at the beginning of words) and a dark l; high intonation at the end.
4. Secondary Gotland diphthongisation, å-like pronunciation of the long o; sharply falling intonation.
5. U pronounced as the central vowel (u), acute accent in many compound words, sharply falling intonation at the end of sentences.
6. In parts of the area short u pronounced as the central vowel (u), dark l and main stress on the last element in some compound words; relatively moderate falling intonation early before the end.

DIALECTS

Dialects (grek. 'diálektos' = speech, manner of speaking) are the variants spoken within certain geographical areas of a language. The variants may occur in pronunciation, vocabulary, phraseology and so on. Dialects developed in an agrarian society where districts were relatively isolated from one another. They run the risk of disappearing in an urbanised society with great population mobility and national media coverage.

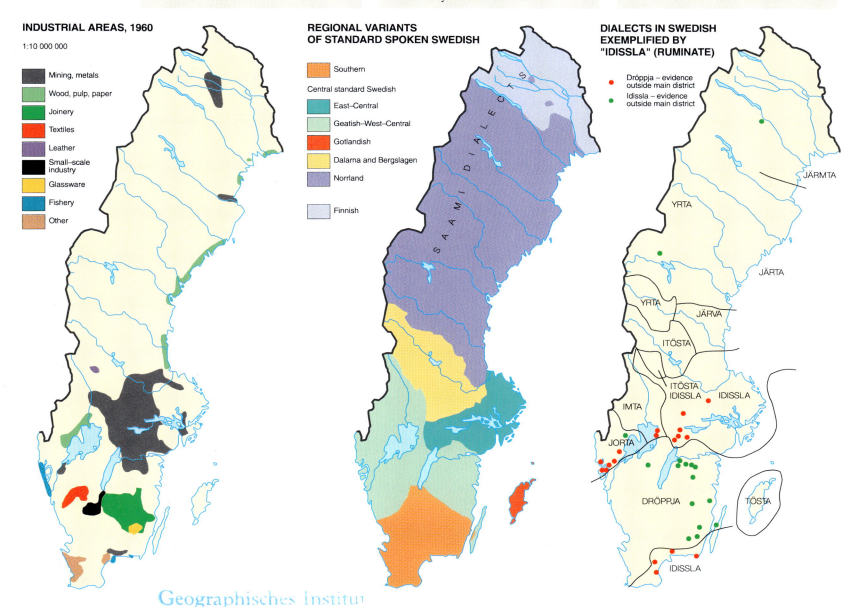

Sweden's Cultural Landscape—a Regional Description

Urban and agrarian features are central for the classification of the landscape. A landscape is considered agrarian if it has not been affected to any visible degree by urbanisation and industrialisation since 1850. Where the opposite is the case, urban and industrial landscapes form the basis of regional divisions and determine their boundaries.

The aim is to divide Sweden into some 50 regions for educational and practical purposes. This is needed, for example, when decisions have to be made concerning conservation. More of the regions are in the south of Sweden and fewer in the north, the reason being quite simply that the landscape is more varied and more affected by cultural influences in the south than in the north.

The way in which the regions are described is not systematic but rather impressionistic. The boundaries are seldom clearly defined but are more like transitional zones. Where the lines are drawn and how the regions are characterised is based on many years' research into the Swedish cultural landscape. Features that are common to many regions have not been included systematically in all the descriptions. Red, wooden cottages are an example of this. Five criteria in particular have been selected to characterise the regions.

Österlen from the north with Rörum in the foreground, "Apple Land" round Kivik to the left, the forest-clad slopes of Linderödsåsen and beyond, the plain between Simrishamn and Ystad

THE NATURAL LANDSCAPE

The natural landscape includes the major features of the landscape (topography and geology) and its soils (surface covering) that have encouraged cultivation. The location of the region above or below the highest shoreline is also usually noted if this is significant for settlement. The hydrological features of the landscape also play a major role.

CHARACTER OF THE VEGETATION

In the first place we note the relationship between broad-leafed and coniferous forest and how dense the forest is, but also other important types of vegetation such as grassland, bare heaths and the like. The types of crops that are cultivated and the topographical location of cultivated land also affect the character created by the vegetation.

SETTLEMENTS AND FORMS OF LAND USE

In the first place we consider the settlement structure of the landscape, its economic features and degree of urbanisation. The form and location of agrarian settlements is studied as well as land use in rural districts and the ways in which cultivated land has been structured.

REGIONAL FEATURES

In the first place we concentrate on cultural features that have strongly influenced settlements and the landscape. In some regions these features are being lost as the landscape is abandoned or changed.

NAMES AND BOUNDARIES

As far as possible we have tried to use place names that are traditional and firmly established in the regions. Where appropriate we have let the boundaries follow administrative boundaries. Regional names which are less definite like Österlen and Roslagen have been used but do not form the basis of regional boundaries. These names are given in italics on the map.

The plains of southern Skåne. A gently rolling landscape. The soil is fine-grained and calciferous. The southern plains are Sweden's most fertile farmland. Competition for land is intense. The non-urbanised part of the plains consists of large fields and the relics of shore meadows, with holiday homes along the coast. Agrarian settlements are characterised by the scattered farms created by the *enskifte* of the 18th and 19th centuries. Here and there old villages stand round a school and a whitewashed church with stepped gables. Red-brick or whitewashed half-timbered farmhouses are a characteristic feature, with barns and stables built of granite. Long, low buildings with steeply-pitched roofs are traditional.

In the urbanised part of south-west Skåne the towns lie close together. Like Lund, several towns have medieval town centres. There is a dense network of roads, including several motorways. The open landscape surrounding the nuclear power station at Barsebäck is criss-crossed with power lines.

South-east Skåne is more rural. The open plain is well cultivated and scattered with farmhouses and churches, in many places offering splendid views of the coast and the sea. Old shipping and fishing villages are now used for summer holidays. The architecture consists of isolated whitewashed farmhouses built at an angle or enclosing a courtyard, and of villages with low cottages lining the streets. Red brick is a characteristic feature of small central places and railway communities which expanded around 1900. The plain contains some hilly areas covered with beech woods and lakes.

Lake and horst district of inner Skåne. This area comprises Romeleåsen, the low-lying landscape round Lake Vombsjön and the Ringsjö lakes and the northern parts of Österlen. In the past broad-leafed forest and pastureland were predominant on Romeleåsen, but nowadays there are spruce plantations. Many of Skåne's large estates stand on the ridge and the area surrounding it. To the east the region ends at Fyledalen.

The open arable land in the north of the area is the Skåne of smallholdings. Here we find dense agrarian settlements and many small villages, but there are several estates here, too. The region has many railway communities and former railway junctions—relics of the once dense railway network.

To the north and the east lies more forested and rocky ground on Linderödsåsen, including Stenshuvud. The Kivik district is famous for its fruit and soft fruit, and the Brösarp district for its open grassland.

Dawn breaks over Brösarps Backar, a pasture landscape of national interest in eastern Skåne.

East of Helsingborg the plain has been transformed by motorways, with a clover-leaf junction at Kropp.

North-west Skåne. The Bjäre peninsula and Kullaberg are dominant heights in an otherwise flat area of intensively cultivated land, using highly mechanised agricultural methods to grow specialities such as early potatoes and greenhouse produce. The agrarian buildings are fairly scattered, a feature dating back to the old land divisions here.

The port and industrial town of Helsingborg is also the meeting point of some of Sweden's most important roads, including the E4 and E6 motorways. The roads here are a dominant feature of the landscape.

The coast of the Sound is very urbanised, including quite a few holiday home estates.

The Bjäre peninsula has an undulating, highly cultivated landscape and specialises in early crops, thanks to its very favourable climate. A few beech woods stand on the heights. Along the coast to the north and west there are still shore meadows used for grazing. The landscape is dominated by agrarian buildings, but along the coast there are holiday cottages, especially round Skälderviken.

Forest area of northern Skåne. The whole of this area lies above the highest shoreline and the soil is mainly till. The landscape is hilly with plenty of lakes and is cultivated to a varying extent round both villages and isolated farms. There are plenty of broadleafed woods, but large areas have been planted with spruce. The stone walls round the fields are a characteristic feature. Most of them were built as a result of the land reforms of the 19th century.

The northern part of the region, Göinge, consists mainly of districts colonised in the Middle Ages, with a low level of cultivation and characteristic isolated farmsteads. There are still large areas of broad-leaved woods, principally beech. Villands Vånga is famous for its fruit orchards.

Kristianstad plain. This is an open landscape with easily cultivated soils and intensive cultivation. There are protective belts of forest planted along the sandy coast. Agriculture concentrates on commercial crops, mainly potatoes. Most of the many scattered industries, dairies, distilleries, sugar works and starch factories, are now closed down. There are plenty of large estates with manor houses, farm buildings, avenues and parks.

Listerlandet may also be included in this region. Its topography is characterised by long, narrow drumlins on whose crests houses have often been built. There is still grazing ground to the south. Some of the farms are mink farms. To the north there are long villages running round the arable land on the bed of the former Lake Vesan. This open plain is the result of one of the few successful attempts to lower the level of lakes in Sweden.

Blekinge. The old national border between Sweden and Denmark is the northern limit of this region. Hamlets are found here above the highest shoreline, mostly consisting of isolated farms or groups of farms which have grown up as a result of the late division of isolated farms surrounded by a landscape of meadows and grazing land that is well preserved in many places.

Towards the south valley settlements with relatively large differences in height, well-preserved villages and hamlets are more common. In the zone towards the more cultivated areas, crofts stand close together on geometric patterns of plots dating from the 18th century.

Mainly north of Highway E22 we meet relatively well-defined districts which have developed in the sediment-filled fissure valleys which run north and south. Some examples are the Ramdala plain, with its large estates formed in the 18th century, the oak and beech landscape round Johannishus and the valley of the Bräkneån with its large farms.

In the coast zone there are fishing villages, abandoned quarries, and farming on meadows and grazing grounds. Much of the Blekinge coast, however, has been taken over by summer cottages and holiday homes. In the centre, Karlskrona, established as a naval base in the 1680s, has Sweden's most characteristic Baroque town plan.

Southern Halland. The Laholm plain is fairly flat and has sandy soils. Cattle farming is extensive here. Cultivation is intensive, but large fields are a relatively late phenomenon. Here, as in neighbouring districts, one-field farming was predominant, with large stretches of meadows. A protective belt of pine trees was planted along the coast in the 19th century. The coastline has been strongly affected by holiday homes.

The inner part of the area is sparsely cultivated, with mainly isolated farms. The forest plantations are fairly recent. Previously there were extensive heaths here, which have been preserved in a few places like Mästocka.

Further north, too, the region is agricultural, with many holiday homes along the coast. Inland the West Coast railway line created a number of railway communities, and at the junctions of the E6 and along the country highways there are supermarkets and industrial premises.

The cultivated districts lie in the river valleys running down from the highlands in the east. In this transitional zone with its many lakes there are broad-leafed woods, mainly beech, but also some spruce plantations. The Småland border country above the highest shoreline is characterised by isolated farms, a low level of cultivation and bogland. Coniferous plantations have recently been planted on former heathland.

Northern Halland. The coastline is famous for its cliffs. The great Fjärås ridge formed in the Ice Marginal Zone marks the beginning of the forest districts to the east.

The coast is scattered with holiday homes, but here, too, there are older settlements connected with shipping, in which the old Captain's Houses, as they are called, are a well-known feature. The area behind the coast is agricultural, with a good deal of cattle farming. The settlements are in the form of villages or scattered farmsteads created by land reform. Towards the Västergötland border there are spruce plantations on former heaths, but also oak and beech woods.

In the north the area is affected by its proximity to Göteborg, containing many stables and other semi-urban buildings. This is particularly true of the Onsala peninsula. Ringhals nuclear power station and Värö papermill are landmarks on the Särö peninsula.

Central and southern Småland. The southern part of this area, which corresponds to the old Värend district, lies above the highest shoreline, but the plains in the centre are formed mainly of lake sediment. In the south there are fairly small height differences, while in the north the landscape is

The coastline of the archipelago at Tjust in the north of Kalmar County is a landscape of fissure valleys.

more hilly. In the central districts and round the big lakes large, open fields are common. Spruce forests dominate the eastern parts in particular.

The agricultural settlements are loose-knit, irregular villages in the central districts and isolated farms, mostly abandoned, on the periphery. Sirkön and the area south of Åsnen have specialised in growing fruit.

Furniture manufacturing and the many glassworks have set their mark on the eastern part of the region. There are few large towns. The main railway line to the south, however, has a few small towns along its route. Another area, corresponding to the old Finnveden and Njudung, is mostly situated above the highest shoreline. It has relatively small height differences. Spruce forests fill the western part, but large areas are also covered by bogland. Only in the Lagan valley and in the district north of Lake Bolmen is there any open landscape. There are no large towns but many small ones like Anderstorp and Gnosjö, whose small industries produce varied articles and components.

To the north the agricultural settlements are often found on high ground with fine till.

Northern Småland and Hökensås. This region is part of the South Swedish highlands, with large height differ-

ences and dramatic scenery here and there, as in the landscape round Jönköping. The eastern shore of Lake Vättern and the island of Visingsö are fairly intensively cultivated, with many fruit orchards. Elsewhere there are islands of arable land in the forest-clad landscape. The settlements are mostly small hamlets consisting of two to four farmsteads, in Småland often on geometrically-patterned plots. The land is also cultivated there along rivers and lakes. Jönköping-Huskvarna is the largest town, where some of southern Sweden's most important roads meet.

North-east Småland. This region lies both below and above the highest shoreline. Particularly in the north there are relatively large height differences. There is scattered cultivation in small villages or on isolated farms surrounded by cultivated vegetation (pollarded trees). In some places, however, there are large villages, some of which have geometrically-patterned plots dating from the 18th century. In the Emån valley there are extensive stretches of arable fields and meadows, the latter related to the meandering river and its tributaries. On both sides of the valley place names ending in -*rum*, -*ryd* and -*måla* indicate that the district was colonised in the Middle Ages.

Visingsö, connected with medieval Swedish kings and Count Per Brahe, seen from the north.

Öland. The whole of the island stands on limestone rock which has created a hydrographical system of wetlands, marshes and underground rivers. The landscape is very flat, which leads to great variations in soil moisture.

Öland is agricultural in character, with intensive cultivation along the coast. There is some specialisation in onions, kidney beans and sugarbeet.

The inner parts of the island are covered by Stora Alvaret (a heath) of formerly culturally-influenced but now overgrown grazing ground with a thin covering of soil and rocky outcrops. The Mittland forest is one of Sweden's largest unbroken stretches of broad-leafed forest with some forest meadows. This forest is of relatively recent date and is in fact an example of natural reforestation. In many places the settlements are in the form of long linear villages along the Littorina and Ancylus ridges, often with regular plots created in the Middle Ages. 19th-century land reforms did not lead to farms being moved out of the villages; instead, the land was divided up in a herring-bone pattern with buildings and the main roads as the spine. The houses are often built of plastered stone. A characteristic feature is the many stone walls enclosing the pastures along the shore and on much of Stora Alvaret. There are the remains of shore meadows which have been in continuous use as grazing land for many centuries in the south of Öland.

The Hanseatic town of Visby has a ring wall, merchants' houses and church ruins dating back to its flourishing period in the Middle Ages. In the centre, one of the medieval churches, the cathedral of St Maria, formerly a German merchants' church.

Coastland of Southern Småland. This region lies below the highest shoreline. South of Kalmar there is a district of large, modern farms, with large fields. North of this district the coast is more broken, with broad-leafed woodland and large estates, of which the wooden manor house at Strömserum from the 1750s at the mouth of the Alsterån is an example. Along the coast there are the remains of grazed shore meadows and quite a few holiday homes. To the west there is a sharp transition to the coniferous forests inland, which have only a few islands of cultivation round isolated farmsteads.

The medieval city of Kalmar has a fortified 17th-century town plan. Kalmar is surrounded by a network of major roads.

Coastland of Northern Götaland. This district consists of a comparatively narrow band of islands off a broken coastline whose deep bays are part of a fissure-valley landscape running from north-west to south-east. There are still old, red wooden buildings built a long time ago by fishermen standing on the islands.

The deep fissure valleys are fairly well cultivated, while the rocky landscape between them is covered with forest, including broad-leafed trees. At the end of the bays and along the lakes there are towns and villages which had early industries.

Gotland. The island has limestone bedrock with very few height differences apart from cliffs along part of the west coast. It is well known for its agriculture. Districts with intensive farming alternate, however, with large forests. In the south we find the bleak, open landscape of Storsudret. Pine forests are dominant along the coast and on Fårö. In the centre of the island and in the south-east there are broad-leafed woods and wooded groves, including meadows and pine trees. Gotland also has extensive wetlands, or former wetlands, and quite a few marshes, some of which used to be grazed. The settlements are traditionally isolated farms, many of them built of stone. The more than 90 large medieval limestone churches are a characteristic feature of the landscape. The coastline in the north and east has been scarred by the limestone industry. There are enormous quarries at File Hajdar near Slite. The medieval town centre and walls of Visby are unique parts of the architectural heritage of Sweden. Along the coast and on Fårö there are many holiday homes.

Forest area of Southern Östergötland. This region lies both below and above the highest shoreline. Hills and fissure valleys create great height differences. There is open landscape round the large lakes. Along the rivers Svartån and Stångån there are well-defined "micro-settlements". The north has a landscape of oak woods and large estates. In the south we find coniferous forests with mires and rocks. This region has few towns, all of then small.

Western plain of Östergötland. This region consists mainly of a fertile plain, flat or slightly undulating. Omberg and Holaveden rise above the surrounding landscape. It lies almost completely below the highest shoreline and the soil is calciferous clay till and glacial clays.

The main crops are cereals and rape produced on large farms in a highly-rationalised agrarian landscape. Large grain silos and storage barns make striking silhouettes on the skyline. Here and there we find the remains of a former geometric pattern of village plots. To the south old meadows and pastures are more frequent, though most of them are now overgrown with broad-leafed trees.

Small towns with well-preserved medieval streets and ancient buildings are found on the plain (the most remarkable one is Saint Birgitta's Convent at Vadstena); in the zone round the plain later industrial towns have grown up where there are waterfalls.

Eastern plain of Östergötland. This landscape lies below the highest shoreline and is characterised in the north by relatively intense cultivation with areas of dry land clad with juniper bushes, forest-covered moraines (Vikbolandet) and large forests. Both bogs rich in orchids and steppe-like dry meadows are found here.

The agrarian districts have small villages grouped on moraines which show traces of medieval geometric patterns. The area is more forested to the south. Linköping and Norrköping give an urban character to much of the region, together with the main roads that criss-cross the landscape. The well-preserved early industrial buildings in Norrköping are unique features of the region.

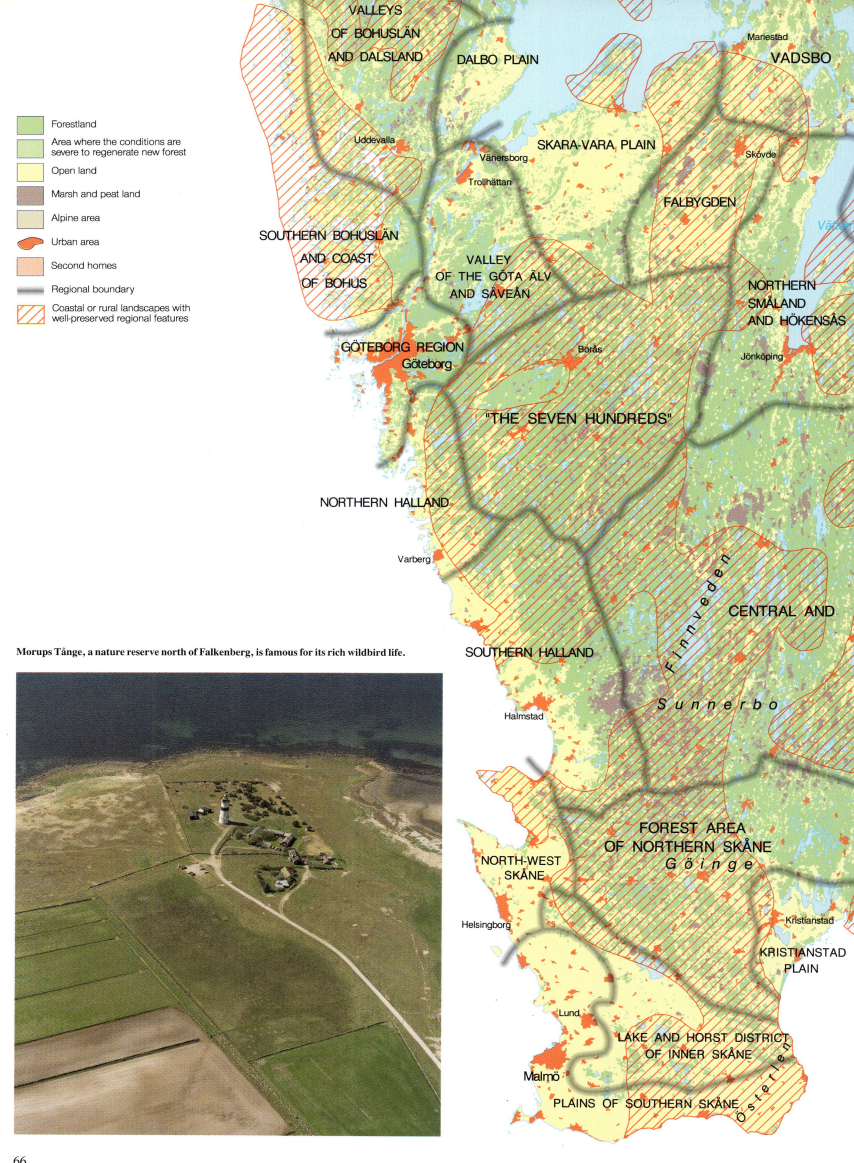

Morups Tånge, a nature reserve north of Falkenberg, is famous for its rich wildbird life.

Legend:
- Forestland
- Area where the conditions are severe to regenerate new forest
- Open land
- Marsh and peat land
- Alpine area
- Urban area
- Second homes
- Regional boundary
- Coastal or rural landscapes with well-preserved regional features

The deep harbour at Oxelösund was established in 1876 to export iron ore from Grängesberg. The ironworks, now one of the largest in Sweden, was founded in 1913, and the town grew in size. The port developed rapidly, with a ferry terminal and other facilities.

Öland's shore meadows have existed for a very long time. From Bläsinge, in the middle of the east coast of Öland.

Cultural Landscapes
– a Regional Description

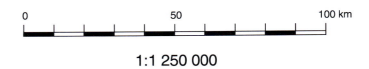

1:1 250 000

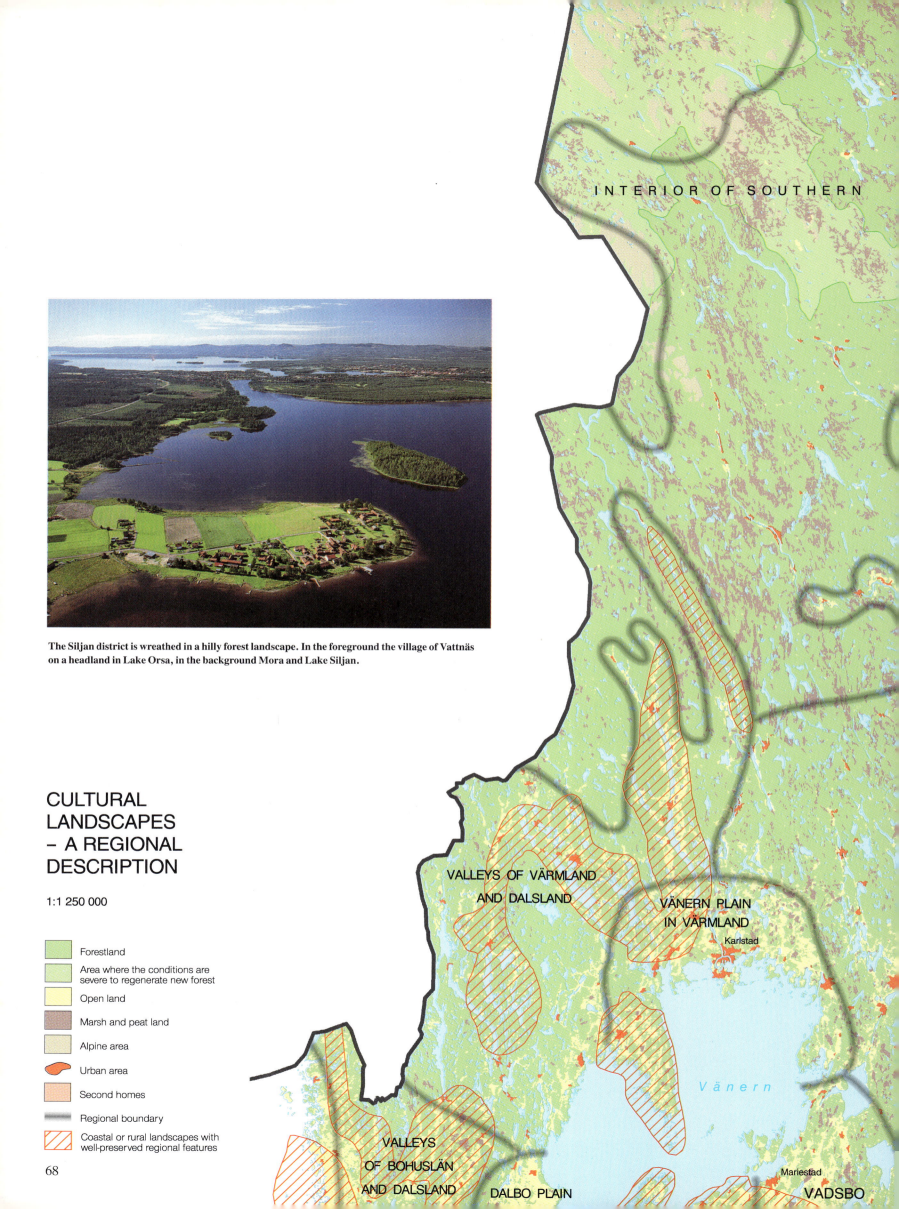

The Siljan district is wreathed in a hilly forest landscape. In the foreground the village of Vattnäs on a headland in Lake Orsa, in the background Mora and Lake Siljan.

CULTURAL LANDSCAPES – A REGIONAL DESCRIPTION

1:1 250 000

- Forestland
- Area where the conditions are severe to regenerate new forest
- Open land
- Marsh and peat land
- Alpine area
- Urban area
- Second homes
- Regional boundary
- Coastal or rural landscapes with well-preserved regional features

68

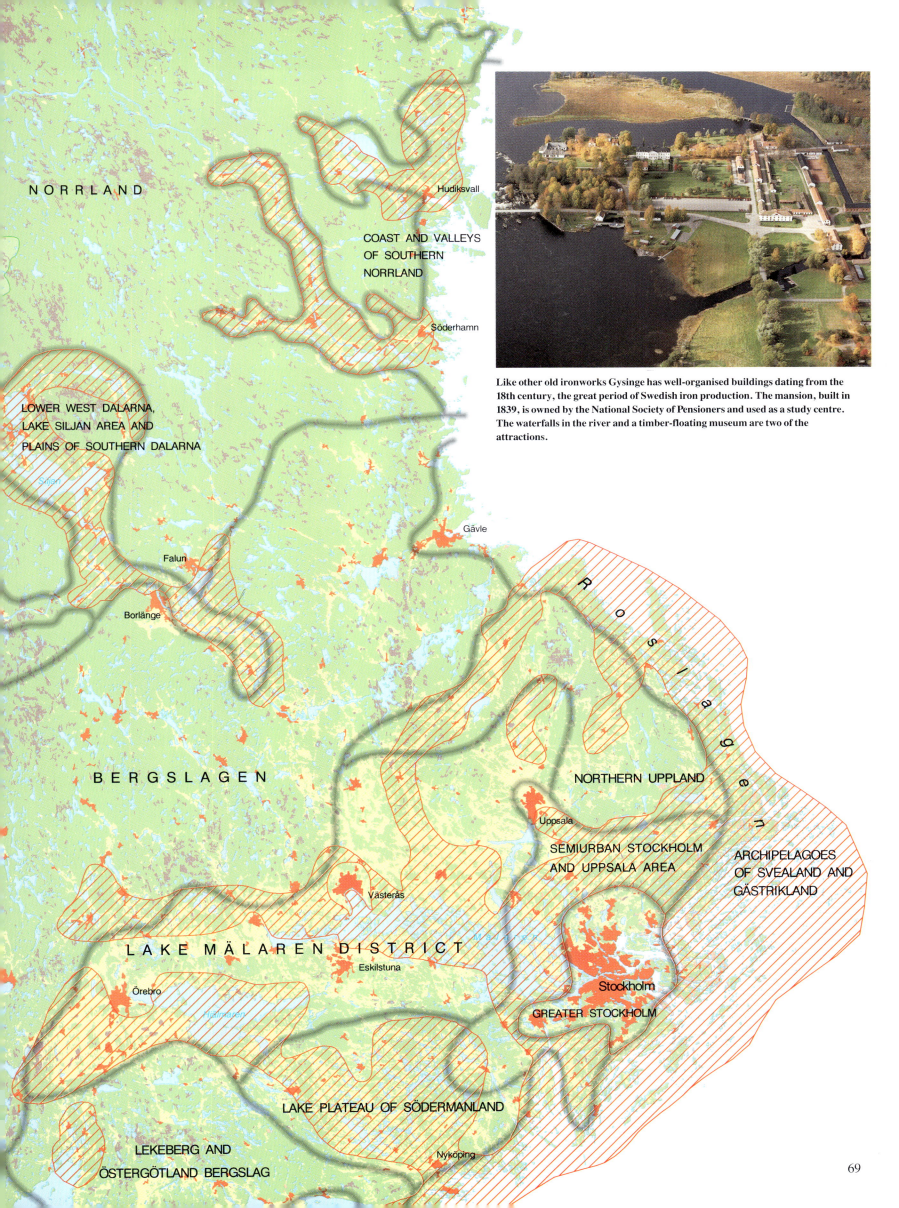

Like other old ironworks Gysinge has well-organised buildings dating from the 18th century, the great period of Swedish iron production. The mansion, built in 1839, is owned by the National Society of Pensioners and used as a study centre. The waterfalls in the river and a timber-floating museum are two of the attractions.

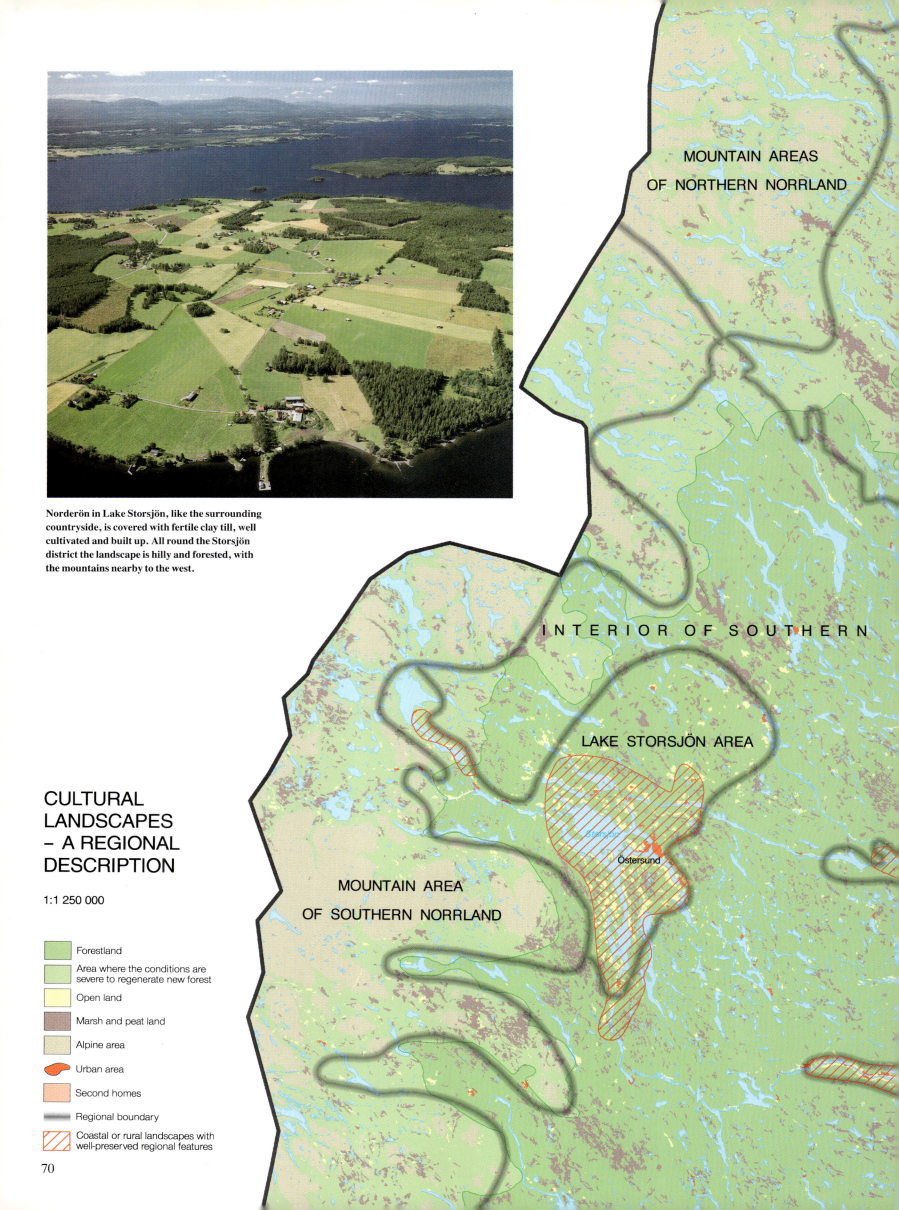

Norderön in Lake Storsjön, like the surrounding countryside, is covered with fertile clay till, well cultivated and built up. All round the Storsjön district the landscape is hilly and forested, with the mountains nearby to the west.

CULTURAL LANDSCAPES – A REGIONAL DESCRIPTION

1:1 250 000

- Forestland
- Area where the conditions are severe to regenerate new forest
- Open land
- Marsh and peat land
- Alpine area
- Urban area
- Second homes
- Regional boundary
- Coastal or rural landscapes with well-preserved regional features

MOUNTAIN AREAS OF NORTHERN NORRLAND

INTERIOR OF SOUTHERN

LAKE STORSJÖN AREA

MOUNTAIN AREA OF SOUTHERN NORRLAND

Östersund

One of the Sundsvall districts's oldest and largest forest industries, Vistavarv, is at Timrå; it was originally a shipbuilding yard, then a steam sawmill after 1851, but since 1905 mainly a pulp mill.

CULTURAL LANDSCAPES – A REGIONAL DESCRIPTION

1:1 250 000

- Forestland
- Area where the conditions are severe to regenerate new forest
- Open land
- Marsh and peat land
- Alpine area
- Urban area
- Second homes
- Regional boundary
- Coastal or rural landscapes with well-preserved regional features

Nature trails, Saami camps and tourist centres mark the presence of human beings in the mountain world. Hikers in the Kebnekaise mountains, with the highest peak in Sweden, 2,111 m above sea level, just outside the picture to the right.

Upper Norrland. The landscape here is flat and covered with vast boglands where many of the rivers of upper Norrland have their sources. In the far north of the region the landscape becomes tundra-like. To the east it runs into the highest shoreline.

The southern limit, towards north Norrland's lake and forestland, has been determined by historical colonisation. North of the limit Finnish colonisation has been going on ever since the 17th century, while Saami and Swedish colonisers from the coast have colonised the lake and forest districts, a difference which is reflected in the place names.

Mining district of Lappland. Upper Norrland has Sweden's largest deposits of iron ore, which have been intensively exploited during the 20th century. Since the end of the last century a mining industry has grown up in Gällivare-Malmberget, Aitik, Kiruna and Svappavaara. Gradually an urban landscape has emerged in the wilderness. *Malmfälten* (the mine fields) is therefore often treated as a regional term. When, as today, the mining industry is in recession, great efforts have been made to find alternative industries. The best-known of these is the space centre at Kiruna and the Esrange rocket base. Several of the traditional townships (Jukkasjärvi, Vittangi) have as a result been able to keep their populations, despite the depopulation of the rest of the interior of Upper Norrland.

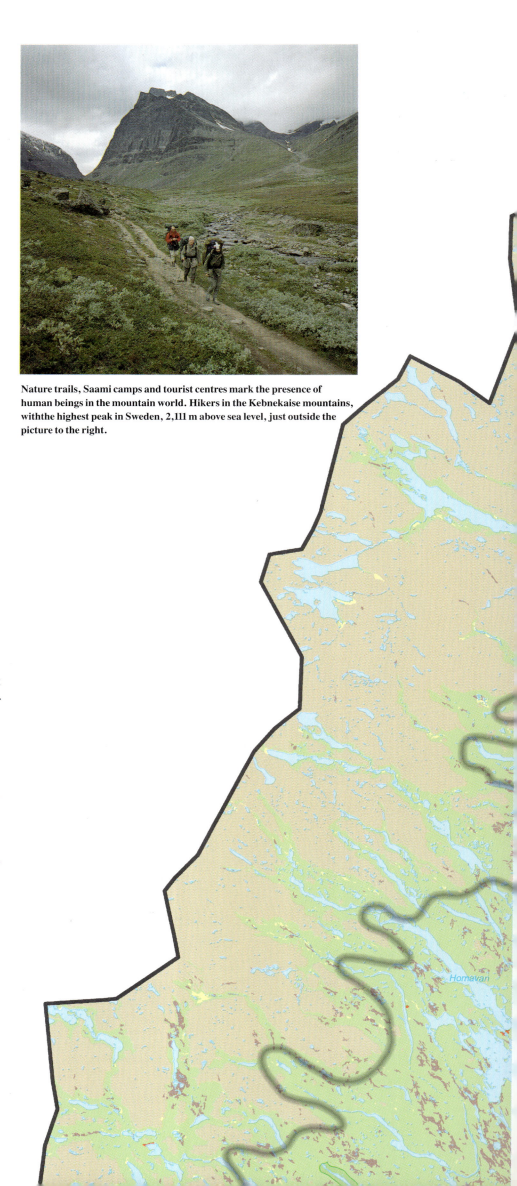

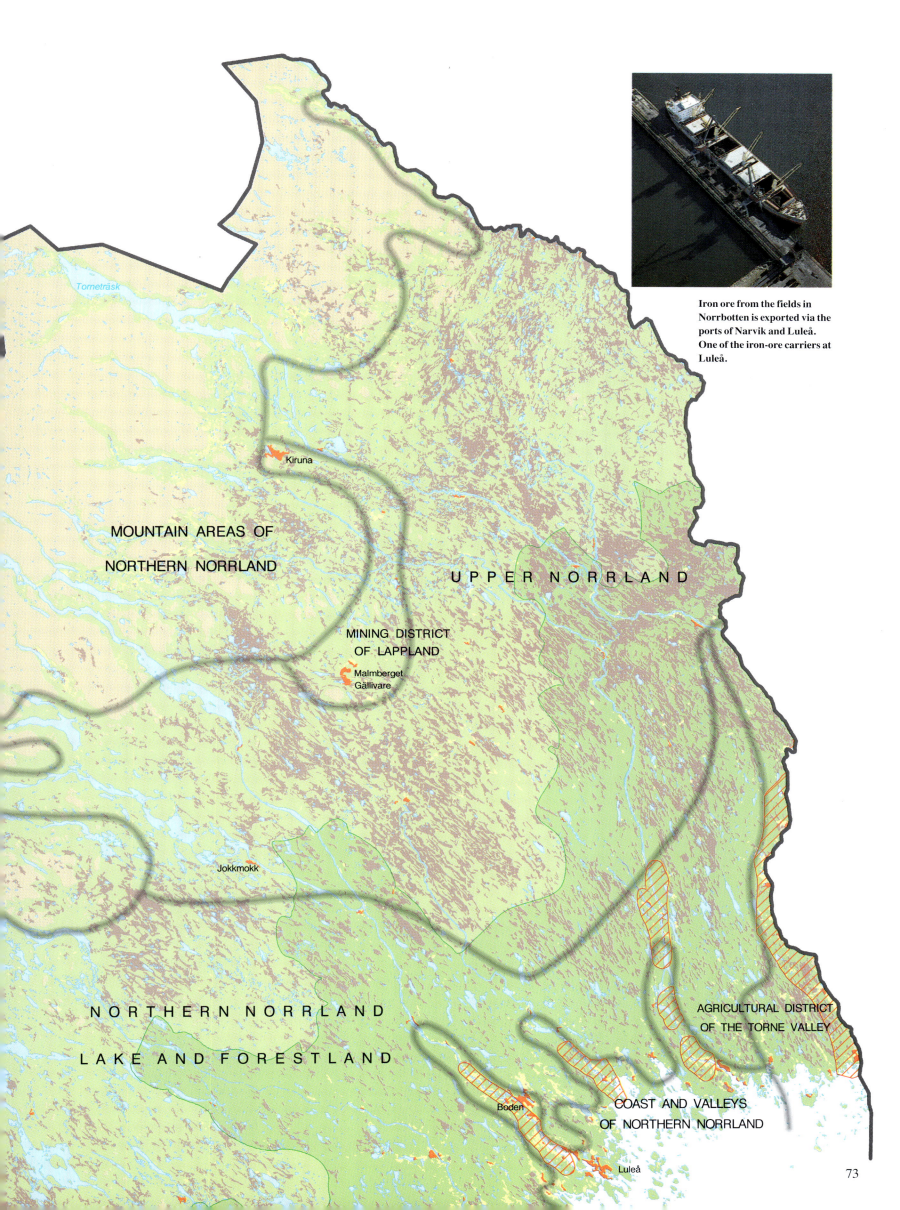

Iron ore from the fields in Norrbotten is exported via the ports of Narvik and Luleå. One of the iron-ore carriers at Luleå.

Lövgärdet in the north of Göteborg is one of many well-equipped metropolitan suburbs which were created at great speed in the 1960s and 1970s.

Göteborg region. The historic core of the second largest city region in Sweden comprises the harbour and the city defences. The roads running into the built-up area create an urban-sprawl landscape which is reinforced by the heavily developed valley of the Göta Älv. The centre of Göteborg has a well-preserved, Dutch-influenced town plan dating from the 17th century, with a canal system that has been partly filled in. The surrounding urban districts may be divided into three zones. To the south and on the small islands we find extensive areas of holiday homes which are more and more becoming permanent dwellings. To the east, towards Bollebygd and Landvetter, there is a typical semi-urban zone with permanent dwellings and "horse farms" within commuting distance from the centre. To the north, on Hisingen and along the Göta Älv and in the Säveån valley, we find a partly industrialised landscape.

Southern Bohuslän and Coast of Bohus. Southern Bohuslän and the islands of Hisingen, Tjörn and Orust still have typical unforested infields or pastureland between bare rocky hills. A shortage of timber made stone walls the general way of enclosing fields. The clay plains in the valleys are fully cultivated and good conditions for arable farming resulted in concentrated agricultural villages in many places, several of which, in spite of land reforms, have retained their old character. The fishing villages in the coast zone are a unique feature of the region. As a result of changes in fishing conditions, these villages are undergoing a functional change. The area also has the relics of an extensive stone-quarrying industry.

Valley of the Göta Älv and Säveån. Here one gets the impression of a "dynamic" natural landscape. Mighty hills, a gully landscape and in particular the natural processes along the Göta Älv leave a lasting impression on the observer. The landscape is open and cultivated and the agrarian settlements consist of medium-sized villages. The river valleys are industrialised. Above the highest shoreline there are a few isolated farms and settlements on hilltops.

"The Seven Hundreds". Since the early 20th century south Västergötland has been called "the Seven Hundreds" (*Sjuhäradsbygden*) and is associated with pedlars of textile goods. Most of the region lies above the highest shoreline. The old arable land is to be found mostly on the hilltops. Since the 19th century stone walls have been used to enclose fields and as land reform in the 20th century was moderate, many of these walls are still standing. Old farming methods concentrating on milk production, combined with relatively fertile soils, are reflected in the semi-open grazing grounds containing some broad-leafed trees. The character of the smaller towns comes from the palmy days of the textile industry, when quite a number of church villages developed into small industrial towns.

Viskadalen, which lies below the highest shoreline, together with other valleys, is a contrast with the rest of the region. There are sediments here, and the farming villages climb the steep sides of the valleys. The industrial buildings in the upper Viskadalen are a striking feature of the valley.

Vadsbo. This region has large lakes in a flat, open landscape, in many places offering broad views. Small villages are a characteristic feature of the settlements, which are often surrounded by an old, well-preserved cultivated landscape with some broad-leafed trees. The southern part of Tiveden forest lies to the north.

Falbygden. This region is characterised by the table hills covered with broad-leafed forests and rich soils in the plains. There has been permanent settlement here since the Stone Age, as witnessed by the many chamber graves. Thanks to the calciferous clay till cultivation is intensive and from many points there are splendid views across the landscape.

There is a scarcity of water and the agrarian settlements, often large villages, are located by rivers or springs. To the south-west we find remarkable remains of large, often freely-grouped one-field villages. The rest of the district has its roots in medieval amalgamated villages, previously based on a three-field system. These villages may still be recognised in the landscape in spite of land reforms.

The table hills have been exploited extensively for raw materials: diabase, limestone, slate and sandstone. The most evident feature is the industrial landscape round Billingen.

Skara-Vara plain. This region has large open fields, where the sea and lake sediments of the Lake Vänern basin provide good conditions for extensive grain production. The open nature of the landscape is the result of 19th-century cultivation. Before this the plain had a heath and scrub landscape with small islands of arable land round the villages. The settlements have always been in the form of comparatively large villages, and in spite of extensive land reforms in the 19th century when farms were moved out of the villages, several of them have been preserved. Some of the church villages and certain railway communities have grown into towns, principally along the Herrljunga-Uddevalla railway, which was built for the exports of oats in the 19th century.

Dalbo plain. This is one of the few fairly clearly-defined districts on the plains round Lake Vänern. In the past it had characteristic isolated farms and hamlets, and it still retains a small-scale character with its scattered but compact settlements.

Valleys of Bohuslän and Dalsland. This region differs noticeably from surrounding districts with its well-defined, often quite broad valleys running from north to south, or lakes (Bullaren), surrounded by forested highland (for example Kynnefjäll). Agrarian settlements in the form of isolated farms and hamlets dominate.

Valleys of Värmland and Dalsland. North Dalsland and south-west Värmland are characterised by a fragmented natural landscape containing large, irregularly-shaped lakes surrounded by forest-clad heights. The cultivated areas are limited but have a well-preserved cultural landscape, particularly in south-west Värmland.

Brandkärr in Nyköping dates from about 1970.

The valley of the Klarälven provides a good example of the interplay between nature and cultivation.

Sergels Torg in central Stockholm in June 1982 was the result of plans drawn up in the late 1950s for rebuilding the city centre.

There are examples of radical farm division in the region, which has resulted in a landscape of many farms, with sparse, late village settlements and isolated farms. This region was strongly affected by emigration to America right into the 20th century. The landscape round Lakes Rottnen and Övre Fryken has more impressive countryside, famous for its fairy-tale-like manor houses. The narrow, meandering course of the Klarälven between Lake Vingängssjön and Edebäck is unique among Sweden's river valleys. The landscape is reminiscent of Norrland, with great height differences. Natural processes still in progress have set well-defined limits to land use along the river valley. There are settlements on higher parts of the river forelands upstream, with cultivated land on the lower parts. The sharp divisions between river sediment, glaciofluvial deposits and till do not correspond to any traditional boundaries, since the early valley villagers used the pastureland and shealings on the highland.

Vänern plain in Värmland. Here early isolated farms developed into compact cluster villages as a result of land division in the 18th and 19th centuries. Many of these villages have retained their character to this very day. Other isolated farms developed into small manors. The Vänern plain has a typical central Swedish character thanks to its landscape of small fields.

Lake Mälaren district. This region is defined here as the agricultural districts within the drainage basin of Lake Mälaren. This is a typical fissure-valley landscape, a mosaic of low-lying, cultivated clay fields, higher till areas and glacial deposits in very varied patterns. Its eskers are the most characteristic features of the Mälaren valley, together with dry, grazed slopes scattered with juniper bushes. Mälardalen is very rich in prehistoric remains and its settlements consist of small villages often shaped by land reform. Place names are stereotyped with endings in -*sta(d)*,-*by*, or -*tuna* from the expansive period of the Iron Age. We find estate landscape in particular on the northern shores of Lake Mälaren, with park-like vegetation. The Hjälmaren district and above all the Närke plain have clay till and a drumlin landscape, as well as the clay mud exposed by extensive lake drainage.

Lake plateau of Södermanland. Central Södermanland has been called "the glorious Garden of Eden". This epithet is Selma Lagerlöf's and refers to the varied and park-like fissure-valley landscape, rich in lakes and natural beauty. Large estates with their open fields and farmworkers' cottages are a dominant feature of the landscape. Here and there the manor landscape is replaced by well-preserved, small farms in an almost archaic environment. Forest plantations on arable land are, however, becoming frequent.

Greater Stockholm. In spite of extensive clearance of old buildings in inner Stockholm in the 1950s and 1960s, many historical areas have been preserved, illustrating the gradual growth of the city since medieval times. The urban landscape round Stockholm comprises some 20 municipalities, from Södertälje and Västerhaninge in the south to Upplands-Väsby in the north, a distance of almost 60 km. In an east-west direction the region is marked off by the islands and holiday homes to the east and the still agrarian islands in Lake Mälaren to the west. Greater Stockholm is expanding along the main roads and railways, especially northwards towards Arlanda airport. Here we find ribbon development of office premises and high-tech industries.

Greater Stockholm has large residential areas and traditional industries in the south and suburban houses and expansive industries in the north. There are still untouched areas between the main roads and railways, an unusual feature for a town of Stockholm's size. A number of Sweden's oldest and most important industrial towns stand round Lake Mälaren. Sigtuna is one thousand years old and had a predecessor at Birka.

Semi-urban Stockholm and Uppsala area. The landscape is marked by the city for many miles outside Stockholm. Good roads and other forms of public transport have made it possible for the city's businessmen and office workers to live in attractive rural environments. Agriculture is declining as wages and the price of land rise. Houses are modernised and extended; horse paddocks fenced in white, golf courses and club houses take over the farmland.

We also find in the Stockholm area

Storms can create havoc in the forests, as here in Gästrikland. Many trees were felled in various parts of Sweden in the great storms of 1967 and 1969.

Winter on Röder in Stockholm's outer northern archipelago

some of the cultural landscapes proposed by Sweden for UNESCO's World Heritage list: Drottningholm, the parishes of Markim and Orkesta, and Birka-Alsnöhus.

The area round Uppsala might well form a region of its own, characterised by a sharp borderline between town and countryside, but the town's expansion southwards towards Arlanda airport has created a semi-urban zone which has joined up with the corresponding zone in Stockholm.

Archipelagos of Svealand and Gästrikland. Off the coasts of Svealand and Gästrikland we find an island landscape consisting of thousands of islands, islets and skerries, which are to a large extent covered with cultivated broad-leafed woods and the remains of meadows and pastures. The island villages were often large and well populated. Pure fishing villages are relatively uncommon but are to be found here and there along Gävle Bay. Since the Second World War the region has become depopulated, and today there is only sporadic farming combined with every possible kind of work, on Gräsö and Arholma, for example. Today the islands are totally dominated by holiday homes, marinas and small shipyards and outdoor recreational life. Modern telecommunications have made it possible to move commercial activities out to the archipelago.

Bergslagen. In this hilly and forested area various kinds of minerals, principally iron ore and sulphides, have been mined ever since prehistoric times. Today practically all mining has ceased. The basis for the limits of this region is early 17th-century ironworks legislation. The various places at which iron was produced were said to lie "within" or "without" the mining district of Bergslagen.

North Uppland forms a region of its own, mainly consisting of the Dannemora ironworks, including extensive areas of farmland that seem not to fit in with the picture of an ironworks district. Within Bergslagen itself there is also farmland, however, round Nora and Lindesberg, for example, that was once inhabited by Bergslagen farmers who took part in iron production. In southern Dalarna there are Finnish districts consisting of small isolated farms in forest clearings. In olden times the forests throughout Bergslagen were very over-exploited.

Lekeberg and Östergötland Bergslag. This area also comprises Tunaberg's Bergslag in Södermanland and is a forest and ironworks zone that separates Mälardalen from the Östgöta plain. Mining and iron production have a long tradition; some of Sweden's oldest ironworks are here, a few with well-preserved old industrial buildings. Today the traditional industries no longer operate, but in a few cases the towns live on through forest industries or in one case glass production. In Åmmeberg and Zinkgruvan zinc ore is still mined.

Northern Uppland. This region drains mainly to the north and the east; contacts with Mälardalen have always been weak. Here we find the well-cultivated Tämnarådalen, the central Oland Hundred and the clay till district of Estuna. The large, open field landscape of the latter district is only to be found elsewhere in Cambro-Silurian districts. In other respects the region is characterised by a small-scale field landscape in which land use and soils correspond closely.

This region also includes Uppland's Bergslag, where the Walloon ironworks (with a remarkable 18th-century layout and buildings) processed the ore taken from Dannemora mine.

Lower West Dalarna, Lake Siljan and plains of southern Dalarna. Sediments from the Dalälven have been deposited along the former sea loch south of Stora Tuna. Here and there the region is criss-crossed by large gullies. It is characterised by intensive cultivation below the highest shoreline, and the settlements are reminiscent of those in Mälardalen.

The surface of Lake Siljan is at about the level of the highest shoreline, and in this calciferous area some high land has been cultivated. As a result of a special inheritance system the cultivated land round Siljan has a special pattern: large, compact villages of red timber houses surrounded by a narrow belt of fields but extensive meadowland, often on hillsides, and complementary land use in the form of shealings.

Coast and valleys of southern Norrland. This region comprises terrain below the highest shoreline in the valleys of the Ljusnan and the Voxnan, the Dellen district and the coast district north of Hudiksvall. The river valley landscape consists of glaciofluvial and fluvial deposits and has been colonised upstream. The historically central districts lie within the Hälsingland coast, where the largest settlements are found. The magnificent 18th and 19th-century wooden buildings in Hälsingland are a remarkable feature. At most places in southern Norrland there is still a well-preserved cultivated landscape, especially in the Ljusnan and Voxnan valleys and round Dellen, where it is still possible to distinguish between the central places and the outlying districts cultivated later.

Coast and valleys of Central Norrlans. The coast is often steep except at the mouth of the Indalsälven, where an unusual and extensive delta landscape has evolved, partly as a result of the flood disaster at Ragunda in 1796. In the south, round the estuaries of the Ljungan and the Indalsälven, an urban industrial landscape has developed round traditional forest industries with Sundsvall at the centre. Northern Ångermanland has a well-preserved cultural landscape in the river valleys. The Nordingrå district, called Höga Kusten (the High Coast), is also notable for its cultivated fiord landscape surrounded by high mountains. The highest shoreline here is almost 300 metres above sea level. There are a number of well-preserved fishing villages along the coast which originated with the seasonal fishing practised by people living in Gävle.

Coast and valleys of Northern Norrland. Here we find agrarian settlements along the major rivers. The industrial sites at Skellefteå mining district are also a striking feature.

The valleys of the Skellefteälven, Pite älv, Lule älv and Råne älv are cultivated below the highest shoreline. The Lule älv and Skellefteälven valleys in particular have an open cultivated landscape along their lower reaches, but also an industrial urban landscape.

Along the Kalixälven, which has not been dammed, we find a cultural landscape where traditional farming has been replaced by soft-fruit farms.

Vindelfjällen in the upper reaches of the Vindelälven. Where the coniferous trees thin out on the slopes of the mountains the mountain birch forest takes over, to be succeeded by bare rock.

Interior of Southern Norrland. This region has typical Norrland terrain, with settled valleys surrounded by mountains of fairly equal height. Several districts were well developed as early as the Middle Ages, others have prehistoric roots. The Saami culture found here may also be prehistoric. Much of the grassland and shealings of the cultural landscape has now been covered with plantations, but agrarian central districts (large villages) are found in Härjedalen and Jämtland. In the area between Dalarna and West Hälsingland and in north and West Värmland there are the remains of Finnish settlements.

Northern Norrland lake and forestland. A landscape with few botanical species, endless coniferous forests and bogland but also large lakes makes up the characteristic features of this region, which has been permanently inhabited far up the river valleys for several hundred years. This is also the district of large Saami villages, surrounded by vast winter grazing grounds. Saami culture has its core district in Sweden in this region, as revealed by the place names, which are often Saami in origin. The Swedish population has penetrated deeper and deeper into the country ever since the 16th century. During the 18th century *lappmarksgränsen* (the Lapp boundary) was established, above which no new cultivation was allowed.

Colonisation continued above *lappmarksgränsen*, however, with characteristic sites on southern slopes running down to rivers and lakes. The last wave of colonisation in *Pite lappmark* did not ebb out until the early 20th century. Large drainage and irrigation schemes were launched to improve hay production. A new boundary, the limit of cultivation, was drawn to protect reindeer husbandry.

Mountain area of Southern Norrland. This region principally comprises the bare mountains, which used mainly to be reindeer pastureland but also contained old mines. Old, permanent agrarian settlements are only found at a few places, for example in the upper valleys of the Indalsälven, Ljungan and Ljusnan—incidentally, the only places in Sweden where prehistoric farming settlements meet the mountains.

Today much of this area is given over to tourism in the form of modern skiing centres and holiday villages.

Lake Storsjön area. The district round Lake Storsjön itself, with its calciferous clay till, is highly cultivated and has long been settled. Up until 1645 this district was part of Norway, whose agrarian settlements were traditionally isolated farms. As a result of a series of land divisions and land reforms, mainly in the 19th century, the large villages which are typical of the Storsjön area developed along the terraces or heights of the terrain. North of the Storsjön area clay till appears in patches, where, like windows in the forest gloom, we find light, cultivated fields in the landscape, often on hilltops. There is a particularly well-preserved cultivated landscape round Offerdal.

Mountain areas of Northern Norrland. This is one of Europe's largest continuous wildernesses. It has scattered mountain hotels and cabins for tourists, for example at Tärnaby, Hemavan, Ritsem, Riksgränsen and Abisko, but the natural landscape is the dominant feature. Outdoor tourists have traditionally made their way to this region, which today contains the largest national parks and nature reserves in the country. Economic exploitation of the district has long been based on reindeer husbandry above the limit of cultivation. In some places, however, sporadic attempts have been made to mine iron ore. Today the dominant industry is tourism.

Agricultural district of Torne valley. This region is the centre of a cultural district characterised by the Torne valley Finnish language. The boundary is on the coast between Sangis and Säjvis. Here we find Norrbotten's most characteristic river landscape along the Torne älv. Along with the Kalix älv, the Pite älv and the Vindelälven hold a unique position because they have not been exploited for hydro-electric power.

Variations in the river water levels affect cultivation, vegetation and location of settlements in these valleys. In many places the valleys are broad and intensively cultivated, with vegetables grown under glass. The agrarian settlements are in the form of isolated farms organised in special ownership systems along terraces and river banks. The many meadow barns and round threshing barns are a characteristic feature.

The Cultural Landscape: Selected Examples

The Skåne Plain

"A small patch of land called Skåne has been attached to Sweden to show it what the rest of Europe looks like." These words were written by R H Stiernswärd a hundred and fifty years ago. Others say that the boundary between Sweden and the continent runs neither north of Skåne nor through the Sound, but straight across the province from the north-west to the south-east. This is true if you put geology and land forms, soils and land use first.

Many changes have taken place since the inhabitants of Skåne first became farmers some 6,000 years ago. The majority of villages were established in the early Middle Ages, only to be dissolved in the first part of the 19th century by land division. This was the start of much of today's landscape, scattered farms and remains of villages, straight farm boundaries and sharply-angled roads, as well as quite a few rows of pollarded willows.

The relation between natural conditions and agriculture is evident. In the north and on the ridges a harsh landscape only permitted the formation of hamlets and isolated farms, while the better land in the west and south and round Kristianstad became a district of large, open fields, dominated by large villages until the land reform.

The role played by land ownership in the use and the appearance of the landscape is almost as obvious. The districts owned by freehold farmers differ greatly from those owned mainly by estates. The land owned by the Crown, the Church and the municipalities has varied through the years, and this has also affected its use.

Private car ownership and extensive commuting to work by car have meant that town and country have developed into a homogenous urban region in western Skåne, as well as contributing to both open and hidden urbanisation in other areas.

Quite a number of features in today's landscape are the result of rationalisation, specialisation and intensification of farming and forestry methods, and it is a matter of opinion whether the open plain should be seen as a landscape created principally by the economy, by technology or by politics.

The most characteristic feature of Skåne's landscape is its openness. The old Economic map and the air photograph from 1991 show the changes since the time of stage-coaches and a dense railway network.

As late as 1915 agriculture was the dominant industry in the south-west. Remains of villages, the railway town of Åkarp (with its folk high school) and a couple of industrial communities (Lomma—bricks and Arlöv—sugar and railway carriages) lay like islands in a sea of farmland.

Today the towns are expanding. Of Karstorp, Vinstorp and Tågarp only a few houses or trees remain. In the south-east the road to the Öresund Bridge is planned to run between the village of Burlöv and the housing estate to the west of it.

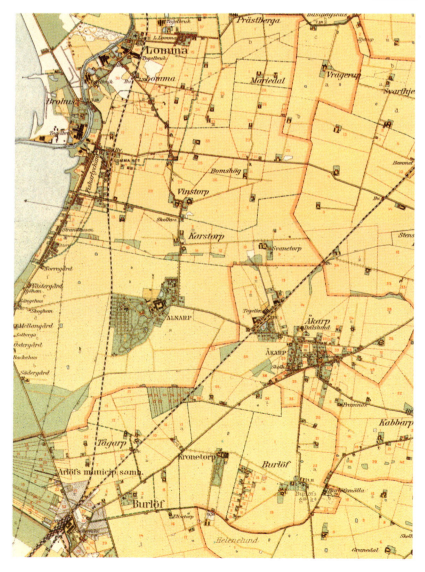

Nowadays Highways E4 and E6 meet at three levels at the Kropp junction in the north-west of the agricultural plain. The E4 cuts across Rosendal's Hage, an open stretch of forestland which, as long as cattle continue to graze here, shows what the national park at Dalby Hage near Lund looked like when it was rescued some 70 years ago. East of the road junction the white church at Kropp rises up to remind us of the Middle Ages.

In the 1930s Österlen had a large number of smallholdings created from the Bollerup estate when it was turned into a trust for the College of Agriculture. Valterslund, Henriksfält and Ingelstads Nygård (nowadays called Gårstad) are typical "Low farms", the result of rationalising the estate in the 19th century and later freeehold farms. Hannas has one of the best-preserved 12th-century churches in the district. The field pattern in the aerial photograph suggests that the majority of houses are no longer used as farms. Agricultural policy has been shaping the landscape for many years.

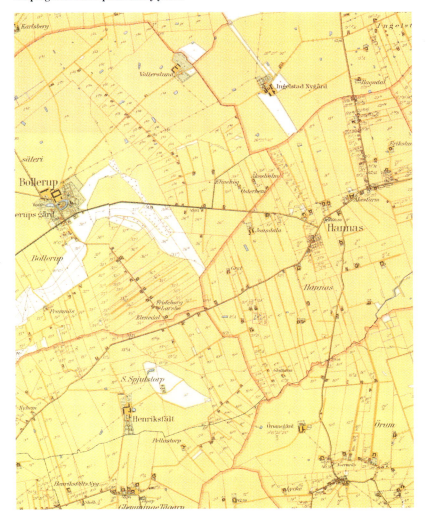 

The old main street in Malmö, Adelgatan, seen from the west, shows the broader part which was once the only market square in the town. Narrow but now broadened lanes led down from Adelgatan to the shore.

Malmö

We do not know the date of the foundation of many of our medieval towns—and this is true of Malmö, too. But when the town charter was confirmed in the 13th century, there were already a considerable number of houses grouped along a sandbank (Malm-ö means sandy knoll). The main street, Adelgatan, ran above the shoreline and widened out into a market square which is still visible today. On one side of the square stood the tower of St Peter's Church, as we can see in the 16th-century drawing by Braun and Hogenberg.

German merchants traded here and because the coast of Skåne sticks out like an elbow into the Sound, they called Malmö Elbogen (the Elbow). Malmöhus castle was surrounded by a moat, as was the whole town. After the Treaty of Roskilde in 1658, when Skåne became part of Sweden, the castle developed into a citadel, at the same time as the whole town was surrounded by a zig-zag-shaped moat round projecting forts. Since military tactics at that time required an open field of fire between the town and the citadel, the medieval buildings west of the red line in the picture were demolished. This line, "the castle cut", is marked today by the straight line of Slottsgatan.

By 1805 this defence system had become obsolete and was abandoned. But a canal was still needed for drainage, so the present straight canal was dug a little further out, so that new gridiron streets and squares (Gustav Adolfs torg and Drottningtorget) could be added on to the old, irregular town. These changes are clearly reflected in the map. One can see how the buildings previously came right up to the castle walls, where two new defence bastions had just been built out into the Sound. In the next phase the old town buildings have been removed from the castle walls and new buildings have grown up to the south-east. This later plan has remained unchanged to the present day. By 1860 large parts of the harbour had been filled in, creating space for new buildings such as the railway station, opened in 1856. It was not only that Malmö Central Station itself was

This etching of Malmö in the 1580s suggests that the town lacked a harbour as yet. The part of the town west of the castle cut (in red) was pulled down in the 17th century.

The three plots of donated land in Malmö have been marked off in this map dated 1955. They were of some considerable importance in the development of the town.

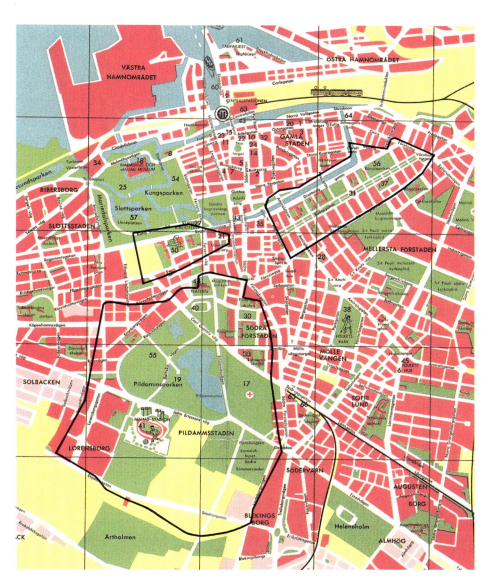

wholly located on a land fill, but all the first stretch of the main railway line north to Lund can also be seen as a long, narrow embankment.

In olden times when the townsfolk of Malmö had their own farms, they often asked the king to give them more grazing land. What they received was "donation land" for common use. A modern interpretation of the common use of this "donation land" in Östra Rörsjön led to the building of public institutions like a grammar school, a fire station, the country administration building and a church (St Paul's) right in the middle of the broad esplanade of Kungsgatan. Västra Rörsjön along Regementsgatan was in a corresponding way used for schools, a town library, indoor swimming baths and parks, but had no private dwellings at all for many years. The third and last area of donation land is Magistratsvången, where Malmö General Hospital was placed and the Baltic Exhibition was held in 1914 (now Pildammsparken). Dwelling houses, however, were not allowed to be built on donation land until after a change in the law in 1965. Thus large parts of Malmö have been developed in accordance with the strict rules for using donation land.

MALMÖ: HARBOUR AND URBAN AREA

The built-up part of Malmö in 1660 is framed by the town wall. Parts of the Sound had been filled in to create a harbour. These fill-ins had grown by 1880. The town now stretches in long bands parallel with the coast along Södra and Östra Förstadsgatan. A hundred years later both the built-up area and the fill-ins have been extended greatly. Industry has taken advantage of the fact that the newly-won land is flat and wholly-owned by the town.

Halland

Halland has undergone great changes; much of what we see today is of recent date. When agriculture expanded, the forests disappeared more and more and were succeeded by vast heaths used as grazing grounds. In the mid–19th century most of Halland had no forestland. On the treeless plain near the coast the sandy soil was exposed to wind and drought and the heathland gave scanty grazing.

The landscape of large, open fields which is to be found in southern Halland today is the result of a transformation during the latter half of the 19th century. A land reform was implemented at that time, and a poor agricultural district still using old crop systems and largely devoted to cattle farming turned into an intensively cultivated arable farming district. The forest began to return to abandoned grazing grounds as a result of planting or natural regeneration.

Fishing in the rivers has a long tradition—Halmstad is famous for its salmon—but most of the fishing villages on the Halland coast are late settlements. It was not until the end of the 19th century that a number of harbours were built and primitive coastal fishing was replaced by effective deep-sea fishing. Today some of these harbours, Bua, for example, have developed into industrial towns.

Halland was Danish until 1645. In this vulnerable frontier country important trade routes led to Sweden. The most famous of them were the Lagastigen and the Nissastigen. Varberg Castle, Halmstad and Lagaholm had strong fortifications.

Falkenberg grew up around the medieval castle of Falkenberghus, today a ruin at the eastern end of the toll bridge. The map dated 1847 shows the medieval town plan, largely preserved to this very day.

Changes were made to the medieval town plan when the railway was built through the town in 1885, as in 1936, when the railway was given a new route and a new railway bridge was built.

In 1850 Falkenberg had a population of 955; today some 17,000 people live in the central parts of Falkenberg. But in the summer the population more than doubles. The Economic map shows Skrea beach with its holiday cottages. As late as the 1920s the whole area was devoted to agriculture.

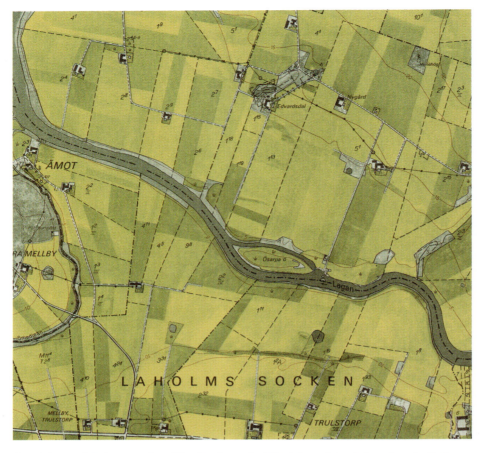

The plain round the lower reaches of the river Lagan is cultivated very intensively and productively. Over-fertilisation leading to nitrogen leaching from arable land (40%) and sewage (15%) has resulted in massive growths of algae, lack of oxygen, the disappearance of seabed fauna and the death of fish in the Bay of Laholm.

The medieval town of Falkenberg has, as shown by the Economic map dated 1966, expanded with industrial and residential estates but above all as a seaside resort along the beaches.

A map from 1847 shows Falkenberg still in its medieval form, with its famous 18th-century bridge.

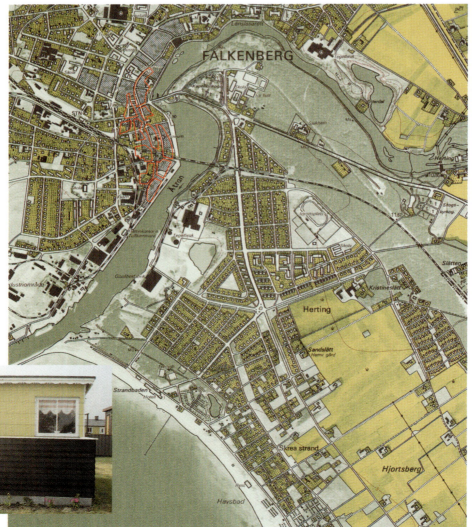

Ronneby became a health resort in the early 18th century, becoming in time the most frequented one in Sweden. The spa buildings and park, among the best preserved in the country, are a conference centre today. Soft Centre, where some 30 companies dealing in computer software are located, is a new development here. Soft Centre also runs research projects, development work and university courses.

South-east of Ronneby is the medieval ruined castle called Hagbards Källare, a relic of the unruly days when Blekinge was Danish frontierland.

Around 1900 well-to-do summer visitors built themselves houses at Ekenäs and on Karön. This area has been well preserved: curiously designed houses decorated with "carpenter's joy", glassed-in verandas and large gardens.

This mid–18th-century map shows Ronneby and its medieval network of streets, but in a long period of decline. Once a flourishing town, Ronneby was reduced to a lower status in 1714 after it had been destroyed by the Swedes in 1564 and lost its town privileges when Karlskrona was founded. It did not regain its town status again until 1882.

Blekinge

In Danish times Ronneby was the most important trading place in Blekinge, partly as a port for exporting firewood, with an excellent position about 15 km from the sea on the Ronnebyån. One of the important roads to Småland also ran from here, as well as the coast road east and west.

North of the town there are several waterfalls in the Ronnebyån, and the "roaring" river is one of the most industrially exploited waterways in the province. Mills, sawmills and industries such as tanneries (Djupadal) grew up here at an early date. For many years the Blekinge leather industry was the foremost in Sweden. The Ronnebyån has its source in Småland and runs through three different types of landscape on its way to the sea. These three, a forest district, a valley district and an archipelago, are characteristic of Blekinge. People have lived longest in the valley district, as there were favourable conditions for permanent settlement at an early date here. Even today most of the towns and villages are located here.

When Blekinge became Swedish in 1658, Sweden gained an important base for its fleet at Karlskrona, which was established in 1680. Most of the population of Ronneby were then ordered to move to Karlskrona. The need for supplies for the naval base led to the creation of the only manor estate in the province, Johannishus.

The agrarian settlements are usually scattered, and the cultural landscape is marked by 19th-century land reforms. Cultivated valleys are separated by forested ridges. Particularly in the south there are broad-leafed forests of beech and oak.

The forest district was not colonised until the Viking Age-Early Middle Ages. Settlements expanded rapidly in the 19th century, when new land was won for cultivation by draining marshes and bogs and clearing till of boulders. Animal products were predominant, and there are still meadows and pastures worked in the traditional way.

GLASSWORKS IN "THE KINGDOM OF GLASS", 1990

Tourism has become an important industry in "Kingdom of Glass", whose reputation for high-quality studio glass has spread throughout the world since the 1920s.

"The Kingdom of Glass"

	Name	First year of operations
1	Kosta	1742
2	Boda	1864
3	Pukeberg	1871
4	Åfors	1876
5	Sandvik	1889
6	Bergdala	1889
7	Johansfors	1891
8	Rosdala	1895
9	Orrefors	1898
10	Lindshammar	1905
11	Målerås	1924
12	Älghult	1933
13	Nybro	1935
14	SEA	1956
15	Transjö	1982
16	Skruf	1981
17	Wilkes studiohytta, Orrefors	1983
18	Hetalåga	1985
19	Sjöhyttan, Älghult	1985
20	Strömbergshyttan Studioglas	1987
21	Gullaskruf, Gullahyttan	1990
22	Nybro studiohytta	1990

"The Kingdom of Glass"

East Kronoberg's County and West Kalmar County are typical of southern Sweden's forest districts, with scattered cultivated areas, often irregular in shape. The soil is mainly poor till with large boulders.

As early as the Iron Age there were small bloomery furnaces here which produced iron from lake and bog ore. During the 17th and 18th centuries some 60 ironworks were built in Småland, where local ore deposits were complemented with mined ore from Utö in the Stockholm archipelago. These ironworks created opportunities for farmers to sell forest products, mainly charcoal but also potash, tar, timber and firewood. Bush-burning was also an important way of increasing the area of cultivated land. The division of farms in the 18th century needs to be seen against the background of the work that was created by exploiting the forests.

New metallurgical inventions in the mid–19th century made it difficult for small ironworks to survive; instead, Småland's "kingdom of glass" grew up in the old "iron country" from the middle of the century. Charcoal for the blast furnaces and forges was replaced by wood for the glassworks furnaces. The industry grew with the help of capital from farmers and expertise from the master glassblowers at Kosta. No fewer than 40 glassworks were established 1860–90.

In the closing decades of the 19th century sawmills and joinery factories were also established, as well as cellulose mills, paper mills and engineering companies. The new railways were an essential component in these enterprises.

We can observe considerable changes in the last few decades. Both the area of cultivated land and the number of farms have decreased dramatically. Most of the glassworks closed down in the 1970s and 1980s. Medium-sized companies have almost completely disappeared or been absorbed into various large groups. In contrast, several studio glassworks with a handful of employees have grown up. The large forestry and engineering companies have also decreased in number. Instead, we now have a range of small industries.

Since the mid–1960s a considerable tourist industry has arisen in "the kingdom of glass".

LESSEBO — FROM CLASSICAL MILLTOWN TO MODERN INDUSTRIAL TOWN

Lessebo, with its 3,000 or so inhabitants, is an industrial centre with its roots in pre-industrial society. In 1658 an ironworks was established on the Lesseboån based on local lake and bog ore. In 1693 a papermill was also built. Until the mid–18th century production was fairly modest; the most

The small farms in the harsh Småland forest districts have been abandoned. Maps from 1949 and 1984 show the changes in south-west Småland. Fields and meadows are once more forestland. The farm buildings remain if it is possible to travel to work in a town, or they become pensioners' homes or holiday cottages.

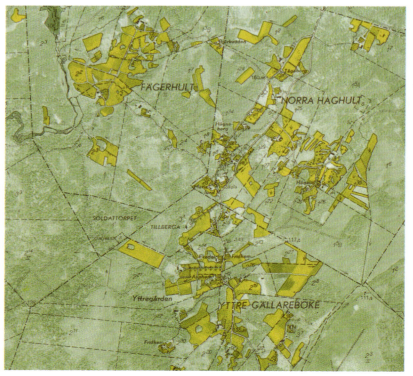

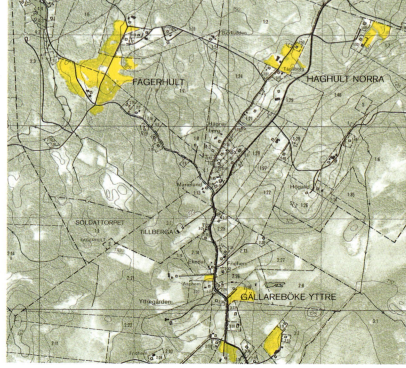

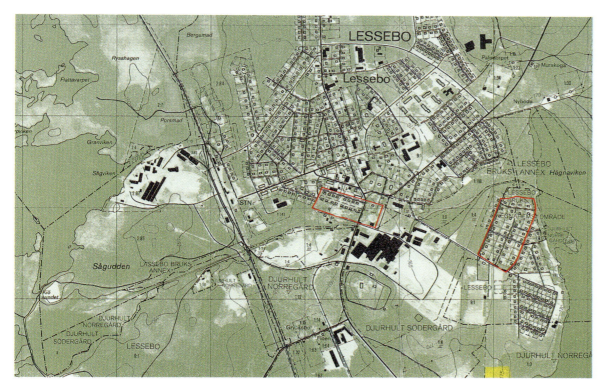

Classic milltown architecture can still be seen in the central parts of Lessebo, but demolition and new construction has destroyed some of the special milltown atmosphere. The outskirts of the town are dominated by private houses which grew up in the 1970s and 1980s, while the number of apartment blocks is quite small.

important customer outside the surrounding district was the naval base at Karlskrona.

In the mid–18th century a milltown started to develop, and in 1745 the Caroline-style mansion was built, surrounded by a well-designed garden. The smiths lived close to the mansion in small houses surrounded by fields and barns, marking the employees' integration of manufacturing and farming.

In 1802 Lessebo was purchased by Dr Johan Lorens Aschan, who made it the centre of a growing empire of mills. The production buildings were completely renovated, the mansion rebuilt and the smiths' houses were placed along a straight street leading up to the mansion. Lessebo had become a classical milltown. The main product became paper rather than iron, and during the 1880s all metal production ceased. In 1878 a modern steam sawmill was built at Lessebo, producing large quantities of sawn wood, most of which was exported from Karlskrona. The location of the mill from a transport point of view was greatly improved by the construction of the Karlskrona-Alvesta railway in 1874.

Lessebo kept its town plan until the early 1870s, when the increasing number of workers demanded new dwellings. Now large barrack-like blocks were erected, containing one-roomed apartments with kitchens. These were placed on the edge of the existing community. Many workers continued to live in crofts and houses within the surrounding district. The small plots of land they cultivated were an important insurance in a society that had no guaranteed labour market.

Lessebo AB dominated the milltown until 1939. The company owned most of the land as well as many of the dwelling houses. It was responsible for refuse disposal, road maintenance, the public baths, laundry and so on. It was not until 1945 that a distinction began to be made between private and public responsibilities, when state and municipal authorities, together with associations and private individuals, took over the various town functions.

Lessebo is dominated by its papermill. The remains of the old ironworks can be seen in the centre of the picture.

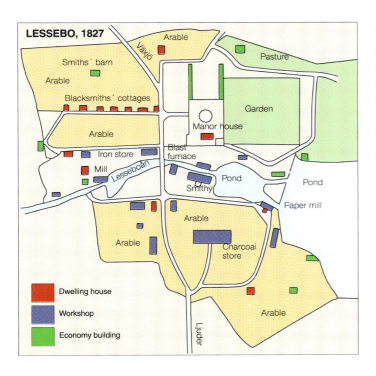

In 1827 Lessebo had traditional milltown buildings. The manufacturing buildings with the great smithy at the centre lie along the source of power—the river Lesseboån. The millowner's mansion has a dominant position, overlooking the smithy road. The small barns housing the blacksmiths' cattle have been replaced by one larger one. Round the buildings lie fields and meadows, indicating the integration of manufacturing and farming. The same is true of the mansion and its wings for agricultural work. All unnecessary and ugly buildings have been removed from the centre of the milltown.

85

Resmo Church on the western cliff of Öland was built as early as 1100. Below it, to the right in the picture, are the linear villages of Resmo and Gynge.

This geological map sheet from 1900 clearly illustrates the sharp contrast between the narrow till plain below the cliff and the grazed heathland.

The map made by the surveyor J E Strömbom in 1822–23 in connection with land redivsion at Åkerby in the parish of Runsten shows the typical linear pattern of Öland villages. Strömbom noted that, mainly on account of the location of the fields, "it was not possible to move any farms away from the village".

Villages and churches (here Stenåsa) stand in a row along the gravel soil of the eastern cliff, which also forms the natural line for the country road.

Öland and the Kalmar Coast

The villages on Öland have preserved to this very day an old-fashioned appearance. There was no settlement dispersal here as a result of 19th-century land reforms. The Öland geographer Abraham Ahlqvist noted in 1822 that "farms are moving out more slowly; the local inhabitants still love to live together in large villages." Reasons given for wanting to stay in the old farms were the severe shortage of timber on the island, the fact that outhouses were often built of stone and that the village had long occupied a favourable position between infields and outfields, and the troublesome scanty supply of fresh water in this dry, limestone landscape.

The pattern of building on Öland is characterised by geometric regularity. The villages lie in straight lines along ridges in the flat countryside, for example below the steep slopes of the western inland cliffs which carried springwater and on the banks of sand and gravel along former shorelines which partly form the eastern inland cliffs on the island. The fact that the farms in a village are often built in a row is closely related to medieval land division. This was introduced as early as the 12th century on Öland. The regular village plots were probably introduced in the 14th century. The idea behind them was that the village should reflect the divisions in the jointly-owned fields, where the part-owners' many parcels of arable and meadow land were spread out in a continually repeated pattern. The farmhouse plots were therefore placed in rows alongside each other in the same order.

The 1820 land division map of Åkerby shows how the rectangular plots are placed at right angles to the eastern inland cliff. The farms are built round a yard and the buildings are divided in the eastern Swedish style into a farmyard and a cattleyard. The length of the village along the street, now 600 m, reflects the generous medieval plot width of 144 Öland ells for each basic unit in the village corresponding to a normal-sized farm. On the cliff west of the village stands a long line of windmills of a simple medieval type. In the late Iron Age and the early Middle Ages Åkerby was not under the cliff but down in the fields, just over a kilometre closer to the shore.

Most churches in the early Middle Ages were placed on the cliff, both on the west and east sides of central and southern Öland.

The geological map shows the dramatic meeting-point at the western inland cliff of the fertile arable district of Mörbylångadalen, lying on marl and clay till, land that is among the most fertile in Sweden, and the naked, treeless, rocky ground of the "alvar" (limestone heath), covered with only a thin layer of till. The "alvar", too, is a kind of cultural landscape, worn as it is by thousands of years of cattle grazing; it was here that the villages' flocks of sheep used to graze or droves of half-wild horses wandered free. The "alvar", like the wide-open stretches of shoreland in East Öland, is now threatening to become scrubland.

The agrarian settlements on the plain on the Småland side of Kalmarsund are of the same impressive age, with their roots in the Iron Age. Whereas the cliffs on Öland offered geographical guidelines for the settlements, here towards the south-east it is the fast-running rivers that fulfil a similar function. Good, easily-worked sandy soils are the basis of Möre's large, open field district, the most important in Småland. The villages in Möre were never "regulated" to the same extent as those on Öland. The infields had their strips in regular pattern, but the farm buildings were less frequently replaced by regular rows.

Places of quite different kinds, characteristic of the Kalmar coast, are the ports of medieval origin which appear as the "vassal states" of the burghers of Kalmar, after it had gained its charter in 1620. They were Bergkvara, Pataholm, Mönsterås, Påskallavik, Dödershultsvik (now Oskarshamn) and Figeholm. This is where the markets for the peasant population living behind the coast gathered, and this is from where the forest districts' products were exported. Mönsterås grew up where a boulder ridge met a sea loch, where road and sea transport could meet. Its first buildings were rows of huts along the country road on the ridge north of the parish church and down by the shore.

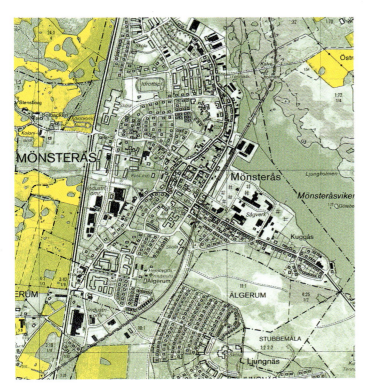

In the 17th century a series of trading places and harbours were established along the coast of Småland as market towns controlled by Kalmar and Västervik. One of them was Mönsterås, today an industrial town.

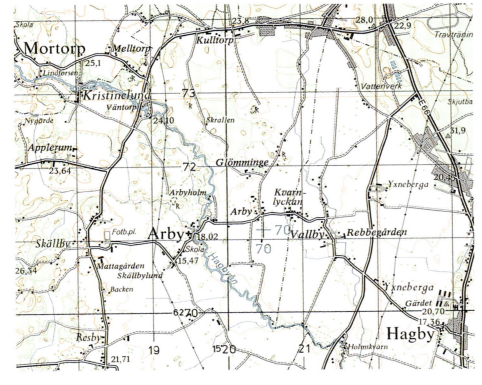

The village names and the large number of churches in Möre, a coastal district seldom more than 10 km broad, tells of a long tradition of cultivation. Most of the churches were built on or near a river.

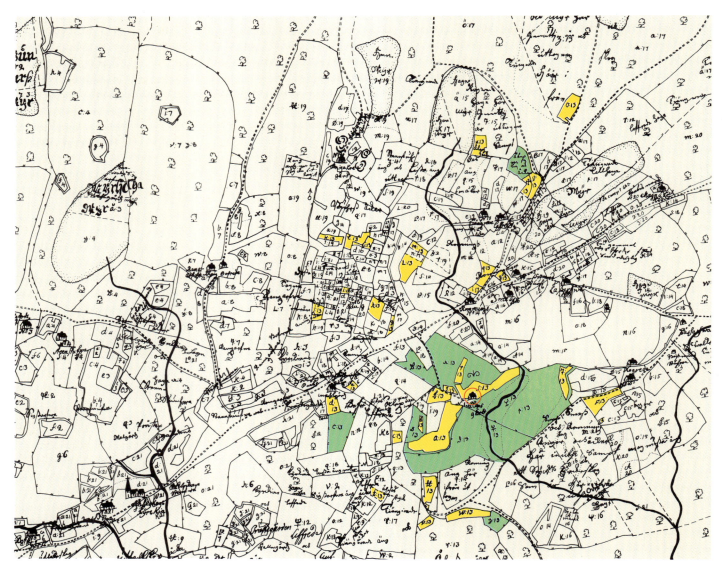

The farm called Ollajvs No 13 is specially marked on this extract from the tax-register map dated 1700 of the central parts of the parish of Alskog on Gotland. Its arable land, yellow on the map, is divided into 21 separate strips, with some concentration in the area closest to the farm. The meadows (green) lie in a large, continuous piece of land with the farm at its centre. In addition there were enclosed paddocks, mainly for grazing horses, at various places in the village. The outfields, mostly covered with forest, lie to the south-east outside the map.

Gotland

The ownership and farming of land on Gotland has always been in the form of isolated farms. Villages as fiscal objects or functional organisations have never existed—only isolated farms. Hamlet-like farmsteads grew up above all in the 18th and 19th centuries as a result of farm division. This compact form of farm settlement, which is still to be seen in the Gotland countryside, has no connection with the village as a form of organisation. Each farmer farmed his own land separately within its enclosures.

After having belonged to Denmark for almost 300 years, Gotland became a Swedish province in 1645. A commission was appointed in 1652 to survey the tax situation. The findings of this commission's investigations are reported in the Audit Book of 1653, which gives a complete picture of all the farms on the island. Land tax was imposed on the farms according to the Danish system called *marklej*. This system was used up until 1747, when it was replaced by the Swedish tax unit called *mantal*. In order to provide a basis for the 1747 reform a complete geometric land register was drawn up between 1694 and 1704.

CULTIVATION

Before the land was reformed and crop rotation was introduced, a three-field system was commonest. Two-field systems were used in a few parishes in northern Gotland and the island of Fårö had a one-field system. A farm's arable land was usually scattered and divided up into a number of irregular parcels. Some 20 fields of varying sizes might be cultivated. The three-field system, which required a large amount of land, usually meant that grain was the main crop. The ratio between arable land and meadow land, about 1:2.25, indicates, however, that cattle-farming was the major type of husbandry on Gotland. Mid–17th-century comparisons between Gotland and geographically equivalent areas in Central Sweden show that the size and potential cultivation of Gotland farms was approximately twice as large as on the mainland. Actual cultivation measured in fields and meadows was, however, roughly the same in both areas. This comparison suggests a sparse population and a low level of cultivation on Gotland.

DESERTED VILLAGES AND LAND DIVISION

The 1653 Audit Book lists 1,540 farms. This number of farms has proved to be more or less constant ever since the middle of the 13th century. Farms have been abandoned to some extent, with the greatest decrease in the 16th century. The number of deserted farms is about 14 per cent of all known farms. The Audit Book lists 58 deserted farms, which corresponds to 3.8 per cent of the number in 1653. Most of the deserted farms were under cultivation but could not pay their taxes.

The parish of Alskog from the east. Ollajvs Farm is just to the left outside the picture. The present division of land is the result of land reform in the late 19th century.

Land division meant that a farm was divided into two or more units, usually as a result of inheritance. Of a total of 1,540 farms in 1653, 215 (13.3%) were divided into 443 units. By the end of the 17th century just over 40 per cent of the farms had been divided; this process accelerated in the 18th century and reached its peak in the 1880s. By then 98 per cent of the farms had been divided into an average of four units per farm. Land division was generally speaking as comprehensive on Gotland as on the mainland.

In contrast, noblemen's estates have never been created on Gotland, nor has there been any pressure at the other end of the agrarian ranking list in the form of croft settlements. The growth in the population in the first half of the 19th century was absorbed within the framework of the freehold farming community. The old fiscal classification of farms as tax-paying, Crown and noblemen's units showed that the freehold tax-paying farmers were in a clear majority. The Crown farmers purchased their farms in the 18th century, so making them tax-paying farms. There were no noblemen farmers at all on Gotland.

LAND REFORMS

Swedish legislation relating to land reform aimed at making villages set up a reform council. But there were only isolated farms on Gotland; each farm was a registered unit and thereby a reform council. There was no legal possibility for two or more neighbouring farms to form a council together and reorganize their landholdings jointly. Thus land reform could not be forced upon a farm unless the farm was about to be divided.

During the period 1760–1860 the *storskifte* reform was carried out at most Gotland farms as a result of farm division. Attempts were made by the county authorities as early as 1771 to force through land reform, using the whole parish as a unit, but this met with stubborn resistance from the farmers. Not until 70 years later was land reform carried out at a parish level, and the special Gotland regulations were abolished in 1859. Instead, the 1827 law of land reform was to apply when redividing land. This allowed land reform to be initiated and during the years 1860 to 1910 98 per cent of the land was redivided. The last great land redivisions took place in the 1950s, and a few units are still undivided.

CULTIVATION SINCE LAND REFORM

In the old days there was a great deal of wetland and many shallow lakes, which are called mires on Gotland. These covered some 10 per cent of the island. Today approximately 35 per cent of the original wetland has been preserved, while the remainder has been drained and cultivated. About 30 per cent of the need for new land was met by cultivating wetland. A considerable amount of the former meadowland, which generally speaking required more work to be cleared, could thus be saved. In Gotland's central cultivated district about 20 per cent of the meadowland has been saved from cultivation. In the districts in the north, east and south of Gotland this figure reaches about 50 per cent.

Gotland's cultivated land is like a patchwork quilt of fields and woods divided into squares by the straight boundaries of land reform. But beneath this system there lies in meadows and grazing grounds another pattern, the relics of an older cultural landscape. The slow growth of the population and a low level of land use have created a very favourable climate for the preservation of the remains of the old cultivated landscape.

A Gotland meadow has a rich variety of wild flowers, including orchids. Many meadows are scythed in the old fashion by the owner or a local historical association.

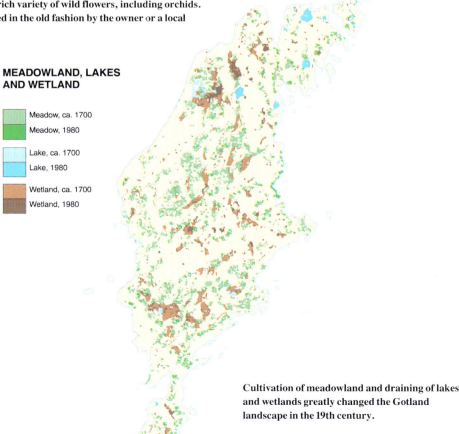

Cultivation of meadowland and draining of lakes and wetlands greatly changed the Gotland landscape in the 19th century.

MEADOWLAND, LAKES AND WETLAND

- Meadow, ca. 1700
- Meadow, 1980
- Lake, ca. 1700
- Lake, 1980
- Wetland, ca. 1700
- Wetland, 1980

South Vättern

From his country palace high up on the cliff at Gränna, the founder in 1652 of the town of Gränna, Per Brahe, had a glorious view of his county. Out in Lake Vättern lies the narrow, low island of Visingsö, where he and before him several of the 12th and 13th-century kings, including Magnus Ladulås, had resided. From the mainland one sees the open cultivated landscape and the enclosed square plantations. The once so common windmills have been replaced by tall, white, three-bladed wind turbines.

Gränna stands on a narrow coastal strip surrounded by fields and orchards in straight, parallel lines. The climate here close to the lake is mild and favourable for cultivation. The farm buildings crouch at the foot of the cliff. The pattern of red farm buildings and white farmhouses is an echo of the plains of Östergötland. South of Uppgränna the buildings lie closer together, gradually merging into the town itself.

Here and there the steep precipices round the east side of Vättern are pierced by deep gullies and valleys. Streams and rivers rush down them on their way to the lake. They often fall from a considerable height, and several of them have been used for manufacturing, which led to the concentrated settlement we have today. Per Brahe established for his own county a papermill, flour mills and textile stamping machines on the river Röttle å, south of Gränna. Even the farmers on Visingsö came here to grind their corn. In 1689 parts of the gun factory at Jönköping were transferred to the river Huskvarnaån. This rich supply of water power was used to manufacture a wide range of small mechanical products for civil use at Huskvarna Ordnance Factory.

King Gustav II Adolf (Gustavus Adolphus) built musket factories along the rapids of the Dunkehallaån, where there were also water-driven flour mills.

The E4 motorway along the shore of Vättern offers wide prospects of the South Swedish highlands' most hilly landscape. Where the E4 passes through Ölmstad, the whole of the South Vättern countryside lies before you. The mighty Taberg towers up in

The landscape round the southern end of Lake Vättern, with the characteristic silhouette of Taberg in Småland in the background, is the dramatic setting for Johan Werner's portrait of Count Per Brahe. The country residence of Brahehus is a ruin today, but provides a magnificent viewpoint and picnic spot on the E4. Gränna was founded by Brahe in 1652 to be the central town in his county.

Huskvarna, in the background, dates back to the 17th century. Rosenlunds Bankar, with its mighty precipice, has never been built on.

Jönköping has expanded in all directions round its medieval core ever since its early industrialisation, which included match factories, now industrial monuments.

the background. The horizon from Habo in the west to Gisebo in the east forms a dramatic line. Deep valleys alternate with steep cliffs. Along the southern shore from Bankeryd in the west to Huskvarna there is a broad ribbon of urban development. The only gap is along the steep embankments at Rosenlund, where it is impossible to build.

The surrounding groups of houses stand further up the slopes, reaching like annual rings higher and higher up each year. Today Österängen, which once separated Huskvarna from Jönköping, is completely built up. The latest estates reach to the very top of Bondberget.

Similar developments can be seen at Bymarken to the west, at Norrahammar to the south and at Hakarp to the east. The oldest areas contain mostly detached houses, while in the new areas there are apartment blocks as well as detached houses.

Rosenlund lies half way between Jönköping and Huskvarna; at a distance it is easy to distinguish its light-coloured clay embankments. Because of their position on the lake these embankments are continuously exposed to heavy abrasion. The waves that sweep in with the north wind hit the embankments with full force, causing continual landslides. Every year some 25 cm of the embankments disappear into the lake, dragging down trees that lie fallen in the clear water. Today this area is used for open-air exhibitions and water sports.

A MEETING POINT

Since time immemorial this district has been an important meeting point for people and goods coming by land or by water. It was a strategic place, the meeting point of the medieval "Erik Tour" and the important Lagastigen and Nissastigen. There is a mound where the medieval fort of Rumlaborg stood, but nothing remains of the fortified castle at Jönköping except a street name.

When the Göta Canal opened in 1832, shipping on Lake Vättern enjoyed a boom. Direct steam-boat lines ran to Stockholm and Göteborg. In the 1850s the main southern railway line came to Jönköping, encouraging new industries, of which match factories and Munksjö papermill were the leading examples. The match factories are now industrial monuments.

The road network expanded in the 20th century. "Highway One" was constructed along the line of the old medieval road and in the 1960s came the broad motorways connected to the European road network. The E4 along the shores of Vättern was voted the most beautiful road in Sweden. Vast land-consuming junctions have been constructed where the major roads meet.

Nowadays the traffic does not cut through the towns but runs on bypasses outside the town centres. The motorway through Huskvarna was built on landfills in Vättern, while round Jönköping the traffic is led in a wide ring south of the town past Ryhov and the old airfield at Ljungarum. A new airfield has been built on the sandy heath west of the town.

These new roads and junctions have created attractive sites for hypermarkets and goods terminals. The old airfield is used by trading companies, transport firms and engineering works that need plenty of space. Several supermarkets have grown up at one of the junctions, where the old artillery regiment had its barracks.

DEVELOPMENT OF JÖNKÖPING

— 1730
1837
1900

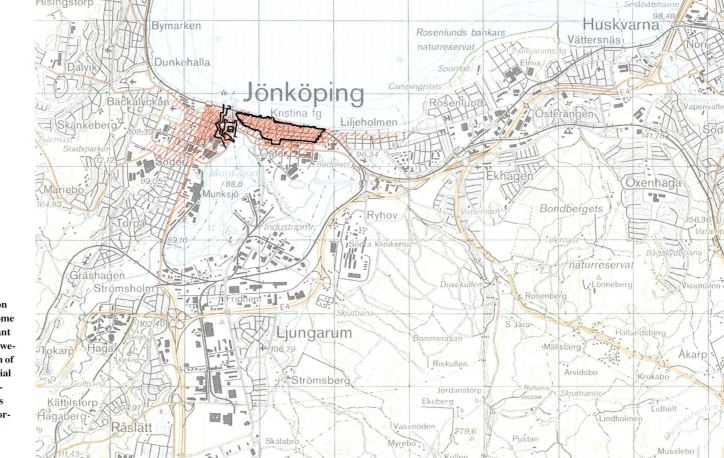

Jönköping's position at the junction of some of the most important roads in southern Sweden has always been of strategic, commercial and military importance. Nothing of its former castle and fortifications remains, however, except in street names.

The old industrial landscape round Motala Ström still dominates the centre of Norrköping. In the background, the lower reaches of Motala Ström, the harbour and Bråviken to the east.

Östergötland

The large fields of the western Östgöta plain belong to large, well-organised farms cultivating grain and oil-seed on soil that is among the very best in Sweden.

The Östgöta Plain

The central Östgöta plain is surrounded to the north by the forest districts of the Östergötland hills and to the south by the north slopes of the South Swedish highlands. To the west the plain runs all the way down to the shores of Vättern, while in the east it meets a rugged coastline dotted with small islands. The central plain is broken up in turn by both shallow and deep river valleys and lakes like the Motala Ström valley running from west to east and the Svartån and Stångån valleys running from south to north.

The bedrock of the central plain, to the west Cambro-Silurian limestone, is covered with fertile clays.

If one travels westwards along the old highway—now the E4—through Östergötland, one follows the main southern railway line as far as Mjölby, which lies at one of the last falls in the Svartån valley, marking the transition from highland to lowland. Mjölby is the town of watermills that became a railway junction. To the north lies the fertile Vadstena plain. This is a landscape of large, open fields. On a fine day one can see on the distant horizon the spires of Vadstena Convent.

The Vadstena plain has always been one of the richest agricultural districts in Sweden, with large, modernised farms, so the architecture undergoes rapid changes. The large farms often have a white or pale yellow farmhouse, surrounded by scattered cottages for day workers and their families. Newly-built double garages in the cottage gardens reveal that the occupants now commute to work in the nearby towns by car. The round barns and stately cowhouses have been replaced by or complemented with buildings with corrugated iron roofs for farm machinery. Another new feature is the high silos, showing that many farms still have large herds of cattle, even though corn and rape are the main crops here.

A number of old railway communities with small industries remind us of the formerly dense railway network. They are more and more being drawn into the commuting belts of towns.

The characteristic silhouette of Omberg stands out above the shore of Vättern. In the district round Omberg's south, beech-clad slopes with its favourable local climate we find many cultural monuments from the Middle Ages.

THE ALVASTRA DISTRICT, 1640

- 🟧 Arable land
- 🟩 Meadowland, pasture
- ⬜ Forest and wasteland
- 🟥 Farmstead
- ✚ Church
- ⬛ Monastery ruins

The Östgöta plain developed into continous arable land in the 19th century after the cultivation of fodder plants had made meadows and pastures superfluous. The maps show the district south of Omberg around 1640 and 1980.

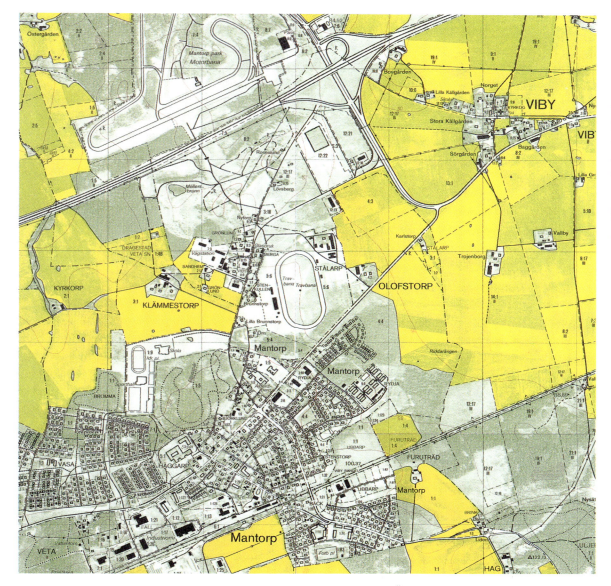

This map dated 1880 shows the district round Viby after *laga skifte* reform and the construction of the railway. The abbreviation Uh stands for a farm that has been moved away from the village.

In olden times Viby church village was an important centre on the Erik Tour through Östergötland. South-west of Viby was Mantorp, a medieval village at the edge of the forest and in the 19th century a large farm. In the 19th century the land belonging to Viby was redivided, which meant that most of the farms were moved out from the village to new sites in the outlying land. Somewhat later the railway was built south of Viby, with a station on Mantorp's land round which an industrial community grew up. As road traffic increased, Mantorp expanded towards the E4. Several public attractions were constructed, including a motor-racing track and a hypermarket. The old church village lost its last central functions as a result of changes in municipal division, 1952–74. The photograph was taken in 1980 facing north-east and shows Mantorp and the plain round Viby.

VIBY AND MANTORP

Viby and Mantorp illustrate the way the plain has been urbanised. Viby church village has its roots in prehistory and is one of the largest church villages on the Östgöta plain. Until the land reform of 1838–39 the farms were gathered close together round the church in the middle of arable land of the finest quality, where the main road from Linköping, the medieval Erik Tour, divides into one road leading to the medieval towns of Skänninge and Vadstena and the present main road to Mjölby. It was a prominent village.

The first revolution came with land reform in the 19th century, when most of the village was dispersed across the outlying land. The second began when the 1853/54 Riksdag voted to build the main railway lines. The southern line was laid just south of the village. The nearest station was given the name of the farm across whose land it ran, Mantorp. Mantorp was a medieval farm, adjacent to Viby to the south-west, on rather poor soil. A railway community developed and when cars became common in the 1950s it expanded towards the main road to the north, which is now a motorway. The third blow to Viby came with the municipal reforms of 1952–74, by which the village lost all its central functions in the old municipality. Today Mantorp is a town with 3,405 inhabitants (1 Jan 1994) and considerable amenities which attract large numbers of visitors. The rerouting of the main road as a motorway north of Viby finally allowed the depopulated church village to sink back into rural tranquillity.

PLACES WITH MORE THAN 200 INHABITANTS IN BOHUSLÄN, 1830

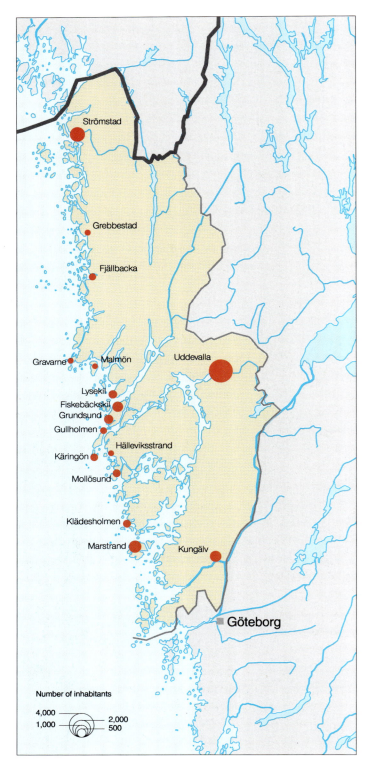

The establishment of the ocean-fishing district in central Bohuslän two decades after the great herring fishing industry had died out, is connected partly with good harbours and partly with the need for large fishing teams. Fiskebäckskil, Sweden's largest fishing village in the 18th century, was in 1830 on the way to becoming the leading ocean-fishing community. Shipping flourished in the 1860s and 1870s, leaving its mark on the architecture of many large and highly-decorated wooden houses. Skärhamn was then only a little coastal hamlet with some fifty inhabitants. The buildings on the islands in the parish of Öckerö had not yet grown together to form "built-up areas". Hönö, with its five groups of houses, had less than 300 inhabitants.

The Bohuslän Coast

The Bohuslän coast and islands face onto the Skagerrak, where they are exposed to wind and waves. Bare rock is the dominant feature of the landscape.

Traces of human activity have been found from the early Stone Age in the archipelago of that time, which today forms the highest points on the mainland and the largest islands. There is proof of permanent, continuous settlement in the present archipelago from the early Middle Ages. The parishes of Öckerö and Tjärnö were formed. Here, as inland, the isolated farm is the usual form of settlement, with agriculture on the larger islands and cattle-farming and fishing on the smaller ones. Remains of "fishing camps" from the Middle Ages and the 16th century have been found along the shores; these were used seasonally in exposed places and inhabited permanently in more sheltered positions.

Some 30 shore settlements from the herring era of the 16th century have been found. The fishing villages of Mollösund, Fiskebäckskil and Lysekil were so large that they formed their own chapel parishes. The inhabitants of the shores and islands made their living by fishing and shipping. The population increased until 1640, but many of the shore settlements were abandoned between 1658 and 1680 when the region became Swedish. The number of tax payers also decreased in other settlements.

The herring returned every autumn in large numbers after 1750, and the settlements in the archipelago increased again. There was a strong demand for herring on the international market. Outside merchants, mainly from Göteborg, built salting houses and when the catches grew, train-oil factories. The managers and the coopers lived at the factories all the year round, the workers during the fishing season. Fishing and transport were the responsibility of the islanders, and the number of fishing villages grew considerably. Six new chapel parishes, Rönnäng, Klädesholmen, Käringön, Gullholmen, Grundsund and Kungshamn, were established. Herring fishing brought prosperity to the local population.

When the herring disappeared, most of the factory buildings were demolished and only a few have survived. Coopers and managers turned to other industries. The fishermen made their living by fishing for mackerel and other small fish from the shore and with hook and line and nets.

Boat-building and shipping, not least on Lake Vänern, became important for the inhabitants of Inland and eastern Orust. Fiskebäckskil developed into a shipping centre in a district which specialised in international shipping.

Increasingly large parts of the North Sea and the adjacent Atlantic were fished in the 19th century from the fishing villages between Åstol and Bovallstrand. Along this part of the coast the classical fishing village developed, with cottages, boat houses and wooden jetties.

Fishing in the Göteborg archipelago concentrated on selling fresh fish. In the late 19th century and the early 20th century West Coast fishing began to go over to seine nets and trawls instead of hook and line. The innovators were the fishermen of Hönö and the other islands in the Göteborg archipelago.

The stone industry grew up initially on Malmön. Its raw material was the granite which forms the bedrock from Lysekil northwards. The stone industry led to the founding of new settlements and affected the growth of existing ones. The largest quarrying villages were Rixö on Brofjorden and Krokstrand on Idefjorden.

The coast settlements are the result of a number of local activities over a long historical period. During the late 18th century the coast and the sea began to be of interest for recreation. Gustavsberg, the Curman villas at Lysekil and the buildings at Marstrand are relics of this period. Since the Second World War many summer cottages have been built, so that large stretches of the coast are exploited today.

The concentration of work places in the towns led to many permanent dwellings being turned into second homes, principally in central and north Bohuslän. During the last twenty years the reverse trend has occurred. As a result of the fishing crisis of the 1960s many villages have become commuter suburbs.

In the 1960s there was an increasing demand for new industrial sites. The refineries on Hisingen and Brofjorden and the petrochemical industries at Stenungsund inflicted great changes on the cultural landscape. This is also true of the motorway that was built through Bohuslän.

The island of Kiddön in Yttre Hamburgsund was built on as late as 1823 by Ingel Axelsson. His descendants were skippers of their own schooners. In 1994 Ingel's great-great grandson lives on the island and helps to conserve the cultural environment there.

As early as the 16th century Mollösund was an important community with its own priest and royal customs officer. In 1586 it was given Mollön and Nedre Tången as a royal donation for hay-making and grazing. In 1773 the buildings lined the street running south, with sheds and jetties down by the sound. By 1839 the cabbage patches closest to the cliff had been built on. A hundred years later the cliffs east and north of the village had been exploited. Today most of the inhabitants of Mollösund live up at Änga (Nedre Tången) or on the cliffs to the south. The old 18th and 19th-century houses are second homes for people who have moved away, their children or other summer visitors. At the turn of the century (1900) Mollösund had a population of 1,000; in 1990 it was 355.

At many places along the coast one sees traces of quarries (Bohus granite). The stone was quarried as near to the quayside as possible. Here at Rixö in northern Bohuslän work seems to have ended only yesterday.

The seaside resort and railway junction of Stenungsund has grown during the past few decades into a town with a population of 10,000 and become one of Sweden's petro-chemical centres.

95

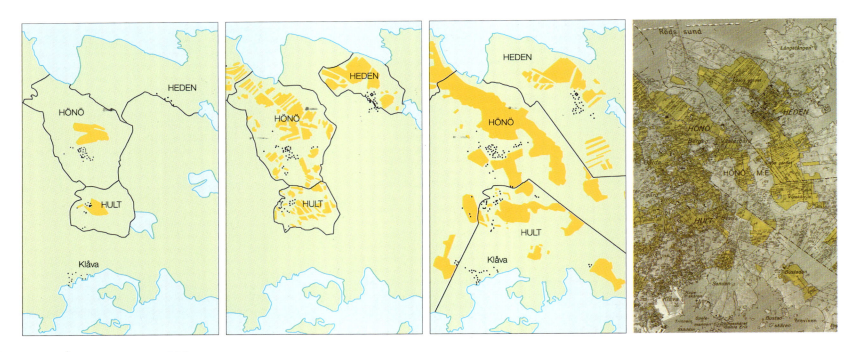

Hönö — An Island Community

This series of maps shows how Hönön has been exploited since the early 19th century and how the area of arable land first increased, then decreased until it completely disappeared in the mid–20th century when Hönö was fully exploited. From the left the maps show fields and buildings around 1800, after the land reforms of 1824–28 *laga skifte* and in 1934.

During the heyday of the great herring-fishing era, the outfields of the five farms on Hönö were redivided. Two maps of the infields dated 1801 show the small area of arable land. The buildings are grouped close to the infields with the exception of a small cluster on the common shoreland of Klåva. The new opportunities for cultivation resulting from the division of the farms were taken and the village expanded. At the same time the area between Hönö and Klåva was built up.

The inhabitants of Hönö introduced several new techniques in fishing, and during the years 1900–65 it was Sweden's largest fishing village. After the Second World War in 1945 the arable land was left uncultivated and the fields were used for building. As a result of the fishing crisis in the late 1960s the fleet of trawlers was sold and Hönö became a commuter town.

By 1900 the former arable land had been completely built up. In the north-west of Hönö there are many foundations which may have been used as bases for fishing from the shore or perhaps even for net fishing for herring.

Göteborg and the Göta Älv Valley

SWEDEN'S GATEWAY TO THE NORTH SEA
- Swedish territory before 1645
- ● Town
- ● Early township preceding Göteborg
- ★ Fortress
- ☆ Deserted fortress

Göteborg was founded in 1618–21 in frontierland where towns and fortresses often changed in status. Kungahälla in Norway and Lödöse in Sweden were the oldest of them. Bohus Castle, built in 1303–08, was able to control the trade route to Lödöse. The Swedish countermove was Nylödöse, founded in 1473. Gustav Vasa established Älvsborg and Karl IX Göteborg on Hisingen. Both were soon destroyed by the Danes.

The heart of Göteborg is at the site on the Göta Älv chosen by Gustav II Adolf (Gustavus Adolphus) in 1618. The town had several predecessors as the west-coast port of Sweden. Göteborg was founded when Sweden controlled only a narrow corridor out to the North Sea. The town site included two small hills, but most of the town was built on marshland, with canals, embankments and fortifications. The town owned low-lying areas south of the moat as well as donation land belonging to its predecessor, Nylödöse, to the north-east. The embankments lost their importance for defence early in the 19th century and became parks. The land south of Nya Allén was planned and built with brick houses, and the outlying areas with wooden houses and houses with a ground floor of brick and two wooden upper floors (*landshövdingehus*). Outside the town limits on the high land at Landala and Masthuggsbergen wooden houses were erected without planning. The suburb of Majorna grew up to the west towards the river mouth. When Majorna was incorporated with Göteborg in 1868, it had 9,000 inhabitants. Örgryte was incorporated between 1883 and 1922 and in 1906 the parish of Lundby. By then the shipbuilding industry had moved across the river. Typical working-class districts grew up on Hisingen. Large brick houses were built on the heights south of Götaplatsen and to the east in the 1930s. After the Second World War the high ground at Guldheden was exploited with tower blocks instead of long, low apartment blocks. Göteborg cannot expand to the south and the east, so its growth was mainly in the south-west in the 1940s. The incorporation of Frölunda meant that Göteborg got access to large areas of building land and a long stretch of coast. Västra Frölunda was built up in the 1960s.

Industry in Göteborg expanded in the 1960s and expectations were high. In 1967 the city absorbed most of Hisingen and Angered and Bergum in the north-east. Land was purchased and Göteborg planned a new town within the city limits with a population of 150–200,000 and a centre at Angered, which would take the pressure off central Göteborg. The new town was connected with the old centre by means of a light railway.

The large height differences in the hilly areas and the clay in the Lärjeån valley led to a change in these plans. The plans for a large-scale industrial estate on Hisingen motivated an expansion of housing north of the Nordre Älv in what was then the municipality of Hermansby. The demand for industrial land decreased and in the early 1990s large parts of Hisingen were not developed. This is also the case with Bergum.

At the same time as building reached its peak within Göteborg's limits there was a considerable expansion of its suburban areas, not least in Mölndal and Partille, to which Göteborg's built-up area extended. The coast to the south was developed after the 1960s when people began to live permanently in old summer cottages and newly-built detached houses. Today the people of Göteborg live not only along the "Gold Coast" down to Onsala but also outside the official Göteborg region in Varberg, Mark, Borås, Alingsås, Lilla Edet, Uddevalla and Orust.

The older parts of Göteborg have been undergoing a renewal since the 1960s. This is focussed at present on the north shore of the river, which used to be the centre of shipbuilding and port industries.

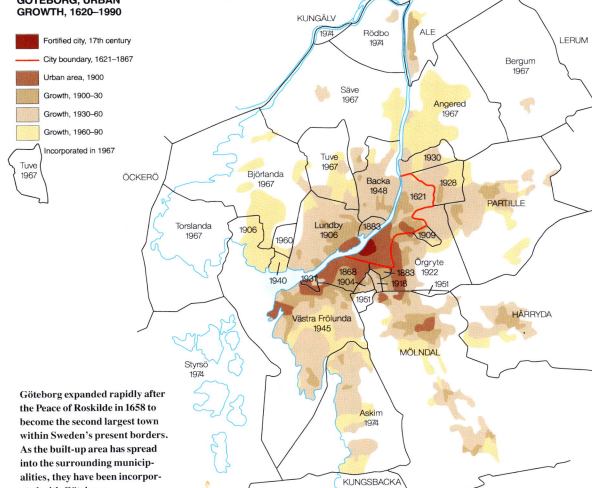

GÖTEBORG, URBAN GROWTH, 1620–1990
- Fortified city, 17th century
- City boundary, 1621–1867
- Urban area, 1900
- Growth, 1900–30
- Growth, 1930–60
- Growth, 1960–90
- Incorporated in 1967

Göteborg expanded rapidly after the Peace of Roskilde in 1658 to become the second largest town within Sweden's present borders. As the built-up area has spread into the surrounding municipalities, they have been incorporated with Göteborg.

Stora Hamnkanalen was Göteborg's first port. To the left, on the north bank of the canal, stands the headquarters of the Swedish East India Company, now the city museum, Kristine (the German) Church, and the City Hall. In the background, Brunnsparken.

Docks and shipyards took over the banks of the Göta Älv during the 19th and 20th centuries. The docks have moved further out and the shipyards have been closed down. Today the former shipyards are being redeveloped. In the background, the town within its canals with the tower of the Cathedral in the centre and the red building of the Skanska Group on the river bank. The new opera house now stands next to Göta Älv Bridge.

The docks today are on the Hisingen side of Göteborg, beyond the Älvsborg Bridge towards Nya Älvsborg. The photograph looks south-west towards the river mouth. In the foreground, the Volvo-Torslanda factory, in the background, the modern Skandia Docks and to the left the lofty span of Älvsborg Bridge.

A map dated 1855 shows the built-up parts of Göteborg and the suburb of Majorna. The regular street pattern within the canals is clearly visible, as is Allmänna Vägen as it winds through Majorna. Some of the canals were later filled in.

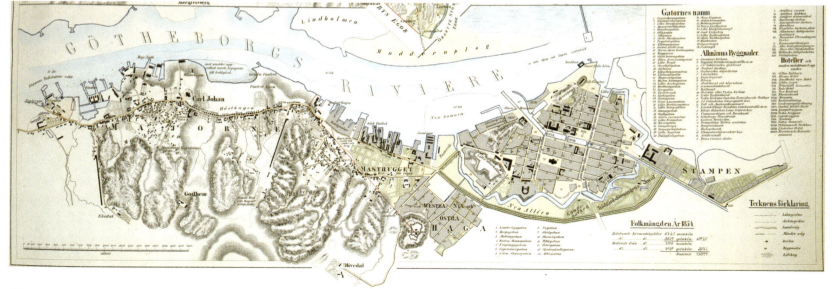

Above left, the view to the south-west along the river valley, showing Bohus Castle and Kungälv.

"Governor's Houses", built with stone at street level and two wooden storeys above, are a well-known feature of Göteborg. Here, a well-preserved district in Majorna.

The major roads lie close together in the heavily industrialised valley of the Göta Älv.

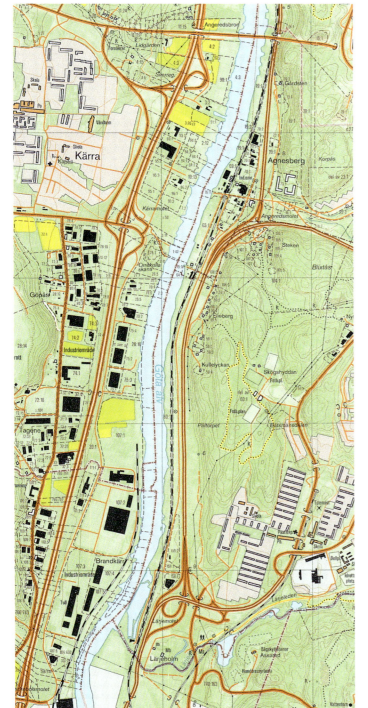

Göteborg's most fashionable street, Kungsportsavenyn, is without parallel in Sweden. The view is from Götaplatsen, the Art Museum and the Concert Hall, down towards the former Kungsporten (King's Gate) by the canal.

N Västergötland
Alingsås

Long is one of the few villages on the Västgöta plain which still has its buildings gathered together in the style that was common before *laga skifte*, thanks to land division according to the "pie principle".

The Västgöta Plain

The settlements round Lake Vänern are situated on the plain in Värmland, Dalsland and Västergötland, where fertile clay has encouraged agriculture since prehistoric times. Västergötland, with its great plains, was also one of the most densely populated areas at the beginning of the Middle Ages. Christianity emerged victorious in the province as early as the 11th century, and the diocese of Skara was the first to be established in Sweden. Progress was slower in Dalsland and Värmland, so these areas lack the strong early influence from the church and the nobility that characterises Västergötland.

The most typical plain landscape is to be found on the flat clay between Vara and Lidköping. Here there are large, open fields worked by isolated farms, the result of a land reform which forced the largest group of farms in the whole of Sweden to move away from the villages. Known prehistoric remains are sparse, presumably because many of them have been cleared away by centuries of cultivation. Today the population is decreasing and farms are being amalgamated to form large, rationalised units.

The Falbygden district is the name given to the special landscape round Falköping. It consists of a high plateau landscape with calciferous clay till on the plains and is one of Sweden's earliest populated and cultivated areas. It is rich in prehistoric remains, including the largest group of passage graves in Sweden. Many small parishes with 12th-century churches bear witness to dense settlement even in the early Middle Ages.

Agriculture has always been and continues to be the main industry,

The Cambro-Silurian plateau in central Västergötland, framed by its characteristic table hills and their forest-clad diabase surface, is one of the oldest agricultural districts in Sweden. A large number of the known stone chamber graves from the agricultural Stone Age are to be found in Falbygden.

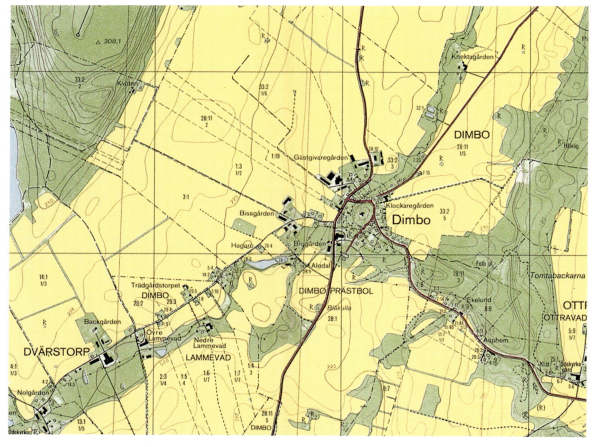

In early times physical-geographical conditions, land use and architectural styles in the clay-till district of Västergötland were similar to those on the plains of Skåne. The farms were often built on low-lying land by a river. In this case the farm is in fact named after its stream. The village common and the lines of the roads on the 17th-century map of Dimbo can still be seen there. The village has prehistoric roots: east of the village lies the largest cemetery in Skaraborg County, dating back to the Iron Age.

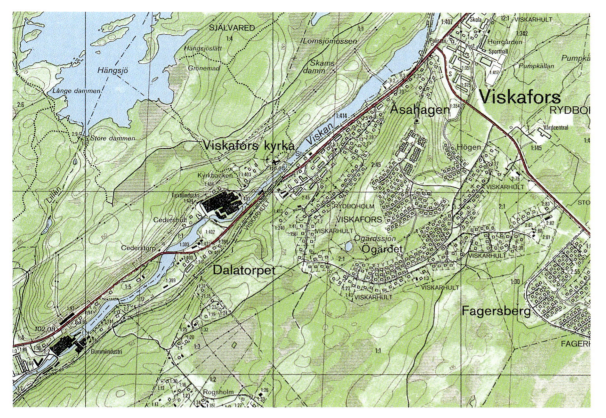

The valley of the Viskan became the centre of the textile industry at an early date, with Borås as its capital. The decline of the textile industry has severely affected the district; many factories are now desolate industrial monuments.

Alingsås was founded by Gustav II Adolf (Gustavus Adolphus) as a market town. During the 18th century it developed into a leading industrial town after Jonas Alströmer had smuggled in a few looms from Holland and established the Alingsås Manufactory in 1724. Its varied textile production flourished for several decades. After only a few years the town (pop. then about 150) was incorporated with the company and twenty years later its factories had 875 employees.

The textile industry has had a dominant position in Alingsås right up to modern times, but its importance has diminished greatly in the past few decades. In 1990 131 textile workers accounted for six per cent of industrial employment.

The gridiron street plan in the centre of the town was developed between the mid–17th century up to the late 19th century, and, in spite of demolition and rebuilding, is still the best preserved example in the county.

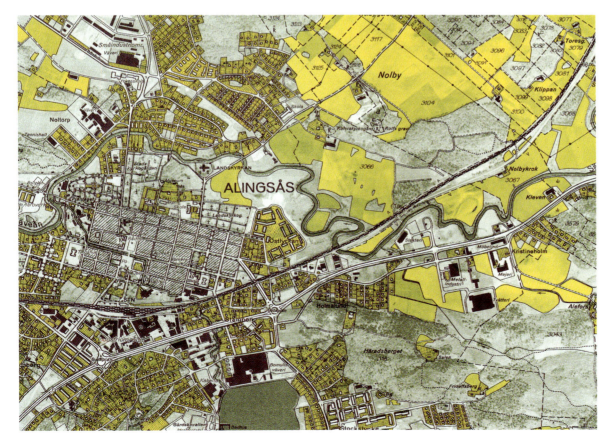

and in comparison with the Vara plain it has also retained many old features of the cultural landscape. Both settlement patterns and land division can in many cases be traced back to the Middle Ages, as shown on 17th-century maps.

The grazing land was called *falorna,* which gave the district its name. This land consists of limestone plateaus with a thin covering of soil supporting a rich and special flora only found elsewhere in Sweden on Öland.

Viskadalen

The Seven Hundreds district consists of the old hundreds of Gäsene, Ås, Veden, Mark, Bollebygd, Kind and Redveg. A textile industry grew up in this part of south Västergötland on the basis of the cottage industry that developed during the latter part of the 18th century from an ancient homecrafts tradition. Trading by pedlars had been made legal in Borås's town charter in 1622.

The textile industry was organised as a cottage industry, in which the purchase of raw materials, which demanded capital, was managed by merchants, who also sold the finished goods through a country-wide network of travelling salesmen or pedlars.

In the early 19th century some forty merchants kept thousands of home weavers employed in the valleys of the Viskan and the Häggån in Mark, where Seglora, Fritsla, Kinna, Skene and Örby were the most important places. This type of work lived on and even expanded towards the end of the 19th century. At the same time craft factories were set up outside farming land along the sides of the valleys. This modern industry was located close to water power in the Viskan valley where communications were good, in competition with agriculture.

This concentration of the textile industry to the Seven Hundreds district in particular, but also to the county of Älvsborg in general, increased during the 1980s. More than 30 per cent of all those employed in the textile and clothing industry worked in this county in 1990.

Increasing competition from countries with cheap labour, as well as other factors, has, however, led to the closure of many firms. Employment in the textile industry decreased from 114,000 in 1950 to 15,000 in 1990 in the whole of Sweden.

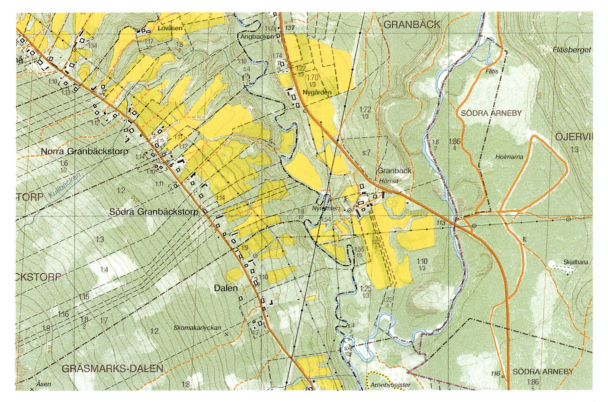

Håbol in Dalsland

The forest districts of Dalsland and western Värmland were not generally inhabited and cultivated until the Middle Ages. The first farmers settled on the sediment in the river valleys and by lakes. Agriculture was primitive in both Dalsland and Värmland for a long time, and was complemented by forestry and trading in wooden goods, above all with Norway. The settlements in Värmland developed into village-like clusters as a result of the division of what were originally isolated farms.

The population of Sweden increased in the 19th century, so agriculture could no longer support everybody. Many people were forced to leave home and find work in towns or in other countries, particularly North America. This was especially true of marginal farming districts where the growth in population had strained agricultural resources to the limit. The forest districts of Dalsland and Värmland were in this category, and the population has continued to decline to this very day.

One of the parishes in Sweden that was struck hardest by emigration was Håbol in north-west Dalsland. Between 1880 and 1950 the population decreased by 64 per cent; from 1881 to 1927 98 crofts and 30 farms were abandoned in this parish.

Two maps illustrate the changes in the district. The Hundreds map of 1894 shows a line of farms along the narrow valley south of Sandsjön. East of this cultivated district, where many of the farms are several hundreds of years old, there is a hilly forest area in which there are crofts and farms belonging to the villages in the valley. The map from 1964 shows that most of the farms in the valley are still in existence, but all the buildings in the forest area have gone. Some of these small farms are said to have been inhabited and worked as late as the 1920s, and traces of houses and clearings are still clearly visible, framed by the dark forest. The forest has begun to encroach on the farms and crofts and their previously open fields that were abandoned at an early date. Soon all that will remain will be the piles of stones once cleared from the fields.

In the high hills of the Värmland landscape the villages are closely tied up with lake shores and river terraces — or to the ridges in the landscape. Granbäckstorp near Gräsmark on Lake Rottnen stands on the upper edge of a terrace of fine sediment which has been eroded at the bottom. The land register numbers show that the village grew up from a few isolated farms.

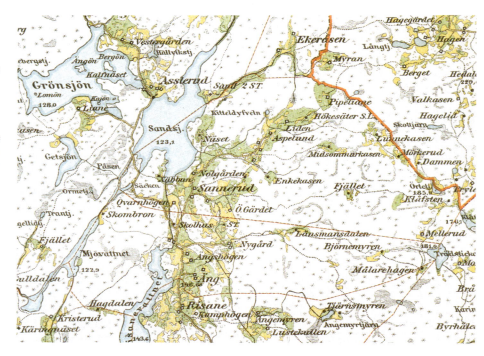

Vedbo Hundred in northern Dalsland has a rugged forest landscape of till. The earlier map, dated 1864, shows how, under the pressure of rapid population growth in the 19th century, cultivation and buildings had moved upwards into rougher country, where mires and clearings might provide hay and some small fields. Most of these outlying crofts had disappeared long before the 1964 map was produced. As late as 1990 there was farming on a small scale down by the lakes.

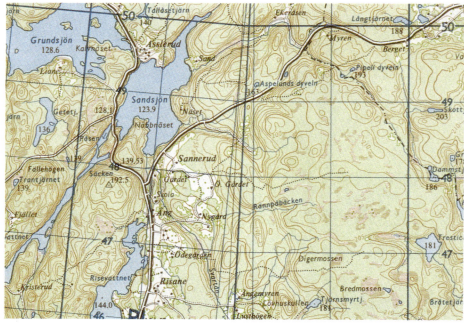

Flatåsen in Värmland's "Finnish" Forests

From the 1580s and for about a hundred years large parts of the central Swedish forests were colonised by Finns, mainly from Savolaks, who farmed by burn-beating. A large number of connected settlement areas in which Finnish forest culture has set a permanent mark on the landscape, architecture and place names may still be distinguished today. These "Finnish" forest districts are found principally in north-west Värmland and in the border country between Dalarna and Värmland, Västmanland, Hälsingland and Gästrikland.

Burn-beating was necessary for the colonisation of these previously uninhabited till areas. Various techniques have been used, but the typical method used by the forest Finns was burning mature spruce forests and the cultivation of rye (Finnish *huuhta*). Some cleared areas were used for settlements and more traditional farming. Many of them became meadows and grazing grounds for cattle-farming. This forest-Finnish colonisation led to changes in the ownership structure; encroachment on the outlying land and forest estates of the old villages led to both conflicts and cooperation between Swedes and Finns.

A typical Värmland Finnish settlement like the village of Flatåsen in Nyskoga stands on a ridge with a southerly aspect on fine till. The local climate was the deciding factor for its location. Among the buildings there it is the smoke-curing hut, the sauna and the grain-drying hut that are most characteristic of the forest Finns.

During the 17th century the forests began to increase in value, especially in mining areas, and laws were passed forbidding burn-beating. This continued, however, in spite of the laws, but mostly on a smaller scale. Cattle-farming became the main occupation, but in parts of the district iron production began to grow in importance.

The population grew rapidly in the Finnish districts, leading to the expansion of crofts, poverty and emigration in the 19th century. The introduction of new methods and new technology in agriculture was slow here; instead, it was forestry that became the main source of livelihood. The old cultivated landscape that is still farmed in the depopulated districts of the "Finnish" forests is therefore of great cultural value.

Flatåsen Farm was established by "Forest Finns" from outside the village of Månäs in the Klarälven valley in the middle of the 17th century. The first clearings were cut and burnt on the long, low ridge, built of nutrient-rich hyperite rock. The first farmstead was established at the top of the ridge and land division and new land clearing led to the growth of the village. The buildings are placed alongside the cultivated land, which runs like a ribbon from north to south, with meadowland in the west. Flatåsen became a church village in the 1870s, when Nyskoga got its own congregation. The church, school and village store made the village a meeting place for the parish, which was notable for its forestry and smallholdings. The 20th century has seen emigration and a declining population in Nyskoga. Today there are no active farmers in the village. The surviving old hayfields are grazed by horses from a nearby tourist centre, which receives a grant for this form of landscape conservation.

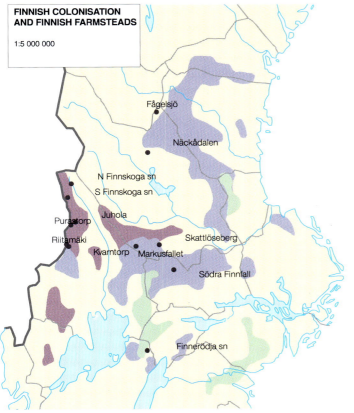

Finnish colonisers from Savolaks opened up the uninhabited forest districts of inner Svealand between 1570 and the end of the 17th century. Their destructive bush-burning methods later conflicted with the needs of the ironworks for firewood and charcoal. Some of the colonisers were sent to New Sweden on the Delaware river in the middle of the 17th century. (N34)

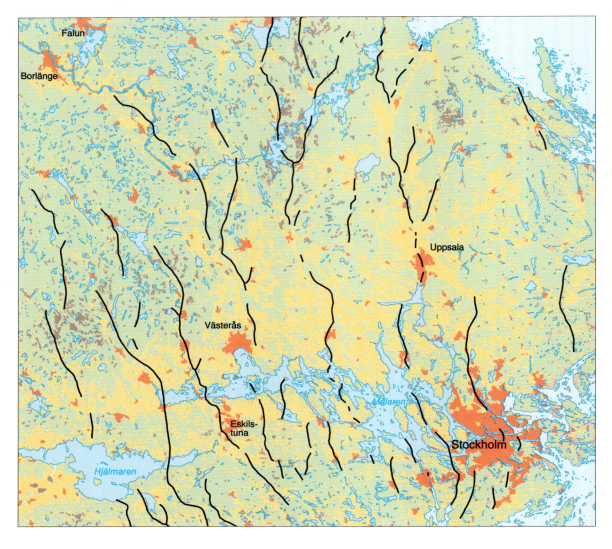

- Forestland
- Open land
- Marsh and peat land
- Urban area
- Recreation settlement
- Esker

The landscape of the Mälardalen consists of a relatively flat, broken surface of bedrock, with height differences of up to a few dozen metres. Where the fissures in the rock have been affected by erosion and glacial ice we see the characteristic clay-filled fissure valleys running east-west and northeast-southwest, widening out into plains where they cross. The ice age left an uneven layer of till on the rocks, whose crowns were washed clean when they were skerries newly risen from out of the sea. The many, often very large eskers are characteristic landmarks in the flat landscape.

The Plains around Lake Mälaren

The landscape round Lake Mälaren, the heart of Svealand, is unified by similarities in the countryside and by the historical links that were once based on shipping on the lake.

A quarter of the population of Sweden live here today. The east part of the area is dominated by the Stockholm region, which has been the fastest-growing region in the whole of Scandinavia in the 20th century. But Stockholm is the youngest of the towns round Mälaren; Västerås, Arboga, Enköping, Sigtuna, Strängnäs and Södertälje are all older.

Stockholm was established not as a natural central point in a densely-populated area but at a strategic point in an island landscape where land uplift had cut off the former sea loch of Mälaren, creating the rapids at Strömmen. The topography in this inner part of the archipelago was not particularly well-suited for town development. Nonetheless, Stockholm displayed boundless powers of expansion, above all in three periods: in the late Middle Ages, when trade with the Hanseatic League and Lübeck flourished; in the late 17th century, when Stockholm was the capital city of a great Swedish empire and the centre of national administration; and since the mid–19th century, under the influence of industrialisation and the railways. The population increased from 100,000 in 1855 to 246,000 in 1890, to 500,000 in about 1920 and to 1,000,000 in about 1960.

The communication networks of today and tomorrow connect all the major areas and are opening up new functional links. High-speed railways, for example, are planned for the 1990s which will reunite the Mälaren region. The concept of regions has attracted renewed interest as a result of European cooperation within the EU, which has led to the concept of a Europe of regions.

The landscape today is dominated by built-up areas and motor traffic. The natural landscape consists of a slightly rolling, broken surface of bedrock, with height differences mostly of some tens of metres. Where the fissures in the bedrock have been hollowed out by the inland ice we see typical fissure valleys running east-west and northeast-southwest which broaden out into plains where they cross. Loose material transported by the ice was deposited in the form of moraines or as glaciofluvials in the form of eskers.

On the beds of the fissure valleys there were rivers, lakes and heavy clay deposited when Mälardalen was below the surface of the sea, pressed down by the ice. We find fields and open grassy stretches in these places today. Higher up, more or less boulder-strewn moraines appear, first with sandy soil which bears the marks of old grazing grounds and then a harsher landscape with larger boulders, today covered with forest. The high points in these areas consist of bare rock.

During the Stone and Bronze Ages Mälardalen had a coast and island landscape. It was not until approximately 1,500 years ago that land uplift began to have an effect in the form of large, drained areas that could be used to graze cattle and grow hay.

North of Mälardalen the fissure valleys penetrate deeper inland and broaden out into large plains, while the landscape to the south is more broken and fragmented. There are consequently large areas of fertile soil, mainly in the north. The settlements in Södermanland are mainly small villages, in contrast to the north shore of Mälaren. The old farming settlements throughout the region often stand on moraines at the edge of forests, along ridges or by streams. In contrast, the many palaces and manor houses which have been a characteristic feature of much of Mälardalen ever since the 17th century often stand by lakes in outlying agricultural zones.

Huddunge is in Västmanland on the river Vretaån. The valley is broad and flat and wholly cultivated. The village is one of those ancient ones that was reorganised in the Middle Ages with *solskifte* and geometric village plots.

This photograph of part of Vikbolandet shows a narrow fissure valley running east-west with a cultivated sediment bottom, lake and typical roads running along the edge of the forest on firm, dry land, often, as here, on the north side of the valley where the snow melts earliest.

Vingåker in Södermanland is situated on an esker which rises above the cultivated clay plain. Where the railway crosses the ridge the village has expanded to become a railway community.

Rösavi is in the municipality of Hallsberg on the Närke plain, where the calciferous clay till provides good conditions for cultivation. The village still stands for the most part on the old medieval site. There is also a cemetery here dating from the late Iron Age.

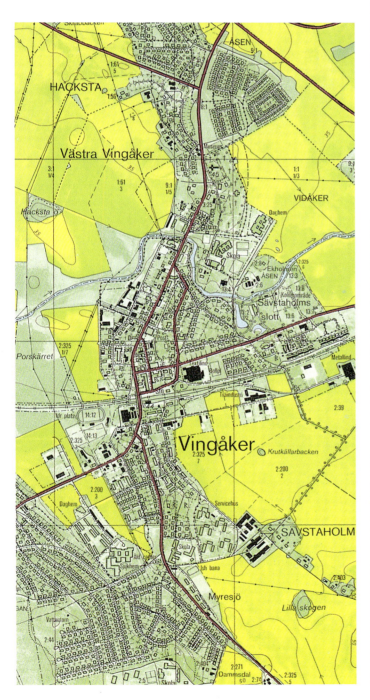

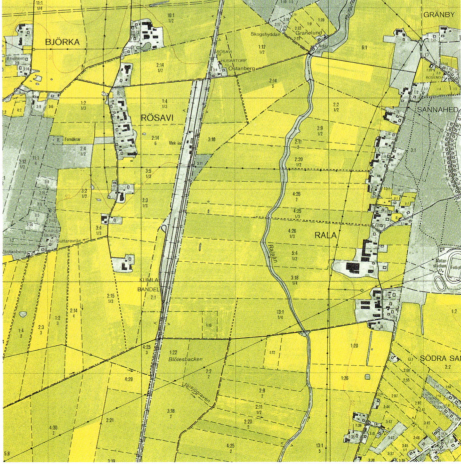

The village of Snåttsta stands on the same site as it did over 1,000 years ago. Runic inscriptions bear witness to this continuity. On a rock is carved: *"Inga had these runes carved for Ragnfast, her husband. He alone inherited this village from his father, Sigfast. God help his soul."*

Inga raised at least three more rune stones. A rune inscription on Svartsjö island tells Inga's story: *"Read the runes! Germund took Gerlög as his wife when she was a maiden. Then they had a son before Germund drowned. The son died later. Then she was the wife of Gudrik. Later they had children. Of them only one lived, a girl whose name was Inga. Ragnfast of Snåttsta took her as his wife. Then he died and his son after him. And the mother inherited her son. Then Inga became the wife of Erik. Then she died. And so Gerlög inherited Inga her daughter. Torbjörn the poet carved these runes."*

Particularly from the Viking Age onwards there has been a great increase in settlement in Mälardalen. This late expansion combined with the structure of the natural landscape has helped preserve many prehistoric remains; today this is the area with the largest number of prehistoric remains in the country. Cemeteries, rune stones and place names bear witness to long continuity in the use of the land. The stability of the agrarian structure and its settlements in this area, where countless farms, villages and even whole parishes stand in the same places with the same names as in the Viking Age, is a remarkable phenomenon by European standards.

West of Sigtuna, on the southern shore of the Håtuna fiord, stands Signhildsberg, an estate which was for many years royal property. Until the late 17th century it was called Fornsigtuna. Excavations near the present manor house have revealed remains of impressive long houses, the largest of them measuring 40×10 m. This place—perhaps of great significance for cult rituals and the administration of justice—was in use throughout most of the Iron Age but in particular during the Viking Age, that is, in the period immediately prior to the founding of Sigtuna in the 970s.

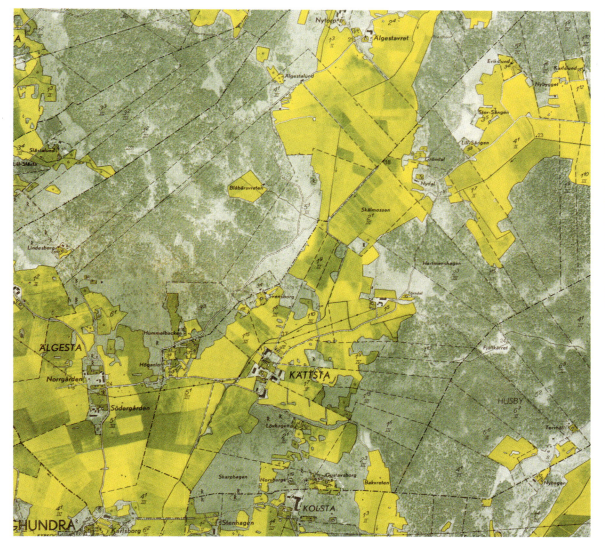

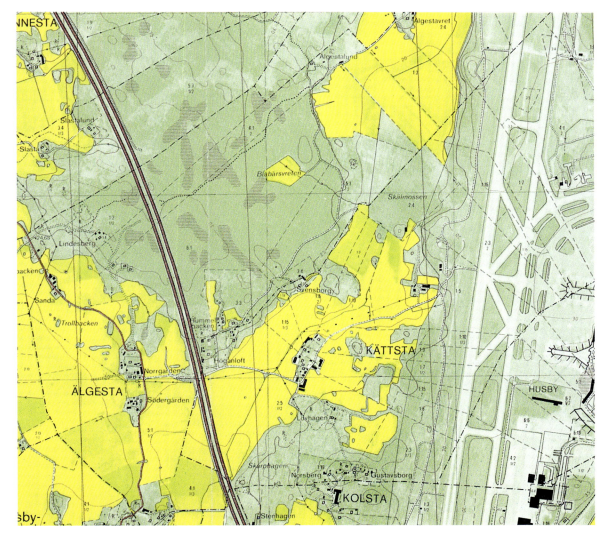

In this district 40 kilometres north of central Stockholm a rich variety of archaeological evidence, field boundaries, rune stones etc. prove a 2,000 years continuity in the agrarian landscape; in a perspective as long as this, the changes have been remarkably few.

New technology and new needs have introduced land use which is quite different and more far-reaching than traditional farming. Communication systems like the E4 motorway and Arlanda Airport form parts of a pattern that has a larger scale than that of the local community.

Land reform in the mid–19th century meant that the clustered villages were dissolved and individual farms were moved out into the cultivated land. During the late 19th and early 20th centuries the old water meadows were also ploughed up. Crofts were built at the edge of the forest and later came holiday cottages. Modern farming techniques on the plains have also created a more monotonous landscape.

But it is modern urban society that most obviously affects the landscape. Motorways, road junctions, airports and new housing areas stand in strong contrast to the traditional, small-scale agricultural landscape. New road systems are laid over a settlement structure with its roots in prehistory and a road network that is often very old, cutting across the old patterns and to a high degree controlling the localisation of work places and housing estates. Golf courses and white-fenced horse paddocks are new features of the near-urban landscape, as well as gravel pits, reservoirs and warehouses of various kinds.

The motorway from Stockholm to Arlanda and Uppsala is the main axis of Sweden's high-tech industries. Since the opening of Arlanda Airport at the end of the 1950s a large number of companies have grown up along the motorway, but even at the beginning of the 20th century industries were moving out to places like Rotebro and Upplands-Väsby along the main northern railway line. In the area between the E4 and the E18, on land belonging to Stockholm, we find, for example, Kista, with Sweden's greatest concentration of electronic and computer companies.

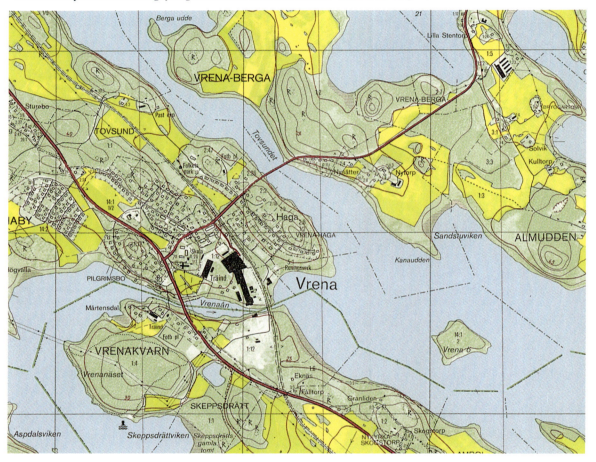

"Here is Danbyholm. Here is Hagbyberga. Here is Hovsta. Here is Åkerö". From Nils Holgersson.

Vrena, dominated today by the forest industry, stands in the middle of a lake landscape where the Vrenaån cuts across a narrow neck of land. The Flen-Oxelösund railway line was laid across this land.

The Södermanland Lake Plateau

No one has portrayed the Södermanland lake plateau better than Selma Lagerlöf:

"Here they've taken a large lake and a large river and a large forest and a large mountain, cut them up into small pieces, mixed them together and spread them out on the earth all higgledy-piggledy. Nothing was given enough room. As soon as a plain began to grow big, a hill came along and stood in the way, and if the hill wanted to stretch out and become a ridge, the plain took over again. As soon as a lake grew so big that it began to escape, it narrowed into a river, and the river wasn't allowed to flow far before it broadened out into a lake. There were changes all the time. Pine forests turned into oak woods, fields into bogs..."

The agrarian settlements consisted of hamlets and isolated farms, but also of estates and manors that set their mark firmly on the landscape.

> Ericsberg is the largest estate in Södermanland. This manor farm was created in the mid–17th century, consisting to begin with of scattered hamlets and farms. The estate grew and by the 19th century it comprised 81 farms, 171 crofts and 26 soldiers' crofts. Today's landscape of large fields is mainly the result of draining and lowering the level of lakes in the 19th century. Today the farm concentrates on forestry. The picture is from "Svecia Antiqua et Hodierna", late 17th century.

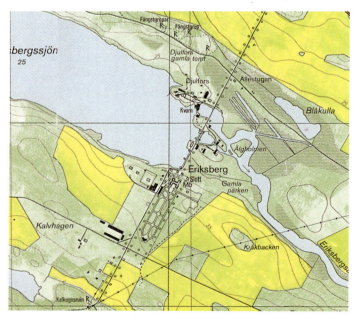

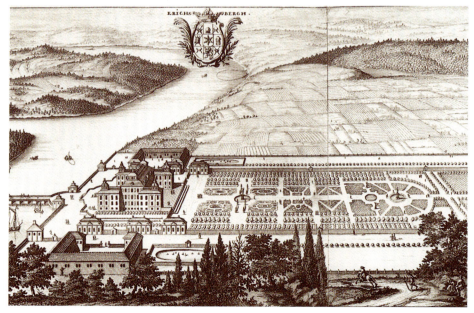

In 1951 Södertälje had a population of 25,266. In the following decades industrial employment grew rapidly. Two of Sweden's internationally famous companies, Saab-Scania (cars and trucks) and Astra (pharmaceuticals) now dominate employment in the town.

By 1982 the population had grown to 60,300. A new town district had grown up in the former agricultural area to the south.

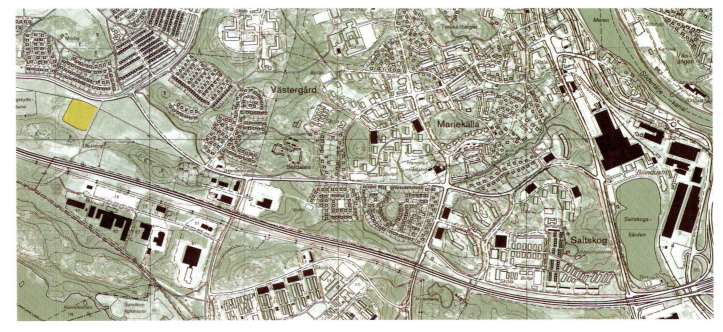

Vrena stands on a narrow headland between Långhalsen and Hallbosjön. With its 13th-century parish church, it has its roots in the Middle Ages. The small farms in the church village were amalgamated in the course of time into one large unit, Vrena Farm. A railway community grew up here in the 1870s after the then privately-owned Oxelösund-Flen railway was built. Sweden's most southerly factory for manufacturing fibreboard developed from Vrena sawmill, the first industry to be established there soon after the arrival of the railway.

Södertälje

Until the 1870s Södertälje was a typical commercial and handicraft town, but at the end of the century it grew rapidly. The canal, the new road to Stockholm and the main railway line together with new industries meant that the population grew from 1,245 in 1850 to 8,027 in 1900.

The Södertälje Canal was completed in 1806–19 and was broadened for larger ships as late as the 1970s. It takes ships of up to 8,000 tons.

In the 1960s the old central parts of Södertälje were cleared, a project that was the most extensive of its kind in Sweden at that time. Percentage-wise, the population of Södertälje grew faster than that of any other town in Sweden. The areas included on the map are all examples of the rapid and large-scale expansion that took place.

The old vicarage land at Geneta was the site of a large-scale building project that produced over a thousand apartments. Västergård and Saltskog, old isolated farms that supplied the town with farm produce, had to give up their land for apartment blocks, link houses and terrace houses. The area to be exploited most recently is Hovsjö, at the bottom of the map, in virgin forestland.

What has changed the landscape greatly, apart from the housing estates, is the motorway to Göteborg. This motorway and the urban freeway from the centre to the western parts of the town, together with their approach roads, have occupied large areas of land.

The changes had begun in the early 1950s with the rapid expansion of industrial premises within the Scania area and the construction of high-rise buildings in the west part of Mariekäll, west of the new school.

All road and railway traffic going south from Stockholm passes through Södertälje. A new railway bridge, the Igelsta Bridge, is one of the longest in Europe. It forms part of the Grödinge line, which reinforces Södertälje's role as a junction.

Stockholm

Stockholm is an unusually clear example of a city that has developed under the influence of and in interplay and conflict with natural conditions, political decisions, economic policies and technical innovations. We shall look at the way one part of Stockholm has developed.

The north-west part of Stockholm contains many of Stockholm's most characteristic elements—but not all of them. Government and royal estates, which have set their mark on the growth of the city to the north and north-east, exist here only in the not unimportant land round the palaces of Haga and Karlberg. The city's "summer zone", stretching from the leisure area on Djurgården out to the mixture of a harsh fishermen's life and the pleasures of the nature-loving upper class in the outer archipelago, is almost only to be found to the east of Stockholm. To the west another very special area—the fertile islands in Lake Mälaren with their fruit and vegetable nurseries, quarries and sandpits, all within a day's boat trip from the centre—is cut off by a fault scarp.

The shores of Mälaren are steep and for many years did not encourage building—until late 19th-century technology and the city's acute need for land solved the problem of building on difficult terrain.

The map from 1932 gives a picture of Greater Stockhom when there was a break in its development. Industrialisation and the brief boom after the First World War are over; there will not be a new period of rapid economic growth until after the Second World War, when a new wave of immigration will lead to a period of rapid building.

Let us begin out in the north-west and move eastwards. There are three small railway communities in Järfälla. Municipal and parish life centres on the church village of Barkarby, where the old Hundreds road to the Mälaren islands and Sollentuna meets the Stockholm road to Enköping. Apart from this centre, the area is still rural, partly because the purchase of Järvafältet by the army in 1905 created a symbiotic relationship between farming and military manoeuvres.

By Lake Mälaren we see glimpses of Hässelby Villastad, a horticultural suburb founded in 1890 close to the Lövsta refuse plant with its railway line and refuse-derived soil. The parish of Spånga stretches from Hässelby to Duvbo and Ör in the east, a conglomeration of suburban homes by the railway stations and still rural land owned by the city of Stockholm or the Crown.

Sundbyberg, a new town (1927), has an inner-city-like network of streets tightly enclosed by rampant industrial estates in Solna and Bromma, now incorporated with Stockholm. Solna is dominated by the working-class areas of Hagalund and Huvudsta, built with private capital at the turn of the 20th century, and the more town-like area of Råsunda, exploited by its own tram company. Solna is also notable for its large areas of government land and institutions, railway tracks, palace parks and cemeteries.

The city of Stockholm stretches out to Ängby, where a project started in 1926 at Olovslund is continuing with small houses built by their owners. A more exclusive area of detached houses is being planned at Södra Ängby. Tramlines run out to the earlier-built suburbs of Ulvsunda and Nockeby. East of Bromma Church lies an airfield and close by, with several railway tracks, a new industrial estate to encourage large factories not to leave Stockholm. There are the remains of old industries along the water at Ulvsundasjön (Svartvik) and Liljeholmsviken. These are factories established outside the city limits of that time, in municipalities not burdened by city taxes and fire and health regulations.

On Kungsholmen the new housing areas of Fredhäll and Kristineberg are just being built. On the hilly ground to the east between the hospitals there are temporary dwellings for the post-war homeless. Västerbron, the first bridge to offer an alternative to the chaos at Slussen, has been drawn in on the map (completed in 1935). Inner Kungsholmen and the rest of the inner city generally speaking reflect the city pattern of the late 19th century.

This map from 1932 shows the centre of Stockholm, "the stone city", the early town-like suburbs of Solna and Sundbyberg and the garden suburb of Bromma. Unbuilt-up areas are mainly old royal land.

The map from 1932 on the facing page shows that the north-west sector of Stockholm was still rural, with scattered garden suburbs.

As late as 1950 Vällingby was still purely rural. Five years later Vällingby Centre (below) was inaugurated on the ridge where Vällingby Farm and the schoolhouse used to stand.

Vällingby was the first large-scale suburban centre, an ABC suburb (ABC = Work, Housing and Centre). From the Underground station outwards the buildings were placed less and less densely, with separated pedestrian and vehicle traffic.

Vasastaden was built up from the late 19th century into the early 20th century in the form of massive tenement blocks that followed the 1866 Town Plan. A new feature was Röda Berget, an area that was designed in the twenties on a more human scale, with co-operatively owned blocks of flats that followed the rocky terrain.

THE TOWN BETWEEN THE BRIDGES, NORRMALM AND VASASTAN — FROM THE CENTRE TO THE OUTSKIRTS

Few big cities have a so clearly limited old town centre as Stockholm. The sandy hill that became Stockholm in the 13th century was surrounded by water on all sides. This was partly what saved The Old Town. The street pattern still reflects a 17th-century town, and certain features go back several hundred years earlier, even though most of the buildings are the result of the almost total transformation of the town in the 17th century, from a modest trading station to the centre of a Baltic Empire.

The medieval street quarters can still be seen in the middle of Stadsholmen — large and irregular, surrounded by the small quarters that mark the oldest town wall, no longer in existence. Narrow paths led down from the wall to the water. As the town grew, these "water alleys" were lined with larger houses and the road running round the outside of the wall became a trading street of increasing importance, culminating in Västerlånggatan's hey-day as *the* shopping street in the 19th century.

The pattern of these narrow, irregular alleys is broken in the west by the strict straightness of the two "New Streets" (*Nygatorna*) — a reminder of 17th-century town planning made possible by the fire of 1626.

The 17th-century town is particularly evident on Riddarholmen, where the Grey Friars' monastery was replaced by noblemen's palaces. The link between the nobility and power is demonstrated by the symbols of authority — the Riksdag building and government offices — which were moved away from the royal offices in the castle or palace, initially to nearby buildings and later to Helgeandsholmen and Norrmalm.

Stadsholmen was fully exploited at an early date. As early as the 16th century there were buildings on the land to the south and north, clinging to the steep cliffs in an unplanned fashion. During the 17th century, when Sweden was a great power, the number of buildings increased, but now the town outside Stadsholmen was to be organised in a strict gridiron pattern. In Norrmalm Drottninggatan (Queen's Street) and Regeringsgatan (Government Street) — the names date from the time of Queen Kristina and the Regency — became the main axes of the expanding town, whose limits were gradually pushed northwards at Solna's expense. Only Klara Church and Jakob's Church retained their positions despite the town plan.

The final conclusion to the supremacy of "The Town between the Bridges" as Stockholm's commercial centre came with the construction of a central railway station in 1872. It was impossible to place this station on Stadsholmen. The nearest possible location in view of the difficulty in laying the track both to the north and to the south was the water between Kungsholmen and Klara. Klara Sjö was partly filled in to create a railway station that did not too seriously impair the environment.

The location of the Central Station here speeded up the process of moving the city centre northwards. The Central Station forecourt was the city's arrival hall, for both rich and poor. Hotels, newspaper offices and confidence tricksters gathered in the Klara district round the station. At the back of the station, towards the water to the west and north, heavy industries were established that were dependent on railway and water transport.

Stockholm's third great period of expansion came during the Swedish Industrial Revolution between the 1870s and the outbreak of the First World War. Stockholm spread across the islands surrounding the Old Town with the encouragement of town-planning regulations that controlled the location of streets and the height of buildings, but in other respects left the land free for private exploitation. In lower-class Södermalm and Norrmalm-Vasastan this uncontrolled exploitation led to a high density of population in large new tenement houses. What was left was Observatorielunden with the Academy of Sciences buildings, Karlbergsvägen — the old palace drive — and Röda Bergen, whose rocky heights were difficult to develop. The large tenement blocks were built with courtyards and houses across the yard, often with a clear so-

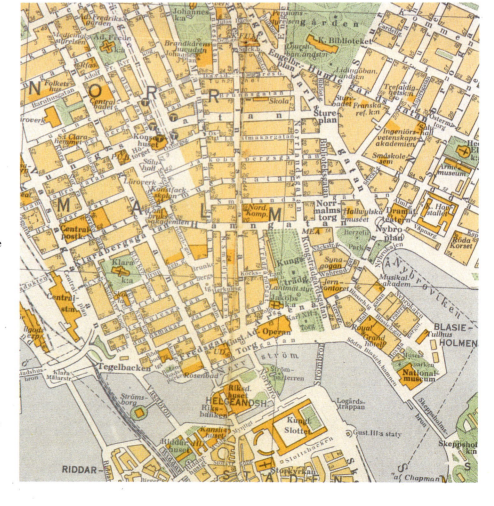

Up to the late 1950s the centre of Stockholm had developed within the street network from 1640, where two gridiron plans met at Malmskillnadsgatan on the high ridge of Brunkebergsåsen. A third gridiron network began east of Birger Jarlsgatan. After 1910 the ridge was cut through by Kungsgatan. The Central Station was built on land created by filling in part of Klara Sjö.

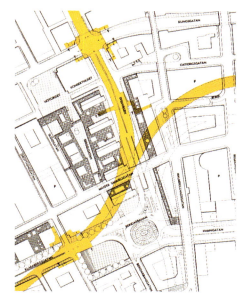

The final rebuilding plan of 1959 for the centre of Stockholm created Sergels Torg. Yellow marks the Underground, the pedestrian precincts are light grey and the terrace gardens dark grey. The terrace gardens proved to be unsuitable for the Swedish climate.

cial segregation between the finer lower-floor flats facing the street and the attic garrets of the yard houses.

In the late 19th century a new factor influenced Stockholm's strict gridiron pattern. Inspired by Haussmann's Paris, Albert Lindhagen attempted to create boulevards and toile squares in his town plan dated 1866. Apart from a few spectacular successes his plan was not carried out, but the city's linear plan was abandoned for many decades to come.

Other ideas were more successful. In the early 20th century architects and town planners turned to their national and European heritage for inspiration. The medieval town with its winding streets and varied architecture became the model for carefully planned districts, often in hilly areas which had previously been ignored for economic and aesthetic reasons; towns were supposed to be flat in an age where inclines of more than 1:15 were impossible for horse-drawn cabs. Röda Bergen in the north-west corner of the map is also an example of an early co-operative tenant-owner project in Stockholm.

Vasastan was the district where many of the generation born between 1900 and 1930 grew up. Cinemas were built in many of the tenement houses, only to be transformed into car salesrooms when cinemas went out of fashion in the 1950s. In the east corner of the map, round the Observatory, we catch a glimpse of "Stockholm's Sorbonne"—the university district which later dominated the whole area until the university was taken over by the state in 1960 and began to move out to royal Djurgården.

During the 1960s another inner-city function materialised. On the map Sveavägen comes to an abrupt halt at the Concert Hall. The area between Hötorget and Brunkebergstorg had long been the subject of heated debates. A decision was made in 1945 to redevelop this district, but it gradually turned into a slum. The plan for a new shopping centre was combined with the extension of the Underground system. The state, the city and commercial interests cooperated to amalgamate small properties into larger ones and a huge, multi-dimensional centre was built at the end of the 1950s, involving underground railway lines, subterranean supply roads to shops and stores, pedestrian precincts and skyscrapers. Many of these projects showed the way forward, but others rapidly became obsolete and could not be changed in this steel, glass and concrete colossus.

The almost complete redevelopment of Lower Norrmalm in the 1960s and 1970s was one of the largest in a city not destroyed by war. As a result of this slum clearance Stockholm got an efficient centre designed for pedestrians, but many historical places of aesthetic and emotional value were also lost in the process.

SUNDBYBERG — "THE FIRST SUBURB"

Stockholm's early suburbs can be divided into two types: planned garden suburbs and spontaneously developed industrial and working-class outer districts. Sundbyberg was intended to be in the first category—but turned into the second. Owners of agricultural land tried to sell house plots on barren rocky ground—but the combination of a main railway line and proximity to water during the rapid industrial expansion of the 1870s soon made industrial exploitation more profitable. The ensuing uncontrolled wave of development was partly brought under control by the creation of an urban district council as early as 1888, after which Sundbyberg, one of Stockholm's ugly suburbs, got its own suburbs, Lilla Alby and Mariehäll. Straight streets, not even deflected by the rocky hills that could not be developed, are a typical feature of Sundbyberg. The plan shown here is a reduced part of the urban district's first "town plan", showing existing buildings, proposed street facades and the like.

Above, "Plan of the Township of Sundbyberg within the Parish of Bromma" drawn up in 1898, revised in 1899. In the photograph from 1922 on the right Sundbyberg still has the air of a newly-built community. The gridiron plan had been applied without any regard for the terrain. Various types of buildings were used.

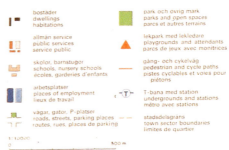

The Vällingby group of suburbs (Blackeberg, Råcksta, Vällingby, Hässelby Gård and Hässelby Strand) were planned in detail in the 1950s. The density of the building was divided into zones based on six Underground stations. Centres and sub-centres, roads and supply systems were developed at the same time as the houses were built. Green open spaces, and separated pedestrian and vehicle traffic created attractive residential areas. Special areas were set aside for industrial purposes.

VÄLLINGBY AND TENSTA — FROM A PLANNED PARADISE TO A SUBURB THAT WENT WRONG

Tensta, built around 1970, has high-rise apartment blocks of a uniform design. Tensta has developed into a multi-cultural immigrant suburb. The 12th-century Spånga Church can be seen in the centre of the map and the photograph.

In 1932 Vällingby was a farm belonging to Hässelby Manor and Tensta a farm close to Spånga Church.

Thanks to far-sighted land purchases in Bromma, Spånga and Brännkyrka at the turn of the century, Stockholm had assured itself of space for expansion. During the period between the world wars the pressure of the growing population only increased slowly. Detached and terrace houses were built for office staff on city-owned land in Äppelviken and Ulvsunda. In 1927 a successful programme was launched in Olovslund (and Pungpinan) for owner-built houses for the working class. Three-storied houses were also built in the inner suburbs. These new, low-rise suburbs were served by tram lines.

When the pressure of the growing population increased after 1945 as a result of a higher birth rate and immigration, the policy of a widespread town had to be abandoned. The new suburbs were designed according to new principles, based partly on London's New Towns.

Vällingby (1955) was the largest example of this new type of suburb, the ABC town (A=*arbete* work, B=*bostad* housing, C=*centrum* centre). Vällingby also represents a detailed plan for a hierarchy of centres, whereby the largest one has a large Underground station with feeder buses, a shopping centre providing almost every service, a church, municipal and social welfare offices, a high school and so on. In and round the centre were grouped residential areas in a falling scale of intensity, linked to the centre by paths. Among and between these residential areas were placed industrial areas and not far away—saved by the curving line of the Underground—were Grimsta Wood and Hässelby Manor for outdoor recreation and culture.

The major problems were to attract shop owners to a non-existent place and to get people to move to Vällingby as the places of work opened up. The shops came, the centre was a success, but the state slowed down migration from the inner city by encouraging people to move to other parts of Sweden. When this policy changed, Vällingby was already inhabited by people who worked elsewhere. Yet Vällingby was a great success functionally, socially and architecturally.

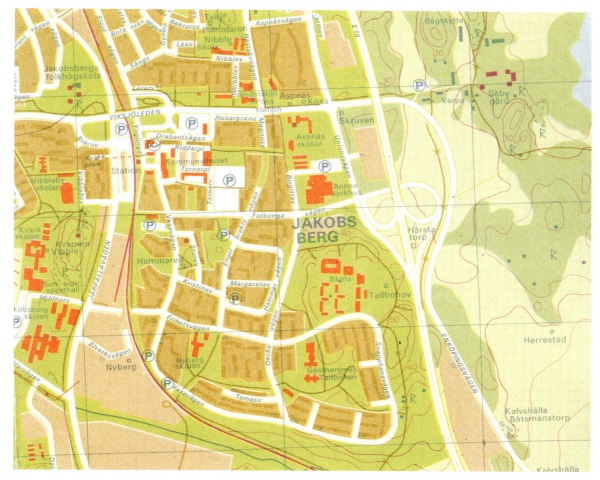

Jakobsberg, on the Västerås railway line outside the city limits of Stockholm, was transformed about 1960 from a railway community with a few detached private houses into a suburb with a large shopping centre and high-rise buildings.

Tensta and the surrounding suburbs of Hjulsta and Rinkeby were developed under somewhat similar circumstances about ten years later. The result was quite different. The starting point was once again a housing shortage, which this time resulted in the government's ambitious "Million Programme"—the number of housing units that were to be built in a ten-year period between 1965 and 1975. When the state sold the military training grounds of Järvafältet to Stockholm and neighbouring municipalities, unexploited land could be appropriated for the Million Programme. The Tensta complex was to copy the successful parts of Vällingby, but adapted to modern, efficient construction technology and stricter demands for land exploitation.

The three suburbs were placed along two types of track—for the Underground and for construction cranes. The density of building would make it possible for all the inhabitants to walk—along well-protected paths—to stations situated in the centre where there were shops, a library and other services. The apartment blocks were placed to suit the tracks of the construction cranes, which resulted in a return to the straight lines of older town plans and a failure to adapt to the terrain. The biggest mistakes were not so much in the physical planning but in the calculations of the time needed to build up the suburb and the social changes involved. Housing was given priority over commercial functions and public transport. It was to take seven years before the Underground was built.

At the beginning of the Million Programme many politicians judged that the expense of owning a house would be too great for most Swedes. But as it turned out inflation and mortgage deductions made it more and more advantageous to borrow money to buy a house. Many of Tensta's tenants soon left their flats and moved to houses in Järfälla and Spånga. The empty flats were filled with the new Stockholmers—foreign immigrants and refugees who value the high standard of the flats and the closeness to friends but are less negative about the lack of countryside and places of work. In the later stages of the Million Programme, when the housing shortage was less acute, planners and construction companies were obliged to change their policies to attract new customers—in nearby Kista the emphasis was on cooperative tenant-owned flats, varied architecture, places of work in the near vicinity and shops and transport systems that functioned from the very start.

JAKOBSBERG—A RAILWAY COMMUNITY WITH GROWING PAINS

Jakobsberg is an example of a station community located on a main line which first developed into a commuter town for Stockholm and then became the centre of a municipality. Vibbla Village was turned into a manor in 1649 by Jakob Lilliehöök. The arrival of the Stockholm-Västerås railway in the mid–1870s allowed the farm to be "commercialised", but there was no suburban development until 1920, when the manor land was sold and divided up into plots for smallholdings and private houses. Expansion was slow. There were still hardly any buildings there as late as the 1930s. By the end of the 1940s there was a small garden suburb east of the railway and a few shops. At this time discussions were being held concerning the incorporation of suburban municipalities with Stockholm. Järfälla happened to own land in Jakobsberg, and about 1950 the area round the railway station developed into a municipal and social centre. But private houses blocked the way for further commercial expansion. A new, privately-developed shopping centre, Nyberg, was opened in 1958 further to the south. Many people believed that the railway station would move there, but neither the State Railways nor the noise from the nearby airforce station allowed this. Instead, and at almost the same time, the municipality launched a complete redevelopment plan for the garden suburb round the station, turning it into the largest shopping centre in the Stockholm suburbs, surrounded by eight-storey blocks of flats. Some of the private houses that were demolished had been built as late as 1953.

The army's sale of Järvafältet and a reduction in flying from the airbase allowed building work to intensify and spread out. During the 1960s Järfälla was at times the fastest-expanding municipality in Sweden. The railway level crossing was a major problem for traffic to and from the shopping centre, but this was solved in the 1990s and the centre has been redeveloped to meet new demands.

Åkersberga

From the 1950s several small towns round Stockholm grew enormously. They often had developed from agricultural districts into second home areas.

Åkersberga in the municipality of Österåker about 25 km north-east of Stockholm developed from being a part of the archipelago with many summer cottages and second homes during the period 1920 to 1950 into a part of Greater Stockholm with a dense urban character since the 1960s. Originally a summer resort turned towards the Baltic, Åkersberga has now become a commuter town centred on the railway station. As late as the 1920s steamboats travelled up and down Åkers Canal and Garnsviken.

When the Roslagen railway was built, the area was opened up for new development. It all started in 1901, when the railway reached Åkersberga. In 1906, when it was extended to Österskär, the great wave of summer cottage development began in Österskär and Tunagård. During the 1960s, the "record years", as they were called, the land belonging to Berga Farm and Söra Farm was developed into an urban area with Åkersberga at its centre. Many summer cottages were converted into permanent dwellings or replaced by proper houses.

The population increased greatly, most rapidly (263%) at the beginning of the period of expansion between 1960 and 1965. During the period 1960–80 the population grew ten times over. Commuting to work is common: more than 50 per cent of those in employment commute, most of them to Stockholm.

Summer Stockholm

The Stockholm archipelago has been a summer paradise for Stockholmers for more than 100 years. Second homes have been built in ever-widening circles throughout the islands, to begin with near the steamboat jetties and then all over the islands as bridges were built.

KOPPARMORA

On Värmdö in the archipelago east of Stockholm second homes are the commonest kind of houses, but permanent dwellings are increasing in number. In general it is farmland and forestland that has been developed. By 1950 a comparatively dense cluster of mainly second homes had been built round Saltarö Farm, while farming continued on the adjacent farm of Kopparmora.

By 1976 the area had completely changed in character and is now almost totally developed. The houses in both Norra and Södra Kopparmora were planned as second homes, but in the south most of them, which had been built to a high enough standard in the 1960s to be permanent dwellings, were converted into all-the-year-round houses, although they had been restricted in size to prevent permanent residence. In 1990 mostly young families lived there, nature lovers who wanted a good area to bring up their children in.

OXHALSÖ

Further away from Stockholm, the small islands in the archipelago have been transformed from fishing and farming villages into recreational areas. Oxhalsö, on the east side of Blidö in the northern Stockholm archipelago, completely changed in character between 1952 and 1980, as the maps show. Most of the cultivated land has been divided up and used for second homes. However, it is forestland in particular that has been exploited, where the houses now lie close together in rows and clusters.

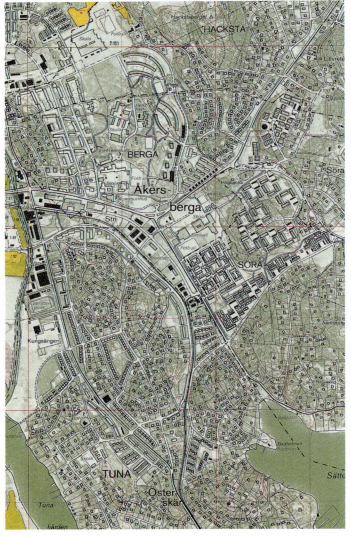

The maps to the left from 1952 and 1978 show how Åkersberga was transformed from a rural district with a small railway station on the Roslagen line and many second homes overlooking the sea, Trälhavet, and its inlets round Österskär, Tunagård and Margretelund, into a metropolitan suburb.

Its summer resort character has been preserved in the old summer cottage areas, but more and more second homes are being converted into permanent dwellings.

The forest-clad islands of the inner archipelago, with their former farming and fishing communities, have been exploited for recreational purposes ever since the mid–19th century in ever-widening rings from Stockholm.

The maps give two examples of recreational development in the Stockholm archipelago between 1950 amd 1980. Oxhalsö in the northern archipelago, where a farming village has successively been divided up into plots for second homes, and Kopparmora on Värmdö, which is so close to Stockholm that many second homes in an area that was developed on a large scale in one phase have now become permanent dwellings.

The bare skerries of the outer archipelago are now protected from further exploitation. Röder in the north of the outer archipelago.

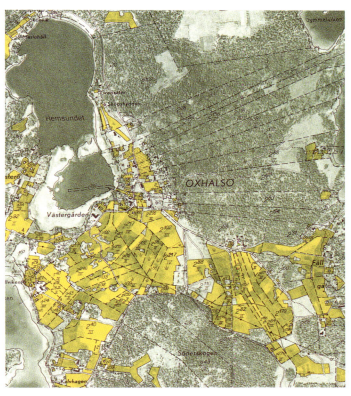

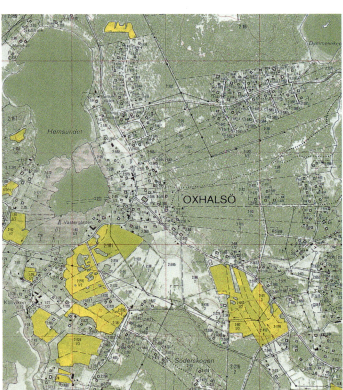

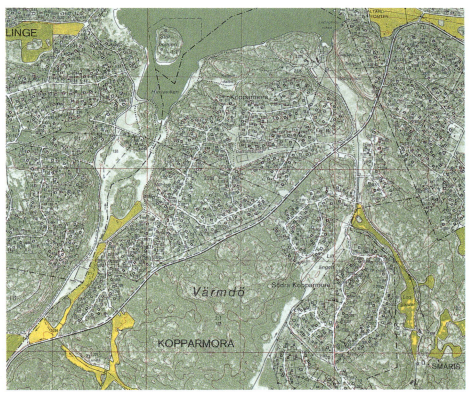

Bergslagen

Until the Industrial Revolution reached it, Bergslagen was divided up into a number of geographically separate mining districts. A mining district consisted of the mine masters and their families and employed workers who did the actual mining and foundry work. The mine masters were mining farmers. There was one or more mine in each mining district, and round them were grouped the ironworks.

The Crown established its own hammer forges, called Crown works, in the 16th century. These were sold at the beginning of the following century to noblemen and merchants who formed a new social class, the ironmasters. Their iron mills were organised differently, with ironworkers, farmers and crofters working for the ironmasters.

The mine masters and the ironmasters co-existed in Bergslagen up to the early 19th century, when the mills were allowed by law to acquire shares in the mine masters' property. The mine masters gradually sold off or closed down their forges completely.

The ironmills had a very low production capacity, however. As a result of changes in technology the total production of bar-iron increased greatly in Swedish ironworks between 1814 and 1914. Many ironmills in Bergslagen introduced blooming steel processes, the construction of blast furnaces improved and rolling mills were built. Larger and more up-to-date plants were constructed at more favourable sites; Sandviken and Domnarvet are examples of this development.

The result was extensive structural rationalisation and the death of many mills in Bergslagen. Between 1850 and 1913 the number of blast furnaces fell from 213 to 117, and the number of ironmills from 440 to 140. This process continued after the turn of the century. In 1913 37 works accounted for more than 90 per cent of Sweden's production of ingot steel. The heart of the industry moved to Norrbotten. In the 1950s there were about 60 iron mines in operation in Central Sweden, of which Grängesberg was the largest. After Stråssa Mine was closed down in 1981 only Grängesberg and Dannemora were left. By 1992 all the iron mines in Central Sweden had been closed down.

The traditional steel companies in Bergslagen were fragmented by the 1970s steel crisis, and the number of jobs and employees decreased.

HÄLLEFORS

Hällefors was set up as a silver mine, but from the 18th century onwards it was a traditional ironmill. Krokborn Park was opened in 1796 as the first people's park in Sweden. The industry has been extensively restructured in modern times; forests and water power have been sold off. Like many other ironmills Hällefors used to be an industrial, forestry and farming company in which the division of work between the skilled steelworkers and the farmers and crofters in the district was obvious. The modern iron and steelworks provided employment for less skilled workers, at the same time as the company became less dependent on the local farming community. Developments after the Second World War meant that the farms and crofts that had acted as a buffer when both industry and forestry went into recession were closed down. Many farmers left their farms when industrial work, and shift work in particular, forced people to live where they worked. More and more women, too, moved away from smallholdings and crofts, which in many cases in Hällefors were replaced by forest-worker camps. The result was that the cultivated land became overgrown and the face of the cultural landscape changed.

The urban area expanded. But in 1989 the steelworks suspended operations. The equipment was sold to China and totally dismantled by a Chinese workforce in the autumn of 1993, leaving a town with a high rate of unemployment.

STRÅSSA MINE IN LINDE

The Stråssa Mine has always been considered to have the largest deposits of iron ore in central Sweden after Grängesberg. The rock, however, is not very rich in iron, which means that the ore has to be processed to be usable.

There were two forges at Stråssa in the 1540s. A mine manager's report dated 1684 shows that Stråssa Mine supplied about 20 of the district's 36 forges with ore.

The Stråssa Mining Company was formed in 1874. A new concentration plant, the largest in Sweden at that time, was built in 1907, as well as

Hällefors in western Bergslagen was one of the old mills that survived the "mill death" and developed into a large, modern high-quality steelworks. This, too, however, was a victim of the international steel crisis and was closed down in 1989. The plant was sold to China, who sent a workforce of 300 men in the autumn of 1993 to dismantle it to be transported to China.

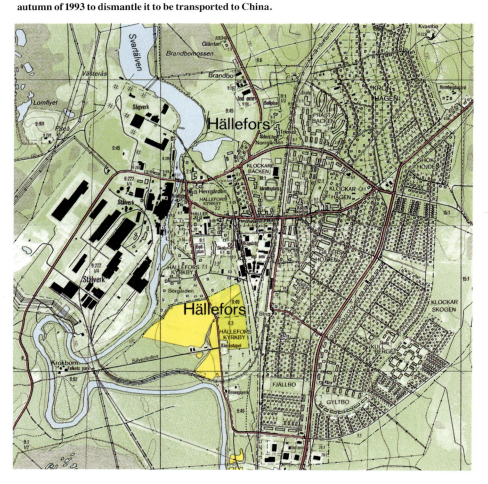

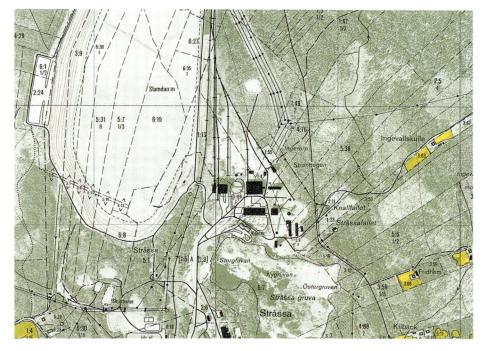

There is a large opencast mine and processing plant at Stråssa which bear witness to the large scale operations of modern mining. All this took place when operations were recommenced after the old mine had been closed down. But mining ceased completely in 1981 and Stråssa is now a tourist attraction, where visitors can see mining technology from different eras.

a briquet plant and a compressor plant. Yet another concentration plant, twice as big as the old one, was built in 1915. Operations ceased in 1923.

The mine was reopened in 1955, since new technology was considered to be superior to that used in the 1920s. The old buildings had been destroyed by fire. When the mine was reopened, a new community grew up with a school, shops, a cinema and a newly-built chapel. Production came to an end in 1981.

Old ironworks were typically small-scale operations. The foundries were placed by a stream whose waterfalls were used as a source of energy. Norn was one of the works that fell victim to the "mill death" when modern steel processes were introduced. It is now an idyllic summer resort and cultural monument.

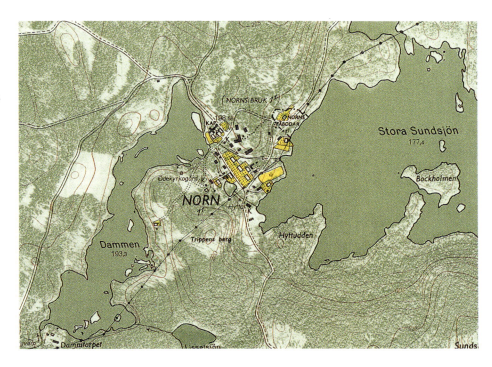

NORN MILL

Norn Mill is one of many examples of an architectural pattern with small-scale industry that was characteristic of Bergslagen, where countless works bear witness to the importance of mining for the standard of living and social conditions. The early ironmills were established round the mines, regardless of any previous buildings there. The forges in Bispberg were placed on the outskirts of the farm area.

Norn Mill stands by a lake, Stora Sundsjön; the blast furnace, forge, workshops, the mansion and workers' houses as well as the 18th-century chapel and the bell tower from 1820 have all been preserved. The blast furnace is typically placed where the river, which runs from Dammen to Stora Sundsjön, has a waterfall.

In 1616 two Finnish colonisers together with a certain Bagge-Jöran from Säter built a water hammer and forge. In 1656, when Hans Steffens founded the mill, it had one blast furnace and four bar-iron hammers. The ore was brought from mines near Norn, and later from the big mine at Bispberg.

The plant was rebuilt in the late 1860s, which increased blast-furnace production dramatically. The forge was finally closed down in 1899. Production ceased in the autumn of 1915.

The blast furnaces at Norn Mill are one of the many monuments to the heyday of Swedish steel production.

Each mill stamped its mark on the bar iron it supplied. NB stands for Norn Mill, the crossed arrows are coat-of-arms of Dalarna.

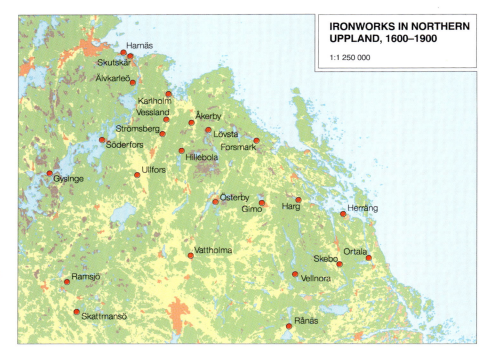

The Dannemora mills in northern Uppland grew up during the 17th century and flourished in the 18th century. They were all in turn closed down in the 19th and 20th centuries. The last to go was the steelworks at Österbybruk.

The Uppland Mining District

North-east Uppland is a region clearly marked by the iron industry. The ironmills were large and carefully planned, with a mansion, church, houses for the smiths and industrial buildings arranged in a regular pattern.

From the mid–16th century up to the end of the 19th century iron was Sweden's major export. The Walloon mills in Uppland were of particular importance for exports. The combination of high-class raw materials and the Walloons' special production techniques in both the forges and the hammer mills guaranteed a world-famous high-quality product.

DANNEMORA

Mining in the parish of Film is mentioned in 1481, probably referring to Dannemora. Silver, lead and copper were mined. Dannemora was owned by the Crown in the 16th century. Forges at Österby and Vattholma are mentioned in 1551, and later bar-iron production. Forsmark Mill was founded in 1580, Ortala Mill in 1590, Leufsta Mill in 1600, Wessland Mill in 1612 and Gimo Mill in 1615.

The Crown's share of iron production was limited after a while, and the era of tenant ironmasters began. Österby, Leufsta and Gimo were leased in 1626 by Willem de Besche, and the following year Louis De Geer joined the industry. During the Thirty Years War the manufacture of cannons and weapons played an important role in the development of the ironmills. After the Peace of Westphalia in 1648 a new market grew up and iron from Uppland was the foremost export during the 18th century. During the following century 20 mines were in operation in various districts.

Dannemora mine's first-class ore was mined until 1992, when the mine closed down. The area round the mine contains features from the 500 years the mine was in operation. Dams, roads, mining villages and crofts bear witness to the mine's influence on the surrounding countryside.

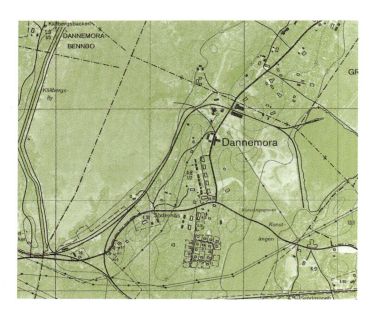

The landscape of Dannemora has been shaped by 500 years of mining. Mining ceased in 1992.

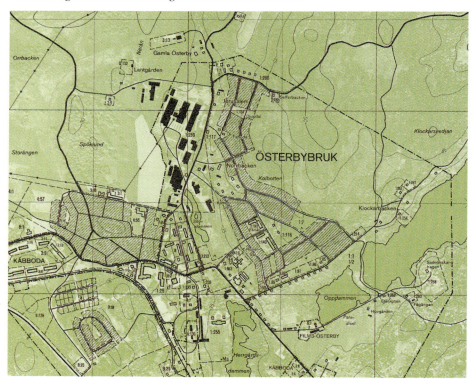

Österbybruk got its classic milltown architecture with a mansion and smiths' street in the mid–18th century. The mill traditions came to an end when steel production ceased. Other industries and a flourishing cultural life have now given the town a new character.

At Österbybruk both the old mill buildings round the mansion, designed by Jean Eric Rehn and with the painter Bruno Liljefors' studio in the park, and its more modern industrial and residential buildings can be seen in this photograph.

The oldest map of Österby is dated 1643, the year in which the De Geer family became owners of the mill's then very modest buildings by a stream in a purely agricultural district.

The Walloon foundry in its old setting is today a unique cultural monument.

ÖSTERBY MILL

The first Walloons to be recruited came to Sweden in 1616 and were followed later by many more. The Walloons were skilled craftsmen who introduced several new techniques. They used a special forging technique to make bar iron. There was a Walloon forge at Österby as early as 1620. Walloon iron from the mill in Uppland was famous in the 18th and 19th centuries as the raw material for steel production. In England, which was the dominant steel-producing country in Europe, Sheffield was the steel centre. All the iron used to make steel in Sheffield between 1701 and 1765 came from the Walloon mills at Dannemora in Uppland.

These mills were extraordinarily profitable in the mid–18th century. Capital was available to modernise the mills, many of which had also been burnt down by the Russians in 1719. Mansions were designed and parks laid out by Sweden's foremost architects.

Österby Mill was particularly well located: it lay close to ore at Dannemora, lakes and bogs suitable for damming water for power and coniferous forests for the production of charcoal. The map dated 1643 shows the rural character of the place when the De Geer family took over.

In the 18th century, when the iron-mills in Uppland were restructured, Österby Mill was also rebuilt according to a strict plan. The mansion, built in 1760–80 by Elias Kessler, stands alongside an artifical lake, Herrgårdsdammen, surrounded by wings, the west wing built in the 1730s and the east one containing the chapel in 1735. To the south lie the orangery and the gardens laid out by Carl Hårleman. The stables and coach houses date back to the early 19th century. East of the lake lie the mill streets and to the north of them the Walloon forge built in 1794. This forge was in operation until 1906. A blast furnace and a roaster were built there in 1880 and demolished in 1977. The mill office dating back to 1730, the steam-hammer forge built in 1860 and a charcoal store have been preserved. There was also an upper hammer mill, consisting of a hammer and steel forge, but this was pulled down in the 19th century and replaced by a cornmill and stables, a charcoal store from 1800 and a malthouse from about 1770, which have been preserved. A crucible steelworks was built in the 1870s.

The railway station bears witness to the era when travel changed in the 1870s. North of the old mill community lie newer industrial buildings, part of Österby Mill's expansion in the 20th century. Fagersta Mill AB took over operations in the 1920s.

In 1972 the mansion at Österby Mill and its buildings were donated to the Bruno Liljefors Foundation. The artist's studio is in the park. In fact, art and culture have always played an important role at Österby. The art collection there once included works by Rembrandt, Roslin, Sergel and Elias Martin, testifying not only to the ironmasters' interest in art but also to their wealth.

The Walloon forge is the only one left in Sweden. It is a very important industrial monument.

Österby was the last place where the old *nyckelharpa* (a three-stringed fiddle played with keys) was still being played when Eric Sahlström gave it a new lease of life in the 1930s. The *Nyckelharpa* Festival is an annual event.

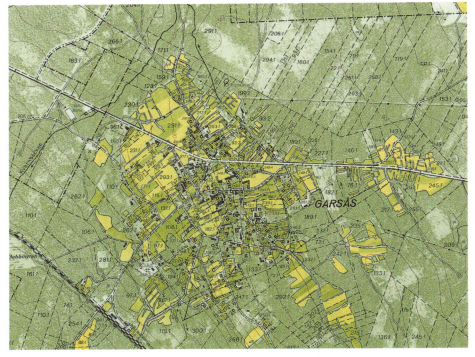

The village of Garsås on Lake Siljan spreads out over the fields in a typical Siljan manner. The fields are divided in the old style; this scattered ownership pattern is a result of agreed land divisions, that is, individual agreements between farmers without the intervention of the authorities.

The ownership pattern in the Våmhus district by Lake Orsasjön is the result of the *storskifte* reform. The land is still very fragmented. The buildings line the roads and have spread out from groups of farms. The decisive factor in the farms' economy is their large but scattered forest property.

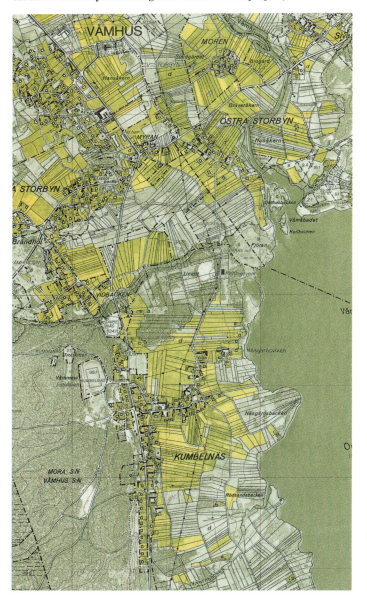

The Siljan District

The Siljan District embraces a fertile agricultural area on Cambro-Silurian bedrock called the Siljan Ring. The open cultural landscape with its traditional architecture, often well preserved, appeals to our romantic concepts of country people's way of living in the olden days in Sweden. In particular Upper Dalarna has often been seen as a district where old traditions have survived. Under the influence of national romantic feelings in the 19th century, writers, artists and ethnologists moved here to collect impressions and facts from a genuine country setting.

Many of the special features of the province are rooted in a social system that differs from that in other parts of Sweden. This is expressed very evidently in the great fragmentation of property and the many farms in the villages. The small, narrow plots in both arable land and forestland were long looked upon by the authorities as an obstacle to rational land use. Attempts at introducing changes, however, met with strong resistance, with the result that traces of old land divisions have to a large extent survived. The *storskifte* reform was not carried out until the 19th century, and still applies in many villages. Other land reforms have been completed or are in progress in our own time.

The explanation of the province's special character lies in the old-fashioned form of inheritance was practised, by which all the children inherited centrally located land, the daughters inheriting half of the sons' shares. In most of the rest of Sweden it was usual for one main heir to inherit an undivided farm and buy off any brothers or sisters. In Dalarna the ownership of a certain amount of land was a mark of considerble social significance: one was allowed to build on one's land and take part in meetings to discuss local matters. The result of this was an enormous upswing in building. In one village there might be as many as 75 farming units and even more households. This fragmentation was, however, to some extent counteracted by the fact that people often chose their marriage partners so that jointly-owned plots of land could be combined to make more easily farmed units. The acreage of arable land per farming unit is, however, still very small, and forestry has become an important source of income. The division of ownership often resulted in many farms being dependent on other sources of income than agriculture. Handicraft skills, for example, were widespread. It was also usual for people to set off on job-seeking journeys, often far outside the province borders. Their destination was Stockholm and the Mälaren district in the first place, and then Norrland. This tradition has continued to this very day, when building workers, for example, have worked from Monday to Friday in Stockholm and then lived in their home village at the weekends.

The typical fragmentation of both infields and forestland in Dalarna can be seen in this photograph of Bonäs, south of Våmhus. The forest properties can be kilometre-long strips only 30 or 40 metres wide.

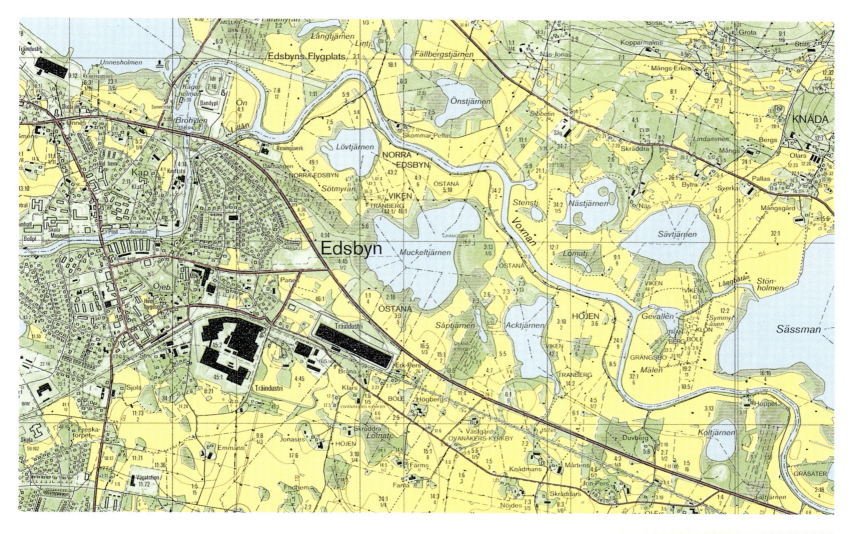

Voxnadalen

During the Middle Ages all Swedish land north of Ödmården was called Hälsingland. Ödmården is the great forest between Gästrikland and Hälsingland.

The Hälsingland valleys of the great rivers Ljusnan and Voxnan and their sediments attracted farmers at an early date. There are traces of settlement at Edsbyn from the early Iron Age, but it was in the Viking Age and the Middle Ages that the district was properly established.

The oldest centre in Voxnadalen was Alfta, a parish of its own as early as the 14th century. Edsbyn is the town which has grown most, developing since the turn of the century from a farming village with small industries into a modern industrial town. The main industries are connected with wood and forest products.

Voxnadalen was a central point on the old trading route, Jämtvägen, which ran from Mälardalen and Dalarna to Norway via Jämtland and Härjedalen. There were a number of market places along this route, one of which was Knåda, north-east of Edsbyn, where the winter fair was held until 1920, when the inland railway line altered the pattern of travel.

During the 18th and 19th centuries agriculture was the main industry, and flax was a particularly important regional crop. In the 18th century two ironworks were established at Voxna, which were soon closed down, however. Towards the end of the 19th century forestry become increasingly important as a source of income alongside agriculture. As at many other places the forests increased in value when sawmills were built along the coast. Evidence of the prosperity that was created in the district lies in the magnificent two-and-a-half-storied timbered houses with beautifully carved porch decorations.

Farm names play a major role in local identity. In Voxnadalen the farms are often called after a previous owner or his occupation. The owner of the farm today uses his own name in combination with the name of the farm. The same custom is observed in Dalarna. The name belongs to the farm and does not necessarily have any relationship with the giver of the name.

The name Voxnan refers to the tendency that the river has to flood, thereby enriching the surrounding water meadows. The small lakes, "sausage lakes", are the remains of the river's old course. Water power was long used to drive sawmills and cornmills and for processing flax. Fishing—eel and salmon—was also important. The Voxnan was used for floating timber right up to the 1960s.

The best-known farm buildings in Hälsingland are the "wooden palaces": two and two-and-a-half-storeyed panelled timber houses with richly decorated porches. These farms and their outhouses often form a square round a courtyard. The farmhouses bear witness to the prosperous times in the 18th and 19th centuries when the forests began to provide an income.

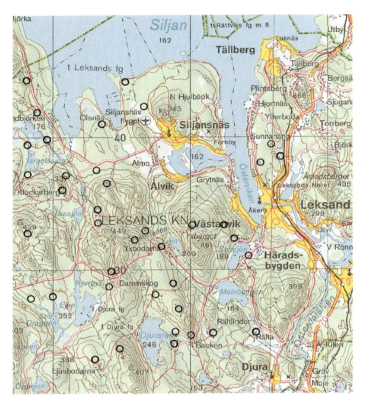

Ljusbodarna was a home shealing with some arable farmland. The part-owners of the shealing came from hamlets in Leksand (almost 20 km away) and Djura (more than 10 km away). The names of the hamlets are given in the ancient blocks of land on the map. A road for motor traffic was built in 1933. The general map shows former shealings in the Leksand district.

Stopsbodarna in Älvdalen has a more modern ownership pattern than Ljusbodarna. The shealings are round the Österdalälven, north of the village of Blomsberg and within its boundaries. The land has been divided up into the long, narrow forest strips that are common in Dalarna.

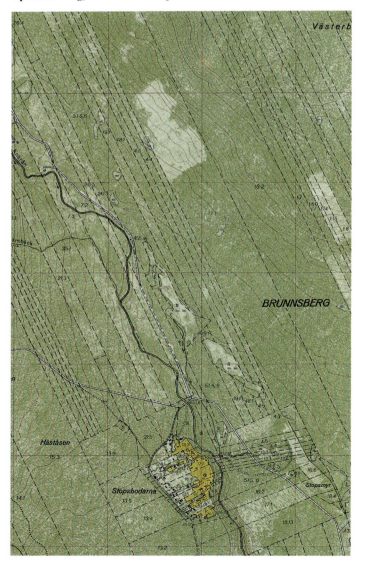

Shealings and crofts

The shealing system is a part of traditional farming methods. Arable farming and cattle-breeding interacted in a system where fields required animal manure. In the western and northern parts of Dalarna, where cattle-breeding and milk were essential but the supply of fodder on the farms was scarce, the farmers were obliged to use resources for grazing and haymaking which lay a long way away from the permanent farm buildings. The custom of taking the cattle to shealings for the summer reached its peak in the 19th century, but began to die out when new agricultural technology introduced artificial fertilisers, cultivated meadows and better seed, and modern dairy technology began to replace the traditional ways of processing milk at the shealings.

Earlier ownership of land at the shealings often survived when they were no longer used for their original purpose. The cottages often became second homes, as has happened with some of the buildings at Ljusbodarna in Leksand. The setting there is well preserved and the fields there are kept open by the shealing association. Some of the land has been turned into forest plantations.

Ljusbodarna was a home shealing with some arable farming. The owner-members of the shealing association came from hamlets in Leksand (almost 20 km away) and Djura (just over 10 km away). The names of these hamlets are given in the old-style, block-shaped plots of land on the map. A road for cars was built in 1933.

Stopsbodarna in Älvdalen has a different, more up-to-date ownership pattern. The shealing stands by the Österdalälven, north of the village of Blomsberg and within its boundaries. The area has been divided up into long, narrow plots as is usual in Dalarna. The fragmentation of fields and meadows, a characteristic of this province, is also seen in the forest. The forest was for a long time a resource exploited by the villages in common. After the great land reform the land was divided into farm plots and common plots. The special rules of inheritance in Dalarna resulted in the pattern of ownership with narrow strips which is evident on the map.

The authorities have attempted to reduce the number of strips to make it possible to work the forest more rationally, but the landowners have resisted them strongly. Land ownership in its traditional form is closely connected with the social system in the district, and hunting and firewood collecting are often felt to be more important than financial profit.

Sometimes it is the home shealings in particular, that is, the shealings closest to the old villages, that have become permanent homes and formed their own hamlets. Particularly in north Hälsingland this expansion has often resulted from people starting to cultivate outfields where previously they only spent the summer months. In old times a farm's land

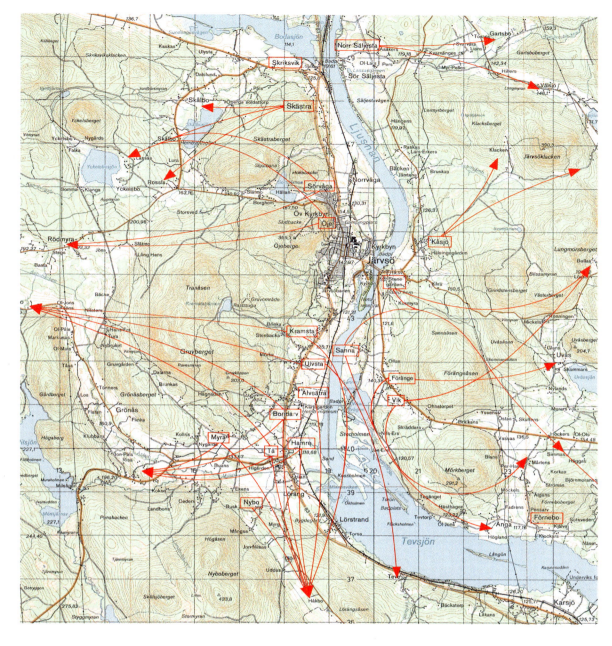

Bodland was a common way of cultivating outfields in Hälsingland in the old days. As with shealings, the fields were cultivated here to provide hay for the home farm. In the 18th and 19th centuries many of these *bodland* became permanently inhabited farms and hamlets. The map of Järvsö shows where the old villages' *bodland* lay.

consisted of three units, the home farm in the village, a *bodland* (shealing with arable land), and a shealing. The *bodland* might lie up to 10 km from the village, while the shealing would be even further away. The *bodland* might be partly cultivated, but they were mostly hayfields. Many villages in north Hälsingland began as old *bodland*. Particularly in the 18th and 19th centuries the *bodland* were permanently inhabited and the former hayfields were cultivated. While the home villages in the central Järvsö district often go back to prehistoric times, the villages whose names end in -*boda* were originally *bodland*, reflecting secondary, medieval expansion.

The *bodland* system was still in use as late as the 19th century. There are records from Järvsö describing how *bodland* were transformed into permanently inhabited villages, a process which would often take place gradually, so that the *bodland* hamlets consisted of both permanent and semi-permanent farms to begin with.

On the outskirts land use changed with time. For example, Skålbo, originally *bodland*, was permanently inhabited in the 16th century but functioned again at the end of the 18th century exclusively as *bodland*, only becoming an independent village in the middle of the 19th century.

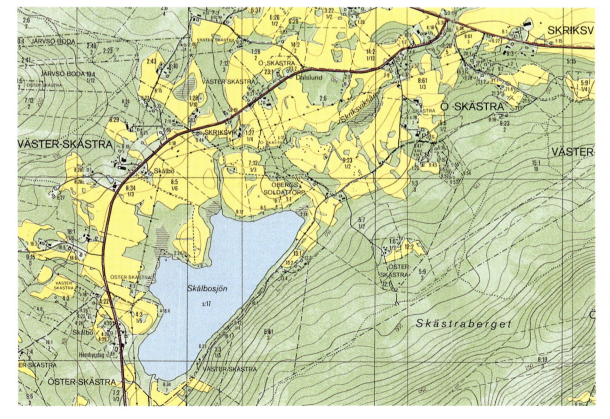

Skålbo, north of Järvsö, was formerly *bodland* but became a village in its own right from the middle of the 19th century.

Clearings in the forest are reconquered by nature.

125

Round Alnösundet

The coast of Norrland south of Västerbotten is the most spectacular part, where the Norrland terrain meets the sea. Agriculture and industry prefer the flatter parts of the landscape. The valleys are the most important areas for agriculture and farm settlements. South of the mouth of the Ljungan the coast is not so steep and a more definite coastal plain has risen from out of the Gulf of Bothnia. The coast of south Norrland and the lower river valleys are agricultural districts with a long history, classified today as densely populated areas with more than two thirds of the land cultivated, comprising Ådalen (the Ångermanälven valley), the area between the Indalsälven and the Ljungan and the Ljusnan valley. These concentrations of agrarian settlements were of great significance for the industrialisation of forestry work in the second half of the 19th century. Most of the sawmills were established in the nearby coastal areas—mainly in Ådalen and the Sundsvall district.

The economic boom in the late 19th century left its mark on Sundsvall that arose from the ashes of the fire in 1888—a town built of bricks and stone as fine as any city. View from Norra Stadsberget across Sundsvall.

INDUSTRY

The coast of the Gulf of Bothnia has in places been taken over by industries based on forest products and iron ore. The first industries dating from the 17th century consisted of ironworks like Galtström and Lögdö. The town of Sundsvall was founded in 1624 between the mouths of the Ljungan and the Indalsälven. The harbour is sheltered by the island of Alnön and as a result of timber-floating and coastal traffic Alnösundet became an ideal place for steam-driven sawmills and timberyards. These comparative advantages helped to give Sundsvall a leading position in the world, first through its sawmills and later through its pulp mills.

The development of freedom of trade and commerce in the 19th century made Sundsvall attractive for investments. Local firms were often taken over by rich gentlemen with ambitious plans. The Dickson family, for example, purchased a water-driven sawmill at Matfors in the late 1820s. It was rebuilt into a more modern sawmill and combined with an ironworks, while the Ljungan was cleared for log and board-floating. The company also acquired Svartvik Wharf and Shipyard at the mouth of the Ljungan, where two steam-driven sawmills were built in the 1870s to replace the one at Matfors. England was the most important customer for bar iron and timber at that time, and sales in London were managed by another member of the family. The company was clearly integrated vertically, with its own forests, sawmills, ironworks, shipyard, shipping firm and sales force in modern style. Timber "lords" like Bünsow, Kempe, Jacobsen, Heffner and Enhörning were, on the other hand, more specialised, which was a characteristic feature of the many small sawmill owners who appeared on the scene too late to acquire any forests of their own.

Tunadal steam sawmill, founded in 1848, was the first steam sawmill in Sweden to export its products and certainly the first steam sawmill in Norrland. As many as 42 steam sawmills were in operation in the district and production reached peak figures of more than 900,000 m^3 in 1896 and 1897. Employment boomed along the coast and urbanisation began to spread.

Before the 1870s the big water sawmills accounted for the dramatic increase in timber exports, producing mainly broad planks from the largest forest trees. Only smaller trees remained, so that the steam sawmills had to concentrate on narrower planks and boards. The value of the timber was raised by introducing planers, and Sundsvall also led the way with this technology (at Mon in 1870). Waste material was used as filling material in the timberyards, fuel for glassworks and ironworks or as raw material for the new pulp mills. Changes in demand and technology led to a series of innovations in wood-fibre processing, from mechanical groundwood mills to chemical sulphite and sulphate mills. Twelve pulp mills were in operation simultaneously for some years between 1910 and 1920, but since there was not enough waste wood at the sawmills or thinning waste from the forests, the pulp mills began to compete with the sawmills.

Changes in demand from Europe and competition from other continents also played a part in killing off the sawmills, a process that started after the turn of the century but accelerated during the 1930s when 15

The sequence of forest-based industries in the Sundsvall district reflects product cycles and the waves of technological innovations that flowed along the Norrland coast.

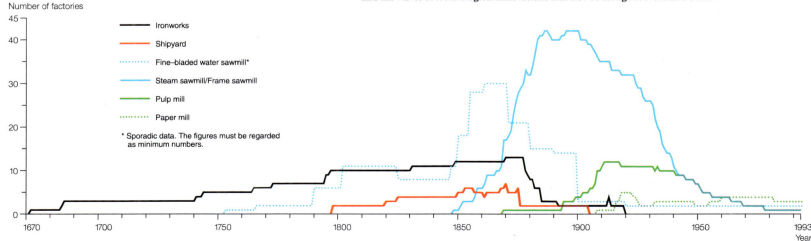

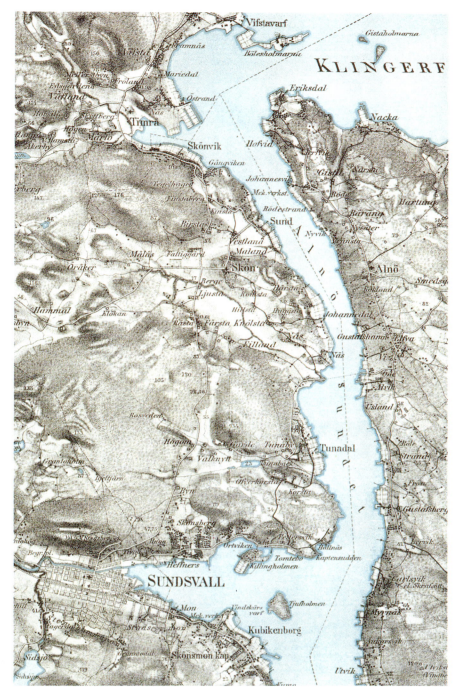

This map dated 1897 shows the steep cliffs along Alnösundet between Sundsvall and Timrå. Steam sawmills with smoke-plumed chimneys, workers' cabins, timberyards, timberstores and small wharves run like a string of beads along both sides of the sound.

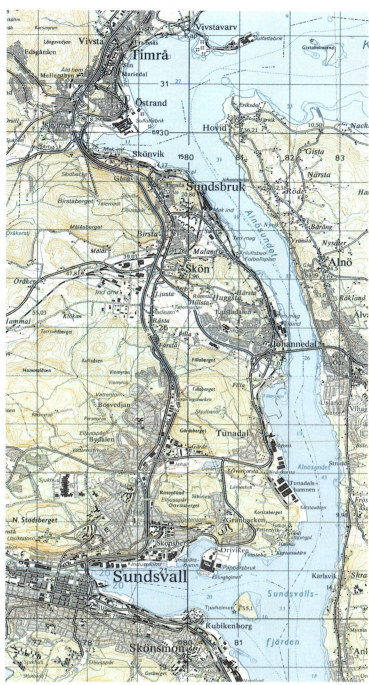

This field map from 1989 reflects the district's transformation within a century from an agricultural area with sawmills into an urbanised district with many roads and railway lines and large-scale industry in the form of the SCA sawmill and terminal at Tunadal, its pulp mill at Östrand and its papermills at Ortviken and Wifstavarf, together with the Gränges aluminium works at Kubikenborg.

The modern mill for LWC (Light Weight Coated) paper at Ortviken was amalgamated with the old pulp factory. In the background, Alnön and the smoke from Östrand and Wifstavarf.

sawmills were closed down. Concentration of production to fewer, larger units, consolidation of ownership and rationalisation have resulted in the situation today, where only one large company (SCA, the Swedish Cellulose Co.) totally dominates the Sundsvall district with one sawmill, one pulp mill and two paper mills.

During the sawmill era Sundsvall was called "the capital of Norrland" and since the fire of 1888 the town centre has been dominated by houses built by the mill bosses and nouveau-riche businessmen. The former sea port functions nowadays as a regional centre with many banks and commercial and cultural activities.

The Bothnian Coast

The highest shoreline is almost 300 m above sea level at Rosstjärnsberget, near Höga Kusten. Today land uplift is greatest along the coast of the Gulf of Bothnia, about 9.2 mm a year, while at Gävle it is only 6 mm a year. The rise in land round the Gulf of Bothnia has exposed rock, boulder till, ridges and drumlins on the convex parts of the landscape, while the sandy and fine-grained material has been deposited in the concave parts, where peat has also accumulated. Thus the coast of North Norrland seldom forms a uniform coastal plain.

The combination of land uplift and drainage schemes has gradually changed the use of the land initially from fishing waters and fairways to lakes and bogs, later to hay meadows and finally from grazing grounds to arable land. Old village names like Hössjö (Hay Lake) remind us of the earlier landscape before lakes and the lower slopes of valleys were drained.

The earliest permanent settlements were probably along the shorelines and river valleys; the conditions for fishing salmon and other species were right, and moose could easily be trapped in the wintertime. Traces of a late Stone Age dwelling site have been found at Stornorrforsen. Only a few of today's villages are low-lying; these cannot have been established very long before the Middle Ages. Sixteenth-century tax returns show that most of the villages on the coast at that time were well populated and productive. Fishing was of great importance as a secondary means of livelihood, as was hunting for and trading in furs and squirrel skins.

Röbäck stands 4 km south-west of central Umeå on a ridge of coarse glacial material about 20 m above sea level; it was a fishing village before the early Middle Ages. Uplift of the flat delta area soon left the village a long way from the sea and farming became increasingly important. Being close to Umeå has meant that today's urban Röbäck is rather like a suburb or dormitory town. To the north, at Backen, at an altitude of 20 m on the same ridge, stands the first parish church (early 16th century) built of stone in the Umeå valley.

In the coast zone, especially out in the archipelago, there are traces of harbour settlements in the form of house foundations, slipways and other stone constructions. By the rate of land uplift, ^{14}C-dating and lichen growth it has been possible to identify dwelling sites from the Iron Age and Middle Ages (500–1500 A.D.).

After 1600 tar production increased in importance in response to a strong demand from abroad. Later in the 18th century many farmers got extra income by making charcoal for ironworks and by sawing timber. When the sawing industry began to expand in the following century, it was once again the local population that provided most of the workforce at construction sites, in tree-felling, transportation and floating, as well as at sawmills, timberyards and wharves. These new jobs provided full-time employment for many villagers who owned no land. The location of steam-powered industries in coast towns and at river mouths as well as at small villages with suitable harbours started the urbanisation process in earnest in Norrland. From the turn of the century the iron and wood-processing industries, and in consequence shipping, were concentrated in the best ports. This process is still going on today.

By the 19th century most villages on the Norrland coast had undergone land reforms. The final reform contributed most to today's agrarian landscape, by moving many farms away from the old village centres and by drawing estate boundaries straight across fields, meadows and forests. The village of Brännland illustrates how the long strips of divided land usually lie at right-angles to the village, rivers and contour lines—both to ensure a fair distribution of land and natural resources and to facilitate drainage with open ditches marking boundary lines. Hay barns were also built as a result of the division of meadowland, but lake drainage and better field drainage soon turned most of the meadows into arable land, so the barns are now in the way of mechanised farming methods.

The Vindelälven meets the Ume älv (seen from the north) at Vännäs, with Spöland in the foreground. The sandy soils here are vulnerable to flooding in the spring. The villages stand on natural embankments but since the disastrous flood of 1938 the farms are protected by artificial dykes. Today the area resembles a polder landscape.

THE EFFECT OF LAND UPLIFT AND SILTING ROUND THE MOUTH OF UMEÄLVEN

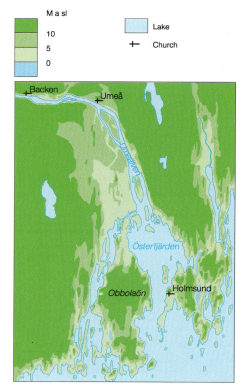

Changes in the coastline during the past 1,000 years show that the site of the town of Umeå lay mainly below the sea until relatively modern times. The river delta is expanding towards the sea as a result of sedimentation and an annual land uplift of about 8.5 cm.

Four thousand years ago at least 60 figures were carved on an island in the wide Norrforsen, at that time close to the sea. Today this cultural monument is just under the 60 m-contour line and more than 30 km from the open sea.

The village of Brännland (right) runs along terraces of sediments. In the background, the Stornorrfors dam. The continuing importance of the river valley for communications is underlined by the present E12 (The Blue Road) and the railway.

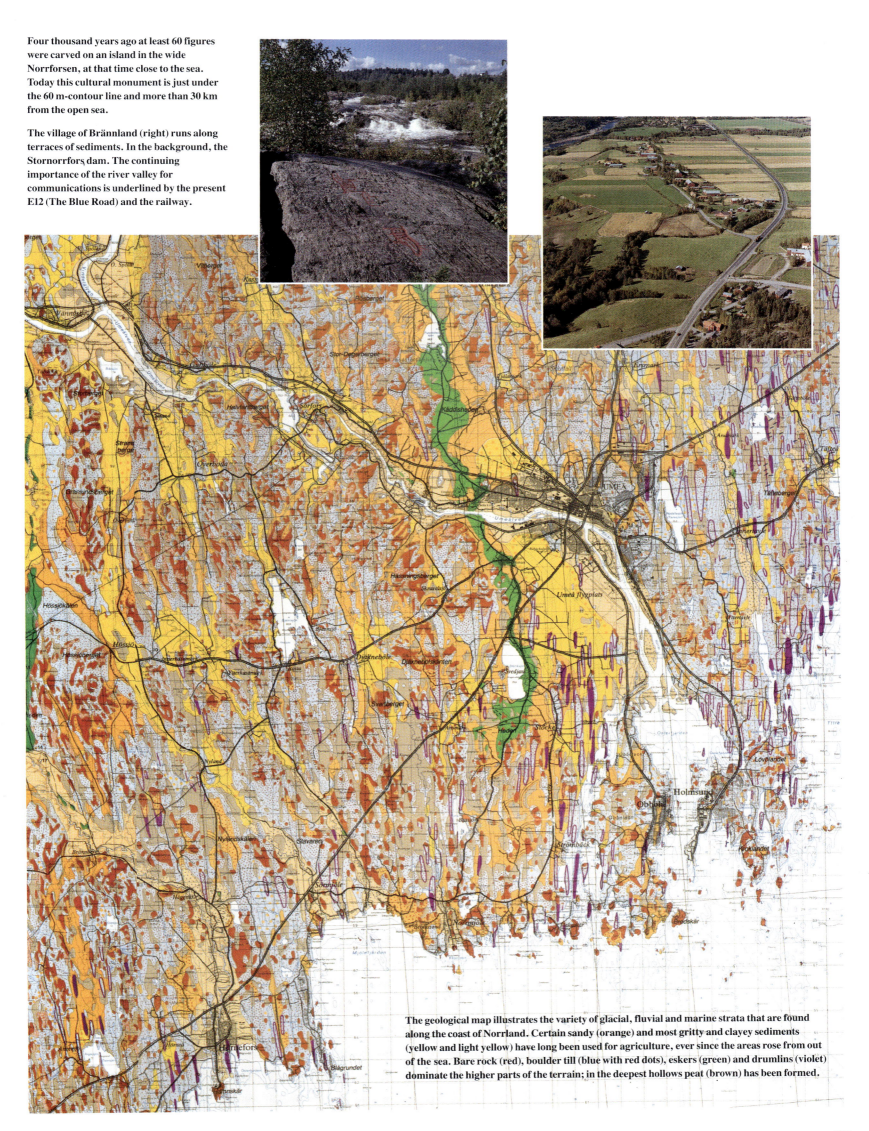

The geological map illustrates the variety of glacial, fluvial and marine strata that are found along the coast of Norrland. Certain sandy (orange) and most gritty and clayey sediments (yellow and light yellow) have long been used for agriculture, ever since the areas rose from out of the sea. Bare rock (red), boulder till (blue with red dots), eskers (green) and drumlins (violet) dominate the higher parts of the terrain; in the deepest hollows peat (brown) has been formed.

Robertsfors

The history of Robertsfors, more than most other industrial towns in Norrland, may be compared to a relay race, in which the changeovers symbolise switches from one industry to another many times in the course of history. Innovations have come to these towns now and then, altering industry and the environment.

The physical arena, the geography, has in general remained the same, but the scenography, the conditions governing the actors' roles, people's work and lives, has been changing all the time. It is mainly technology that brings about these changes, introducing a vital new idea at each changeover.

Wood supplies for Robertsfors sulphite mill in 1948

THE MID–18TH CENTURY

In the 18th century Robertsfors was called Edfastmark and was a traditional agricultural village by the Rickleån, its life-giving resource. The natural meadows were the basis of the economy; a few acres of arable land provided barley for bread and there were plenty of fish in the river, including salmon at times.

The forest was important only for building timber and firewood. The water power in the river drove a watermill with a horizontal wheel. In 1759 there was a coarse-toothed sawmill, which in 1795 was replaced by one with a fine-toothed blade.

THE FIRST HALF OF THE 19TH CENTURY

As early as 1759 Robert Finlay, a Scottish merchant of noble birth, and John Jennings, an Irishman, were granted a charter to build a blast furnace by the Rickleån. The ironworks, which expanded in 1782 with a hammer and a manufacturing forge, was given the name Robertsfors.

The new vertical overshot water wheel drove the bellows for the blast furnace and the hammers. The supply of charcoal as well as water power was an important factor in the choice of site and decisive for regional planning at that time, which favoured the iron industry in northern Sweden, because there was a fear that the forests in the south of Sweden, especially in the mining districts there, would be decimated.

The ore from Utö and other central Swedish mines was transported by wherries from Roslagen to the harbour at Sikeå and thereafter 6 km by land to Robertsfors, where a foundry was also built in 1821.

The mill town social structure at this time was hierarchical and patriarchal. This was reflected in the town plan and the new urban design of the buildings. The first brick houses were built.

The town had become dependent on international economic cycles. The old self-subsistent peasant village of Edfastmark disappeared into history.

The plant at Robertsfors today is a reflection of industrial history. It has been adapted for new types of production. The pulp mill has become a high-tech centre. The town and residential areas are to the right outside the picture.

THE LATE 19TH CENTURY

The era of the ironworks was now past. The blast furnace was closed down in 1883 and the manufacturing forge in 1891. A shift in production from iron to wood took place.

In 1879 the Kempe family bought the mill including the sawmill, which had been built in 1830. The sawing work had been done almost throughout the 19th century with water-driven gang saws, but in 1890 the mill was modernised by introducing water turbines.

At the same time steam power was utilised by putting a steam locomotive to work on the track down to the harbour at Sikeå. This track had been laid in 1820, using oxen and horses as draught animals. It was electrified at the turn of the century and evidently functioned well. This is why the industry stayed in Robertsfors and did not, as was usual in Norrland at that time, move down to the coast.

Forestry expanded greatly. Secondary industries like tar distilling and timber floating improved the local economy. The management also developed the agricultural side of the mill throughout the 19th century, by buying up crofts and cultivating new land. In 1879 the mill owned 23 crofts in Bygdeå and 17 in Burträsk. In 1863 the first dairy in Västerbotten was opened and in the 1890s there was a herd of about 130 cows on the mill farm, which was by far the largest in the county.

THE 1930S

A new shift in production has taken place. The manufacture of sawn wooden goods ceased entirely in 1926. Instead, the labour market was now dominated by the sulphite pulp mill which was built in 1903. It was worked by a steam engine until a steam-turbine generator was installed in 1920. The workers built houses of their own and in 1927 Robertsfors became an urban district.

Social and cultural activities flourish in this prosperous industrial community. Here, Moses in the local drama group.

ABOUT 1990

Yet another shift in production! Paper pulp manufacturing was discontinued in 1948. Twenty years later the mill farm was also closed. The dairy had gone as early as 1911.

In the course of time ASEA took over the pulp mill and converted it into a high-tech centre, with a high-pressure laboratory, manufacturing synthetic diamonds for drillheads in mines all over the world.

The latest product in the broad industrial range at Robertsfors is what is produced at high temperatures by high-pressure technology: strong, hard-wearing ceramic components for industrial precision machinery, for nuclear power plants, for example. In 1994 Cerama AB is a world-famous company.

But popular cultural activities in the form of art and handicraft, theatre and music, have also turned Robertsfors into a modern, multifaceted community. The relay race goes on. What will happen at the next change-over?

The Forest and Bog Landscape

Above the highest shoreline the till lies more or less unsorted. Drainage is by the large rivers running down from the mountains to the Gulf of Bothnia. The long river and lake systems have many rapids and waterfalls—but the most spectacular of them have almost dried up as a result of exploitation for the all-important hydro-electric power. A number of fine stretches of river remain, including the whole of the untouched Vindelälven and individual falls like Storforsen on the Piteälven and Kamlungeforsen on the Kalixälven. There are large areas between the valleys where there is no uniform direction of drainage and countless hollows are filled with lakes or bogs. The character of the forest varies between the dwarf mountain forests of old pine, spruce and birch to the west and the higher forests at lower levels towards the coast, where the climate permits a longer vegetation period.

COLONISERS IN FORESTS AND ON BOGLAND

This region provides a favourable environment for a rich fauna. It was in fact hunting and fishing that attracted people to make their living there for hundreds, if not thousands of years. But a permanently inhabited colony did not begin to grow up in the interior until the late 17th and early 18th century. It was the extensive boglands that attracted settlers in the first place. Cattle-breding was the main source of livelihood. Fishing and hunting were still important, but came second to cattle-breeding. A good supply of winter fodder was the limiting factor for the cattle, and this was provided in large quantities by the bogs. The forests provided summer grazing.

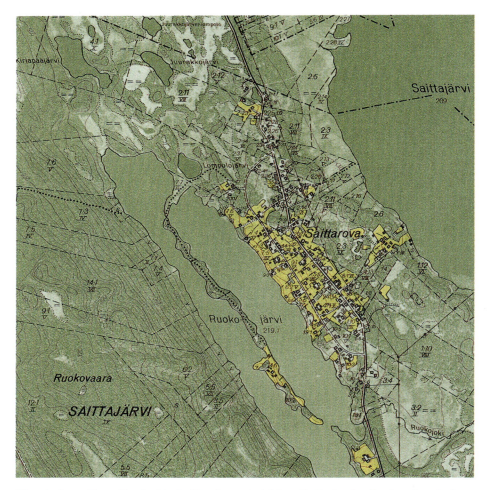

The colonisers of inner Norrland looked for sites protected from the frost on headlands and southerly slopes facing lakes and rivers. Saittarova, some 100 km north of the Arctic Circle, stands on a slope facing south-west on a neck of land between two lakes. Old fields can be seen on a headland jutting out into the lake.

When a new settlement was established, a special group of experts surveyed the land that was expected to provide for a family. Reports were written, and from these one can see how much winter fodder a certain bog might provide. To begin with very large areas were needed to provide enough for each new settlement. But by the end of the 18th century and right up to the 1930s much smaller areas were sufficient. This meant that the area could be more densely settled and populated—thanks to irrigation. By supplying the already waterlogged bogs with still more water, yields of sedge and horsetail could be at least trebled. In the late 18th century irrigation systems were developed using dams and irrigation canals. Resources were also improved by winning land from drained lakes in combination with building these dams and by increasing harvests on water-washed slopes. The large increase in population in the 19th century can mostly be explained by irrigation of the bogs and the flooding devices that were constructed. After the Second World War the old-style cultivation of meadows was gradually abandoned.

Nygård, on a hillside near Stortjulträsk, Ammarnäs—a farm clearing that looks like an island in an ocean of forest.

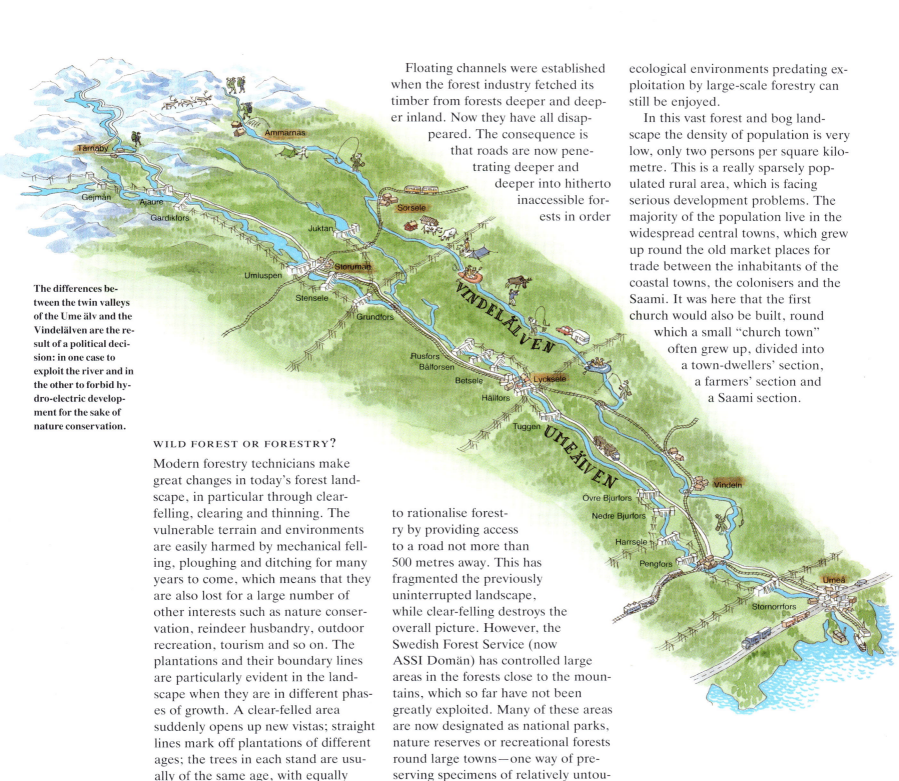

The differences between the twin valleys of the Ume älv and the Vindelälven are the result of a political decision: in one case to exploit the river and in the other to forbid hydro-electric development for the sake of nature conservation.

WILD FOREST OR FORESTRY?

Modern forestry technicians make great changes in today's forest landscape, in particular through clear-felling, clearing and thinning. The vulnerable terrain and environments are easily harmed by mechanical felling, ploughing and ditching for many years to come, which means that they are also lost for a large number of other interests such as nature conservation, reindeer husbandry, outdoor recreation, tourism and so on. The plantations and their boundary lines are particularly evident in the landscape when they are in different phases of growth. A clear-felled area suddenly opens up new vistas; straight lines mark off plantations of different ages; the trees in each stand are usually of the same age, with equally spaced trunks.

Floating channels were established when the forest industry fetched its timber from forests deeper and deeper inland. Now they have all disappeared. The consequence is that roads are now penetrating deeper and deeper into hitherto inaccessible forests in order to rationalise forestry by providing access to a road not more than 500 metres away. This has fragmented the previously uninterrupted landscape, while clear-felling destroys the overall picture. However, the Swedish Forest Service (now ASSI Domän) has controlled large areas in the forests close to the mountains, which so far have not been greatly exploited. Many of these areas are now designated as national parks, nature reserves or recreational forests round large towns—one way of preserving specimens of relatively untouched landscapes, so that certain ecological environments predating exploitation by large-scale forestry can still be enjoyed.

In this vast forest and bog landscape the density of population is very low, only two persons per square kilometre. This is a really sparsely populated rural area, which is facing serious development problems. The majority of the population live in the widespread central towns, which grew up round the old market places for trade between the inhabitants of the coastal towns, the colonisers and the Saami. It was here that the first church would also be built, round which a small "church town" often grew up, divided into a town-dwellers' section, a farmers' section and a Saami section.

Svansele Meadows along the Petikån, a tributary of the Skellefteån, as they looked before and after damming.

The Mountain Region

The mountain region from Dalarna to Treriksröset, a distance of 1,000 km, 50–150 km broad, has a permanent population of only 25,000 people. A feature common to the whole region is the Saami population and reindeer husbandry, and in our time tourism and tourist facilities. Tourism first developed along the railways running through the mountains, in the 1880s to Storlien and in 1902 to Narvik. The later development of holiday homes up the mountain sides came in the 1960s with cars, a more extensive road network and skilifts.

The Swedish Touring Club has been building trails and overnight cabins in the roadless mountain districts for a hundred years. The thousand-kilometre long trail called Kungsleden runs all the way from Grövelsjön to Abisko. The small townships in the mountain region provide services that far exceeds the needs of the local population.

Accessibility has always differed greatly in the northern and southern parts of the mountain region. The mountains in Dalarna, Härjedalen and Jämtland have had permanent farming populations in the valleys and on southern slopes ever since the Viking Age or even earlier. Cattle-breeding, supplemented by winter fodder from forest bogs and shealings, fishing and hunting, have formed the basis of livelihood right up to the present. Most of Sweden's highest farming villages are to be found in West Härjedalen. But iron-ore deposits have also played an important role; we often find relics of iron and copper workings round old settlements. We also find numerous trapping pits from the trapping culture which lived on into modern times. The southern mountains did not divide up settlements; cattle tracks and pilgrim paths connected the then Norwegian villages east and west of the mountain range even in the Middle Ages.

In contrast, the Jämtland and Lappland mountain districts remained Saami territory right up to the 20th century, apart from a few adventurous Swedish mining projects that started in the 17th and 18th centuries. Large-scale mining, railways, power stations, trunk roads and tourist hotels still only manage in a few isolated places to encroach on this mighty mountain kingdom, often called "the last wilderness in Europe".

BRUKSVALLARNA

Here, in the foothills of the mountain region, 709 m above sea level, where the soil is poor and the period of growth short, hay meadows were for many years the main resource. Farmers from Ljusnedal and Funäsdalen had their shealings here, in "Vallarna" (*the Meadows*).

The oldest settlement, from the Viking Age-early Middle Ages, has left traces in the form of Sweden's highest-lying prehistoric graves (Ramundberget). A system of trapping pits running from Bruksvallarna acrosss Ramundberget forms the remains of an ancient hunting method practised here until 1864.

In the 1680s Ljusnedal Mill began to extract copper ore at Mittåkläppen and Ramundberget. The labour force consisted of crofters who had to move to the north side of the Ljusnan, where the mine had the right to exploit the land (hence the name Bruksvallarna, where *Bruk* = Mill).

Mining, after 1755 of iron ore, was not as profitable as had been expected, and in the 1870s the company went over to cattle-breeding on a large scale. When the company was sold to the Crown in 1893, the crofters were allowed to become tenants provided they continued to farm the land. This has helped Bruksvallarna to remain one of the best-preserved farming villages in the mountain region.

Shealings were a necessary part of agriculture in the mountain districts, and the farmers in Bruksvallarna used the vast peatlands for summer grazing and haymaking, for example in Mittådalen, where the largest number of shealings in Härjedalen are to be found.

The farmers, the company and the Saami were soon disputing the right to use the land in and round Bruksvallarna. As early as 1690 the farmers complained that the company was encroaching on their shealings. Later there were conflicts between the reindeer-farming Saami and the settled farmers when the reindeer herds passed through the shealings on their autumn and spring migrations. These conflicts came to a head during the last few years the company was in operation. After debates in the Riksdag and newspapers the Saami were granted the right to graze reindeer on the land when it was sold to the Crown. The question is still under discussion, but after a court case against the Crown which started in 1966, the Crown's ownership of the land was confirmed, as was the Saami right to use this land.

Today tourism is the most important industry. From a modest beginning in the 1930s with tourist services as a sideline to farming, the industry has grown to employ most of the 230 permanent inhabitants. Hotels and holiday camps have a total capacity of about 1,000 beds. There were also 348 second homes in the area.

Upper Härjedalen is a part of Sweden which has many shealings, but very few of them are in use today. The grassland and mires in the mountains were also used as shealings during the short summer, often in competition with grazing reindeer. The geological map describes the soil types. Till, often with large boulders (blue with boulder symbols) is the dominant type; eskers are shown in green, finer sediments (sand and clay) in yellow, peat and mires in brown. Red indicates bare rock.

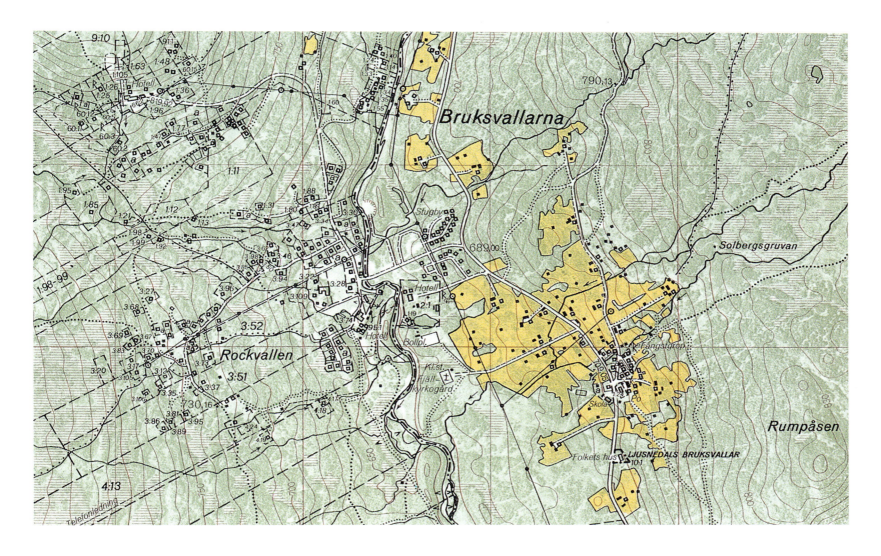

This map from 1976 shows how holiday cottages, hotels and other amenities have already taken over the traditional meadows and farm buildings at Bruksvallarna. In many places winter tourism has created artificial landscapes, where, if necessary, even snow can be made. In the summer heavy erosion is revealed on the ski slopes.

The old grassland of Bruksvallarna is still grazed by mountain cattle and goats. Holiday cottages spread over the slopes round the tourist hotels. The mountain hotel on Ramundberget can be seen in the background. The network of roads is penetrating deeper and deeper into the mountain valleys.

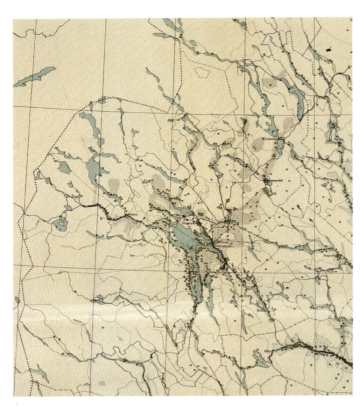

A map of Sweden's arable land dated 1921 also shows the calciferous clay till round Lake Storsjön, as it was known at that time. The importance of clay till for cultivation is quite evident.

The buildings and fields in the old agricultural district at Optand between Ope and Brunflo not far from Östersund have the characteristic appearance of that region. Old maps prove that the district grew up over a long period of time.

The Storsjön District

The district round Lake Storsjön has long been a farming district. Many of the farms have been handed down from father to son for centuries.

When the first permanent settlement was made in the Late Iron Age, it was a small area in the wilderness, an outpost of the nearest district with permanent inhabitants on the Norwegian side. Trading links with Norway were for many years an important part of the farmers' economy and continued after 1645, when Jämtland became Swedish. Norwegian influence is evident in many areas, not least the agricultural settlement structure and the organisation of cultivation.

Today the Storsjön district is one of Norrland's main agricultural areas, where most of the population of Jämtland live. The district's central role throughout the centuries is largely the result of the favourable conditions for settlement and agriculture created by the bedrock, soil and local climate. The Cambro-Silurian bedrock and calciferous clay till provide conditions for cultivation that are very favourable compared with other districts at the same latitude. Jämtland has also played a major role in the trading links between the Baltic and Tröndelag ever since prehistoric times, and as a result the Storsjön district with its favourable conditions for permanent settlement became a central place. Pilgrims passed through the mountain valleys on the way to Nidaros.

Klövsjö

The village of Klövsjö is one of the last of the "living" old-style farming districts in the interior of Norrland. As in the 18th century the farms lie scattered over the limited part of the village that consists of arable land. Mixed herds of cattle—mountain cows, sheep, goats and North Swedish horses—are kept on the farms, which have a few acres of arable land. Of the many old shealings some 15 were

A map of Optand from 1752–55 shows how the buildings stand in groups, with the arable land in long strips on the slopes running down to Lake Storsjön. Large areas are still given over to meadowland, showing that cattle rearing is still very important in the district.

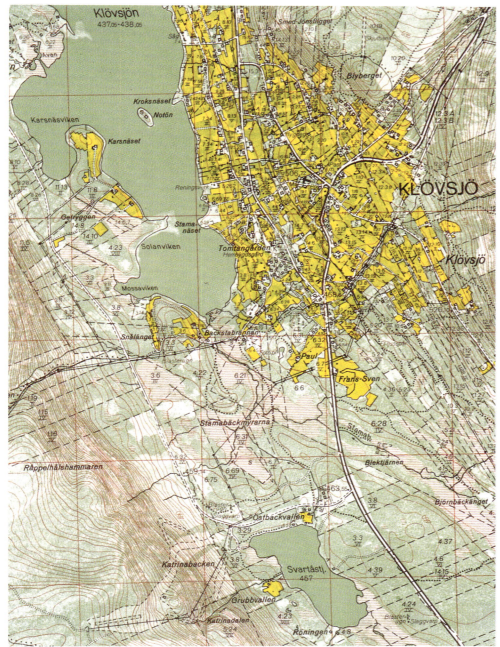

The farms in Klövsjö, each with its small area of arable land, are scattered over the infields. Complete groups of farms have developed as a result of dividing old farms, leading to a denser building pattern.

This parish map dated 1845 is of part of the large outfield area with its shealings and hay mires which continued to play an important role in Klövsjö's economy well into the 20th century.

This photograph of Klövsjö taken in 1979 shows how the infields on sunny slopes run down to Lake Klövsjön. The village has retained many ancient farmhouses and traditional farming methods. The alpine part of Klövsjö with its ski lifts and tourist facilities stands on the steep slopes in the background.

still in use in 1990. Both the number of farms and the number of shealings are decreasing as the elderly farmers retire.

The parish map dated 1845 shows part of the vast outlying area of shealings and bogs where fodder was grown which still played an important part in the farmers' economy right into the 20th century. The fact that cattle husbandry was still the dominant form of farming is proved by the enclosed fields, but also by the large number of barns and cattlesheds.

Slag heaps and bloomery furnaces bear witness to simple iron production in the old days. Today fishing, gathering wild berries and hunting moose are important complementary activities. But it is above all tourism that provides new jobs and fresh income. The village was "discovered" in the 1930s and became famous for its natural beauty, lying as it does on slopes running down to Klövsjön, surrounded by mountain peaks and fells. Modern alpine skiing was introduced in the 1960s. The steep slopes in the south-west which have the best snow have been equipped with extensive lift systems and winter-sport facilities.

Malmberget got a proper town plan in 1908, after which its disorganised shanty town disappeared. It was important for the dwelling houses to be placed close to the places of work in and round the mines.

Malmberget

The Gällivare ironfield was known as far back as the 17th century, but it was not until the 18th century that the deposits were first exploited. This was the century when it was realised what great potential Norrland offered in the form of mineral deposits, forests and water power. The earliest claims in the ironfield included the Baron Mine and the Robsahm Mine, the latter named after a lawyer at the Mining Institute who worked with the owner at that time, Baron Samuel Gustav Hermelin. At that time the permanent population was very small and production was insignificant. Colonisers in the surrounding districts supplied the mines with charcoal, timber and transport.

Bad times came and Hermelin was declared bankrupt in 1812. Mining and iron production ceased almost completely and conditions were serious for the local population. New plans were made after 1817 to exploit the iron-ore deposits. The problem of transport lay at the heart of the matter.

After about 50 years of discussions and planning the Luleå-Gällivare railway was completed in 1887, reaching Malmberget in March 1888. The railway was built by a British company, but was nationalised in 1892. After 150 years the Gällivare transport problem was solved at last. This was all the more important because England had recently succeeded in making steel from phosphorous ore on a large scale by the Thomas process. The phosphorous ore in Norrbotten had thereby gained in value on the international market.

Up to now the ironfield had been owned privately. Ownership had been connected with two farms. In 1887 a law was passed which aimed at clarifying what was Crown land and what was private land. The result was dramatic in Malmberget: the great field with all its mineral deposits became Crown land, so the state became the owner. A solution to the dispute over ownership came in 1907 in the form of co-ownership between the state and private interests represented by the Grängesberg Company and LKAB (Luossavaara-Kiirunavaara AB), which had been formed in 1890. This co-operation lasted until 1957, when the state took over LKAB's shares, while Grängesberg retained a minority holding. Today the company is wholly owned by the state.

The growth and development of the mining community at Malmberget was completely dependent on the

The close connection between mining operations and municipal life in Malmberget became very evident in the early 1950s when it was discovered that the Captain's Seam ran under the built-up part of the town. The centre was affected, including the school, the church, public baths and the People's House, as well as many private houses. All in all some 20 blocks had to be cleared to allow mining to continue, which was necessary if the community was to survive. The risk of subsidence later proved to have been exaggerated, but the effect on the town was still dramatic.

mineral deposits there. An unplanned shanty town mushroomed on the slopes of the mountain as the beginnings of the new town. The extensive mining operations which began when the railway reached Gällivare required, in contrast to the old days, a permanent workforce employed solely for mining work. The first dwellings were built close to the railway and the mines. The houses built by the mining company were not sufficient, however, so they were complemented by primitive dug-outs and wooden huts.

In the late 1890s the population increased by 600–900 persons per year. The dwellings built by the company only met the needs for about one third of the employees.

It was realised at an early date that this disorganised shanty town with primitive sanitary conditions and a great risk of fire needed to be brought under control, but for various reasons no decisions were made until 1908, when a town plan was finalised and building started afresh. Much of Malmberget was developed in the early 20th century. As late as 1955 Malmberget looked like a garden suburb of one or two-storeyed wooden houses, but high-rise brick apartment blocks were built in the 1960s and 1970s. However, a rich deposit, the Captain's Seam, proved to lie under this district, and when the seam was exploited in the 1970s and 1980s many buildings in the centre of Malmberget had to be demolished.

Shacks in Malmberget in the 1890s. There was work to be had, but living conditions were harsh. Malmberget was a unique community in Sweden.

Around the turn of the century the highest paid workers in Sweden lived in this shanty town. It was a Swedish Klondyke — here, one of the shopping streets.

Planning for Future Landscapes

Gävle illustrates the early history of town planning in Sweden. A map of Gävle from the 1640s attributed to Nicodemus Tessin the Elder shows the late medieval, organically developed structure of the town. The typical feature of this kind of town structure is that the street pattern consists of long streets running mainly parallel with the river banks, crossed by streets connecting the river with the inner parts of the town. According to the generally accepted pattern there were as yet no roads along the river banks. It is also possible to see in medieval towns the original country roads round which the town grew up.

A town clearance plan drawn up in the 1640s is also attributed to Nicodemus Tessin the Elder. At this time clearance plans of this type were being drawn up for practically all Swedish towns. The aim was to create a gridiron of uniform town districts which could be subdivided into uniform blocks (in this case exemplified by the district in the top left corner of the plan). Existing buildings and topographical conditions were hardly taken into account — this was an attempt by the authorities to force Swedish towns to adopt a uniform design.

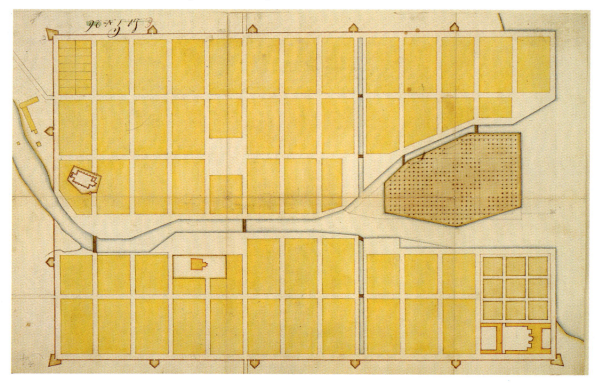

Town Planning from the Bjärkö Rights to the Planning and Building Act

Sweden's earliest preserved municipal law, the late 13th-century Bjärkö Rights, and various medieval province laws contain regulations concerning the way a town should be built; these laws, in a systematised and expanded form, reappear in Magnus Eriksson's Town Law from the mid–14th century. Magnus Eriksson's National Law also contains regulations concerning land and buildings. The Town Law decreed that "public streets" should be eight ells (about 4.8 m) broad, "for the use of both horses and carriages"; this tallies with the fact that most streets in Stockholm's medieval Old Town have this width. The province laws in eastern Sweden and Skåne also contain detailed regulations concerning the division of village land and the placing of farms on regular plots in the village. This created a stable foundation for ownership and land use at the same time as building was controlled. In eastern central Sweden this plan was realised in countless villages in the Middle Ages.

The first great planning wave in Swedish towns came in the decades round the middle of the 17th century. Sweden's newly-won international power status demanded internal reforms and the national government decided to establish a large number of new towns and regularise the existing ones. A large number of plans were drawn up by a small group of engineers and officers in the Fortifications Corps. The aim was to create organised and "trim" town structures; a rectangular gridiron plan was considered to be the way to attain this goal (it is misleading to call this type of plan a Renaissance plan, as it sometimes is). The execution of the plans did not always turn out as expected, but the results were nevertheless impressive. Göteborg, Kalmar, Uppsala and parts of central Stockholm, as well as many other towns and town districts, still bear the stamp of these 17th-century ideas.

There was no such planning wave during the 18th century; the previous century's planning had been imposed

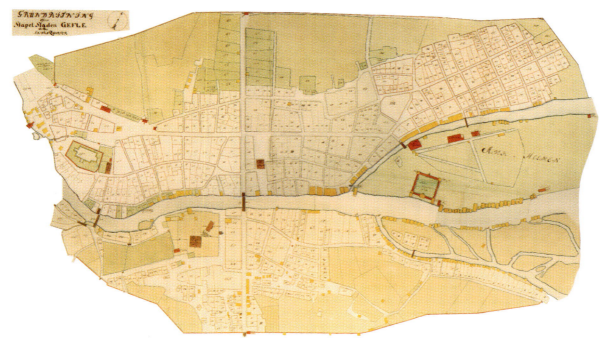

According to a map dated 1747 the town's structure still agreed in the main with the survey carried out 100 years earlier. The only results of the ambitious plans of the 17th century are the straight streets — Kungsgatan and Drottninggatan — which cross at right angles, and the central square.

After a disastrous fire Jonas Brolin drew up a clearance plan whose main features were implemented. Right angles and uniformity were still the guiding principles, but with attention paid to topographical conditions. A broad harbour road is an important part of the plan. The old plan can be discerned under the new pattern.

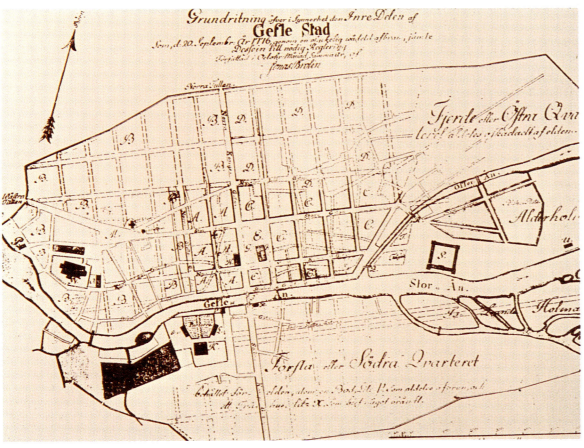

from above, and this was no longer possible in the political system of the "Age of Liberty". The only new town to be established was Östersund. In 1734 Sweden got a new law book which was to have included a section concerning town planning, but for political reasons this never materialised. Instead, each individual town was made responsible for the development of building regulations. Stockholm was first in the field — its first building regulations were issued as early as 1725, followed by revised and extended versions. At first only a few of the biggest towns followed Stockholm's lead, but in the early decades of the 19th century several towns adopted building regulations. Clearance projects were launched as a rule only after fires, as in Vänersborg in 1834 and in Gävle in 1869.

In the mid–18th century a process started, with the aid of various land reforms in 1757 (*storskifte*), 1803 (*enskifte*) and 1827 (*laga skifte*), which was to change the shape of the whole Swedish countryside. This was the dissolution of villages in Sweden.

About the middle of the 19th century discussions were held concerning the introduction of national building regulations, which later resulted in the 1874 Building Regulations. Each town was to draw up and adopt a town plan, and this set in motion a wave of intensive planning. The gridiron plan was still the norm, but now, according to the regulations, it was to include esplanades (broad streets divided into two lanes by an avenue of trees). The plans were usually drawn up by local surveyors and town engineers.

Just before 1900 new town planning ideas began to reach Sweden. Instead of rectangles, the ideal now was to adapt plans to the terrain; instead of straight streets, a varied sequence of streets offering focal points and open places. The foremost Swedish proponent of this school of thought, started by the Austrian architect Camillo Sitte, was Per Olof Hallman. He drew up plans for some 60 towns and townships.

The building regulations of 1874 were not an act of parliament but a regulation issued by the government, so their legal power was rather weak. However, after repeated efforts Sweden adopted a town-planning law in 1907. One of its important innovations was that it was now possible to impose regulations concerning the design of individual buildings.

This Town Planning Act was thought to be radical and progressive when it was passed. But soon additions and amendments were being proposed. Rapid urbanisation, improved standards for buildings and changed attitudes towards the role of the authorities in physical planning resulted in an almost continuous debate throughout the 20th century on town-planning legislation, which was continually being analysed and altered.

Hallman and his contemporaries often drew plans that comprised whole districts, but they were really

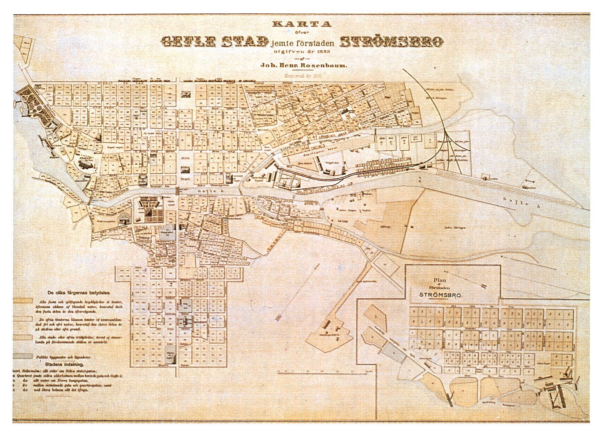

There is a map made by Joh. Henr. Rosenbaum in 1853 in which the town north of the river reflects the main features of Brolin's plan, except for the more monumental form of the square.

Disastrous fires were common enough in pre-industrial wooden towns in Sweden. They provided opportunities for wholesale clearance plans. Gävle burnt down in 1869.

blown-up detailed plans, not general plans in the true meaning of the term. During the years between the wars legally-binding town plans became more and more detailed, at the same time as the continuing growth of urban areas made it necessary to make general plans for communication systems, industrial localisation and the like. The 1931 Town Planning Act, for example, was intended to regulate general planning, but it was only a half measure. In the early 1940s the government enquiry machinery was back in operation and it was soon time for the third generation of building regulations in the 20th century: the 1947 Town Planning Act and Building Regulations. An important innovation was that plans had to be drawn up for all urban development. This made it possible for municipalities to prevent unsuitably located building projects.

In the 1930s a few towns had already drawn up general plans. The creation of the General Plan in the 1947 Town Planning Act encouraged overall planning, even if general plans were seldom adopted. It was evident that municipalities did not want to limit their freedom of action by adopting general plans. In the early seventies the central government authority, the National Board of Physical Planning and Building, launched two new types of general plan: the land-use plan and the municipal general plan, neither of which were supported by building legislation. These general plans were in many cases theoretical exercises that were rather remote from reality. Detailed planning, on the other hand, was often tossed in like yeast into the dough: in other words, the legally binding plans were made after it had been decided what was to be done. This was particularly true in the years when the Million Programme was being implemented, when projects were adapted to suit production methods.

Much of the 20th century has been dominated by planning ideas based on functionalism. The town was seen as an apparatus for communication,

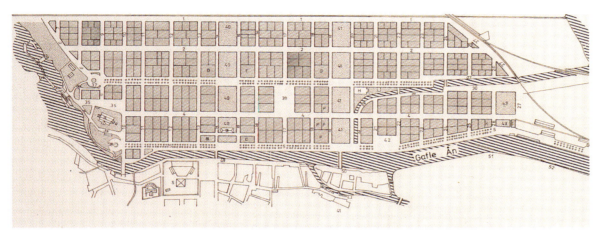

After the fire in 1869 two alternative plans were put forward for renewing the town. The upper one was drawn up by a railway engineer, Nils Ericson, the lower one by Per Georg Sundius. The plan that was adopted for Gävle was a combination of the two proposals. Even though these projects were drawn up several years before the 1874 Building Regulations, they reflected the planning ideals that were to characterise these regulations, with their emphasis on broad streets and boulevards. In the late 1870s plans of this type were drawn up for almost all Swedish towns. Sundius was the leading light in this school of town planning.

Around the year 1900 new planning ideals became popular. Instead of right angles there should be variety and flexibility. The main advocate of these ideas in Scandinavia was Per Olof Hallman. A town plan for Gävle proposed by Per Olov Hallman and Fredrik Sundbärg used the new ideas for new districts, while the old town was left untouched. Their plan was only partly realised. The medieval street pattern south of the river, which had survived all the fires, remained unchanged in the Hallman-Sundbärg plan. Today part of this area forms the cultural monument called Old Gävle.

housing and production. There was little understanding for the values of continuity and variety. The stage was set for traffic routes, Million Programmes, stereotype suburbs and the demolition of old town centres. If efficiency and rationalisation were the key words for the fifties and sixties, the key word for the eighties was perhaps creativity. Every town was eager to create a positive "image" of itself in order to attract the post-industrial society.

Yet another characteristic feature of planning and building in the eighties was that, to a far greater degree than before, it obeyed the terms set by industry, at the same time as the distinction between public and private initiatives tended to weaken. Municipalities bargained with business consortiums over projects they found important, paying for them not in money but by granting the use of land and using their monopoly to allow generous building rights. This is what has been called "pre-planning".

During the rapid expansion of urban areas and the large-scale development of towns in the sixties the legislation on town planning, in spite of many amendments, appeared more and more remote from reality. In addition new laws were passed which affected planning, land use and building in various ways. An example of this is the Nature Conservation Act. Towards the end of the sixties work was commenced on a National Physical Plan which was not justified in building legislation. For this reason and others a thorough reform of building legislation seemed more and more urgent. A commission was appointed in 1968 to investigate the planning system and bring together all the regulations concerning planning and building into one law. It was to take almost 20 years of discussions and investigations before a Planning and Building Act was passed in 1987.

The 1987 Planning and Building Act (PBL) did away with the term "town plan", replacing it with "detailed plan". The General Plan was also abolished. Instead, municipalities were obliged to draw up an *översiktsplan* (general plan) for their whole area. Other important changes were that the state's approval of plans was no longer required and that each detailed plan should be implemented within a period of between five and fifteen years.

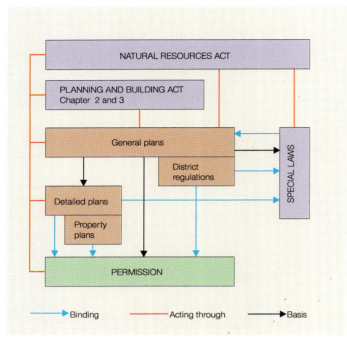

Town plans are adopted at various points in time and according to the laws and regulations in force at the time. Each of them refers to areas of very different sizes, which they deal with in varying degrees of detail. The great majority of plans relate to very small areas; they often change some detail in a previously adopted plan which is still in force. (N35)

NUMBER OF BUILDING PLANS, TOWN PLANS, DISTRICT REGULATIONS AND DETAILED PLANS IN FORCE ON 20 OCTOBER 1993, BY COUNTY

Sections 2 and 3 in the Planning and Building Act state the "general interests that should be observed when planning and locating buildings". These considerations are worded in general terms, allowing plenty of room for local political interpretations. Section 2 also includes a requirement that buildings should be located on land that is suitable for the purpose. Section 3 requires buildings to be placed, designed and painted so that they contribute to the aesthetic quality of the environment and are attuned to the natural and cultural values of the site.

General and Detailed Planning

The development of the cultural landscape and building is governed by the constraints provided by social planning, in particular physical planning. This aims at the long-term use of resources and the co-ordination of various land uses for society's needs. Physical planning deals with the exploitation of land, water and other natural resources, and the localisation of buildings and facilities of various kinds. Housing planning is one important part of the municipalities' responsibilities.

Physical planning is regulated by a number of laws. *The Natural Resources Act (NRL)* which is based on national physical planning is an umbrella law operating mainly through other laws, primarily *The Planning and Building Act (PBL)*. Both these laws were passed in 1987. The overall aim of the NRL is stated in the opening paragraph: "Land, water and other aspects of the physical environment are to be used in a way that promotes their good long-term utilisation from ecological, social and economic points of view."

The PBL regulates the plans that are to be or should be drawn up and applied in various contexts. In addition the PBL includes the requirements that are to be applied to buildings with regard to energy, water, load-bearing capacity, accessibility, appropriateness to the surroundings, enjoyment, hygiene, fire security and so on.

The General Plan is the municipal plan. The introduction of the general plan dealt for the first time with the overall balance of the future development of the whole of a municipality, its land and its water. It is not binding, but for future decisions concerning the use of land and water, natural resources and building it is an advantage if these issues are treated with care and concern in the general plan. A general plan should give the outline of plans concerning the proposed use of land and water in the municipality, changes in and conservation of buildings, and the way in which the municipality intends to satisfy national interests expressed in the NRL with regard to major roads, areas important for nature and culture conservation programmes, the provision of adequate recreational areas and so on. A general plan is a kind of political programme, stating the municipal council's goals concerning the physical development of the municipality.

District Regulations are binding and are used to ensure that the aims of general plans are attained. District regulations may be drawn up for limited areas, but they may also be used to secure national interests.

Detailed Plans are binding; they are used to achieve a balance between public and private interests. These plans assess the suitability of land for building and regulate the building environment. Sometimes it may prove necessary and practical to adopt a *Property Plan* within a detailed-plan area. A property plan may be needed to draw up plans for a project, to clarify property holdings and facilitate the transfer of property, and to plan and construct jointly-owned facilities.

In general *permission* from the municipality is needed before a building is erected, or extensions or substantial changes in the use of a building are made, like converting a housing unit into an office.

Changes in legislation concerning types of plans mean that it is common for legally binding regulations and plans from different periods to apply to different parts of a district. This also affects the way in which building work develops. Each and every part of Sweden's land is subject to restrictions specified in one or more paragraphs of a law or a plan.

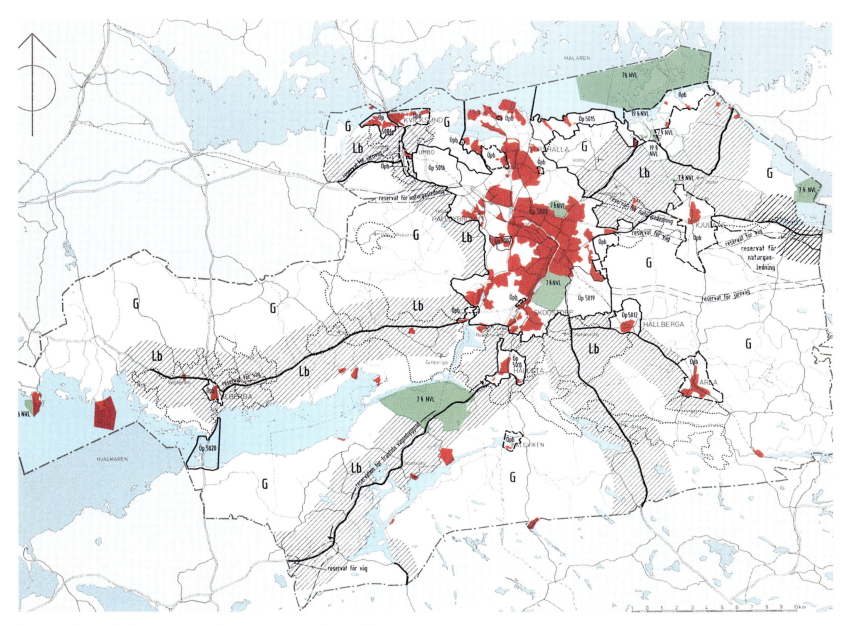

The General Plan for Eskilstuna was adopted by the town council on 26 April 1990 in accordance with the Planning and Building Act. The map shows the restrictions in the town, that is, where there are adopted detailed plans, nature reserves and nature conservation areas as well as land reserved for new roads, railways and natural gas pipelines. This politically adopted general plan acts as an action plan for future planning.

The eastern part of the Kjula plain is of national interest both for nature conservation and for cultural preservation. In the foreground, Barvalappen, a narrow inlet in Lake Mälaren, in the background Sörfjärden, another bay in the lake, and the bird sanctuary of Strand. This photograph was taken facing north-north-west from a hill south of the E20. The E20 is to be widened and perhaps rerouted. The National Road Administration wants to build it close to the south shore of Barvalappen; the town prefers a more southerly route, which instead will conflict with a prehistoric area of national interest. The problem had not been solved in 1994.

ÖVERSIKTSPLAN
FÖR ESKILSTUNA KOMMUN
STADSBYGGNADSKONTORET DEN 1 FEBRUARI 1989

REKOMMENDATIONER–ALLMÄNT

- Antagen detaljplan
- Naturreservat 7 § NVL
- Naturvårdsområde 19 § NVL
- Op 5008 Område med tidigare antagen del av översiktsplanen
- Opb Bebyggelseområde/tätort där översiktsplanen avses fördjupas. Bygglov för nybyggnad endast med stöd av detaljplan
- Lb Landsbygd kring större väg – komplettering med ny bebyggelse är tänkbar på vissa villkor
- G Glesbygd – främst för jord- och skogsbruk. Stark restriktivitet mot ny bebyggelse
- väg/järnväg/naturgasledn. Reservat för ny väg, järnväg respektive naturgasledning. Bygglov för nybyggnad endast efter särskild utredning
- Dominerande åkerområde. Stark restriktivitet mot ny bebyggelse på eller i anslutning till brukningsvärd jordbruksmark

LANDSCAPES PROTECTED BY LAW
1:5 000 000

- Area of particular value for tourism and recreation
- Coastal district and archipelago protected from industry that interferes with the natural environment
- Coastal district and archipelago where industry that interferes with the natural environment may be established if such industry already exists there
- Mountain area
- River protected from exploitation for hydro-electric power

Areas which are of national interest in their entirety for their natural and cultural value are given special mention in Section Three of the Natural Resources Act. (N36)

NATIONAL PHYSICAL PLANNING

The starting point for the concept of national physical planning was a couple of cases in the late 1960s concerning the localisation of heavy industry in a sensitive coastal area in Halland: a pulp mill and sawmill at Värö and the nuclear power station at Ringhals. At the same time plans for a number of other large projects started an environmental debate that resulted in a demand for national planning. The airport at Sturup, exploitation of the Vindelälven for hydro-power and an oil refinery at Brofjorden were examples of projects that brought discussions about the future environment to a head.

The aim of national planning was not to produce a plan for the whole country; instead, national interests were to be expressed in municipal plans. Extensive reports on the natural environment and its sensitiveness provided the background material for the guidelines for the use of land and water which were adopted by the Riksdag in 1972, 1977 and 1981. These guidelines for national physical planning were incorporated in the law concerning the use of natural resources (the Natural Resources Act, NRL) which came into force on 1 July 1987. Apart from the central regulations concerning use, the act includes special regulations for certain areas in Sweden (areas of national interest). It is the duty of the municipalities to follow the guidelines laid down in the NRL in their physical planning. The county administrative boards check that this is done.

The coast of Bohuslän is full of areas worth protecting—here, Hunnebostrand—at the same time as good harbours and ice-free waters are attractive for industry.

Höga Kusten (The High Coast) is the part of the coast of Ångermanland where the mountainous Norrland terrain runs right out into the Baltic, creating a coastal landscape unique in Sweden. Häggvik in Nordingrå.

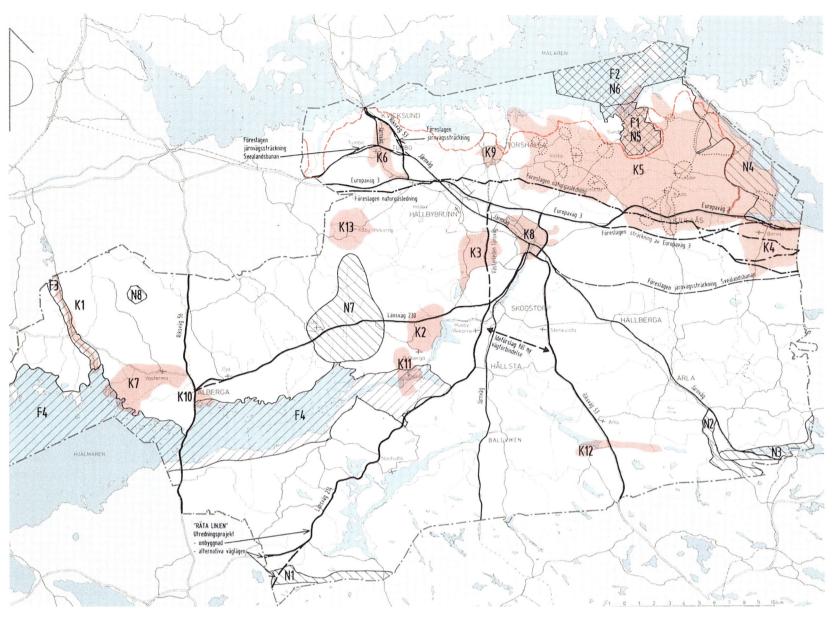

Municipal general plans, here Eskilstuna's, should, according to the Natural Resources Act, register places of national interest and their effect on land use and building plans. Figures refer to detailed descriptions which are found in the general plan proper.

Östra Hjälmaren near Lövön has ideal conditions for boating and bathing, fishing and enjoyable nature studies of all kinds. The lake is also important for commercial fishing. A more detailed general plan protects recreational interests by guaranteeing the right of public access to its shores. Active regional planning is essential.

The farms in the village of Mora did not move away from their medieval village plots even after *laga skifte*. The village stands in Sundbyholm, a nature conservation area.

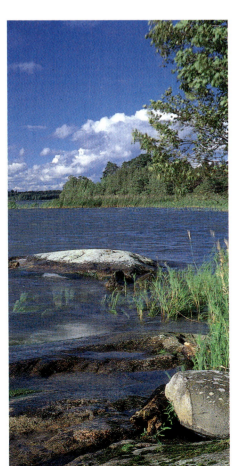

ÖVERSIKTSPLAN
FÖR ESKILSTUNA KOMMUN
STADSBYGGNADSKONTORET DEN 1 FEBRUARI 1989

Allmänna intressen enl naturresurslagen

RIKSINTRESSEN

K1 — Område av intresse för kulturminnesvård med kärnområde
Nummer hänvisar till särskild beskrivning

N1 — Område av intresse för naturvård
Nummer hänvisar till särskild beskrivning

F1 — Område av intresse för friluftsliv
Nummer hänvisar till särskild beskrivning

Mälaren med öar och strandområden

Europaväg, riksväg och länsväg

Föreslagen sträckning av väg

Järnväg

Föreslagen sträckning av järnväg

Föreslagen sträckning av naturgasledning
3 alternativ

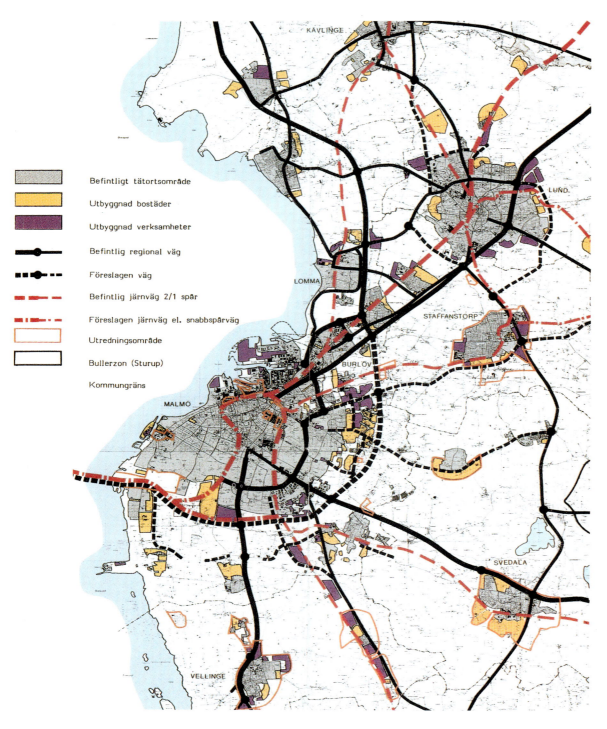

The Municipal Association of South-West Skåne (SSK) coordinates regional planning in south-west Skåne, comprising Burlöv, Kävlinge, Lomma, Lund, Malmö, Staffanstorp, Svedala, Trelleborg and Vellinge. This is an area of 1,600 km², with a population of about half a million.

These municipalities' general plans have been coordinated to facilitate planning across the municipal boundaries. The map shows the state of planning in the Malmö region for the proposed new roads and railways leading to the bridge across the Sound. A number of new industrial and residential areas linked to the new roads have also been planned.

GENERAL PLANNING

In an international comparison Swedish municipalities have a strong position in government, which is reflected in the field of physical planning. The Planning and Building Act has taken a further step by making general planning mandatory, thereby making the enforcement of detailed plans a municipal matter rather than a matter for central government through the county administrative boards. A general plan gives the state, as the representative of national interests, the opportunity to assess how a municipality is dealing with planning and building matters within its area.

What is unique about the Planning and Building Act is that a law passed by the Riksdag can be nullified by decisions made at the municipal level. This can be seen most clearly in matters concerning building permission, where legal requirements can be modified after a vote in the municipal council. The requirements may either be reduced or made more stringent in particularly important areas. In this case the general plan is used as a means of informing a municipality's inhabitants what has been decided, and allows the state to keep a close eye on municipalities that intend to ignore national planning interests.

General planning in its modern form has its roots in the optimistic faith in planning that followed the Second World War. The 1947 Building Act made it possible for each municipality to draw up a general plan which, once it had been adopted by the municipal council, could be confirmed by the state, thus making it legally binding. Only eleven plans were confirmed during the 40 years that the act was in force. Most of these plans were major road projects that needed to be discussed and given legal status for a larger area than would normally be covered by a detailed plan. A good example is the general plan for the motorway north of Eskilstuna.

REGIONAL PLANNING

For certain regions in Sweden it is necessary to have physical planning that extends beyond municipal boundaries. In the Stockholm region, for example, regional planning has existed in one form or another since the 1930s. Initially it was for traffic planning in the expanding metropolis. At present it is the Stockholm County Council that is responsible for working out and adopting regional plans. In the Malmö-Lund region there is a council of nine municipalities that deals with regional planning. The corresponding body in the Göteborg region is a council of eleven municipalities. No formal regional plan, either in the Göteborg or the Malmö region, has been adopted in accordance with the Planning and Building Act.

The aim of this regional planning is to solve major problems which are common to a group of municipalities such as the infrastructure (traffic and public transport, water and sewage, refuse disposal and so on), housing and the labour market during the coming 10–15 years, with long-term forecasts for 20–30 years ahead. It should, however, be pointed out that it is the municipalities that have the final word concerning their land. Thus, if a regional plan is to be realised, the municipalities concerned have to consider it sufficiently important to carry it out.

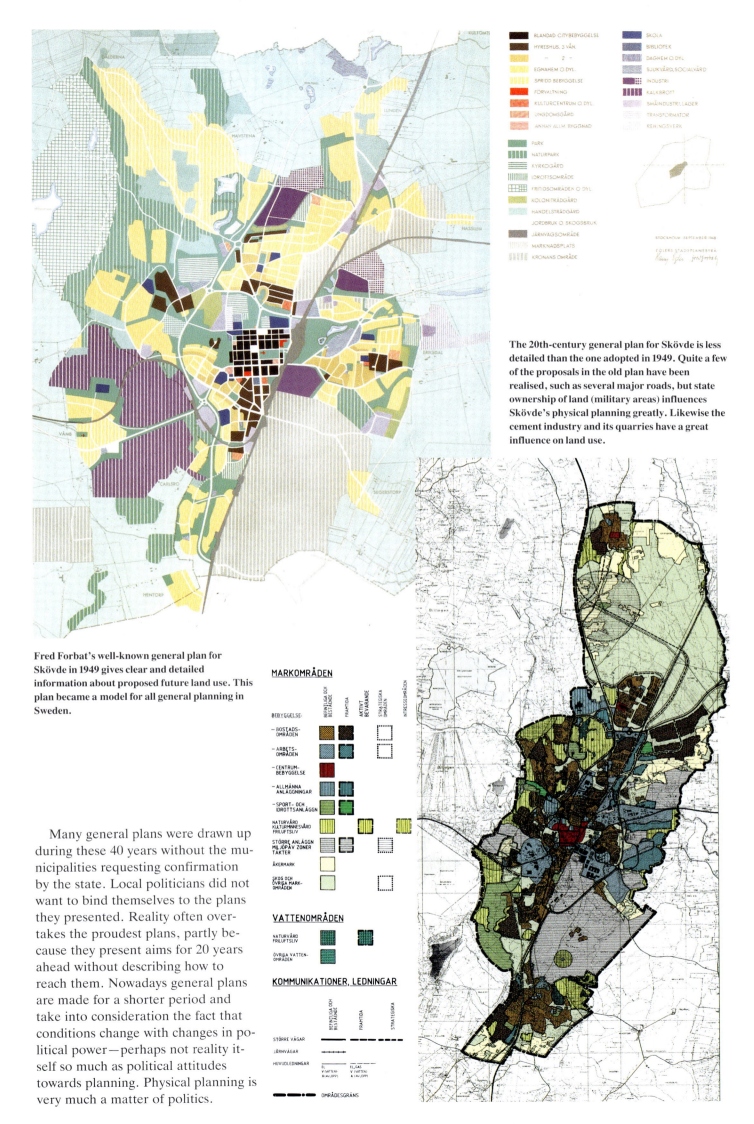

The 20th-century general plan for Skövde is less detailed than the one adopted in 1949. Quite a few of the proposals in the old plan have been realised, such as several major roads, but state ownership of land (military areas) influences Skövde's physical planning greatly. Likewise the cement industry and its quarries have a great influence on land use.

Fred Forbat's well-known general plan for Skövde in 1949 gives clear and detailed information about proposed future land use. This plan became a model for all general planning in Sweden.

Many general plans were drawn up during these 40 years without the municipalities requesting confirmation by the state. Local politicians did not want to bind themselves to the plans they presented. Reality often overtakes the proudest plans, partly because they present aims for 20 years ahead without describing how to reach them. Nowadays general plans are made for a shorter period and take into consideration the fact that conditions change with changes in political power—perhaps not reality itself so much as political attitudes towards planning. Physical planning is very much a matter of politics.

Navestad in Norrköping from the south looking towards the town centre. To the right, the road to Norrköping and Söderköping. To the left, outside the picture, Vrinneviskogen, a recreational area with woods, summer cottages and the garden suburb of Ensjön built in the first half of this century.

Detailed Plans

As soon as a group of houses is to be built, a number of questions have to be discussed, such as how the people living there will get out onto a main road and where water and sewage pipes should be laid, where paths and perhaps a park should be located and so on. In these matters it is advisable to set down the various proposals in a legally binding detailed plan.

A plan of this kind may deal with a group of perhaps 20 houses, but also an estate of the size of Navestad in Norrköping. It need not be restricted to new buildings but can just as well deal with an area that needs to be cleared or be more densely built up. A detailed plan gives landowners an opportunity to clarify certain responsibilities they have in common and the public a chance to make their opinions heard.

A detailed plan consists of a map (the plan) and a description. The map indicates the constraints on building heights and the like. There are more than 70,000 detailed plans in force in Sweden at present, dating from the late 19th century onwards, many of which are out of date and irrelevant, but still in force.

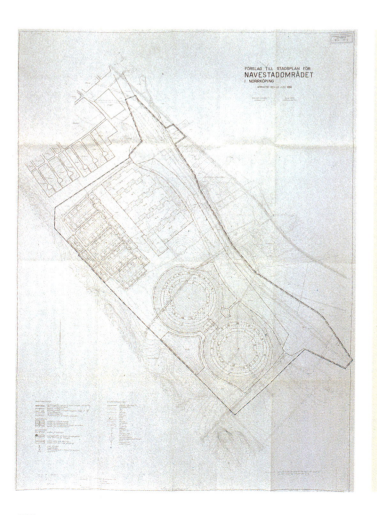

A town plan (since 1987 called a detailed plan) for a housing estate in Norrköping called Navestad. The so-called Million Program was launched in 1964; it was a program to build some million new housing units within ten years. The aim was to get rid of the severe housing shortage. Quantitatively the program was a success: 1,005,578 new housing units were built, 1/3 of which were private houses. Navestad, which was part of this Million Program", consists of three parts: in the north, a densely-built area of 230 atrium houses and 130 link houses, and south of these low-rise buildings apartment houses two to eight stories high containing 1,630 flats. As in many similar Million Program" areas, there was difficulty in Navestad in letting all the flats and other problems as well. Extensive renovation, more green spaces and a better traffic environment have made Navestad an attractive housing estate today.

Between 1,000 and 3,000 detailed plans are passed in Sweden every year. The production of plans is dependent on the state of the economy, since almost half of all plans are concerned with building dwellings. In the early 1990s traffic plans were common. These plans concern small areas—in a third of them the area is less than 0.5 ha and only one third cover areas larger than 3 ha. The National Housing Board, which is the authority responsible for seeing that the legislation concerning physical planning is followed, can also point out that only one tenth of all detailed plans are completely new; nine tenths concern changes to existing plans. Of these most are changes to built-up areas, such as filling empty sites, altering road layouts and laying water and sewage pipes. The remainder reflect changes in the terms for exploiting the property, which make it necessary to rewrite the plans before anything has been built.

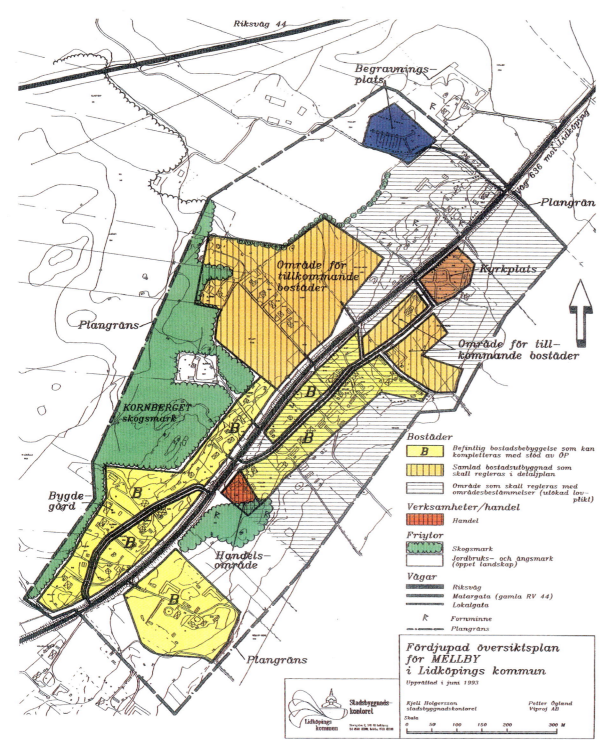

Mellby in the municipality of Lidköping provides an example of a more detailed general plan. In 1993 60 people were living in the planning area. The proposed expansion of about 50 housing units means that the population will increase to about 150 people. The plan proposes stricter rules for granting building permission in Mellby church village by means of area regulations.

The Planning and Building Act gives municipalities the opportunity to cancel detailed plans without any difficulty. Few municipalities, however, have utilised this opportunity to tidy up their existing plans. As long as there is no need for a change which might contravene an existing plan, it might just as well stay in force. However, changes are often made to parts of a detailed plan.

More Detailed General Plans and District Regulations

A general plan may not be adequate for certain areas in a municipality as a basis for future planning; a more detailed plan is needed, so the municipality works out a more specific general plan, but it does not specify building rights and does not oblige the landowner to use his land in accordance with the plan. If a municipality wants to ensure that land is used for a certain purpose without specifying any building rights, it may use district regulations. District regulations are also useful for pointing out where the requirements of the Planning and Building Act for building permission are to be interpreted differently.

The setting of a rural church can easily be destroyed by unskilled renovation or inappropriate new buildings. A strict interpretation of the Planning and Building Act may be applied locally in such areas by means of district regulations. Normally building permission is not needed for many kinds of changes which a landowner may wish to make; the best-known example is that building permission is not needed to build a shed not exceeding 10 m^2 in size. A district regulation can stipulate that all building or demolition work, or changes in land use, must be reported in advance to the municipal building committee for advice on possible changes in a sensitive environment.

Area regulations for Mellby mean that applications for building permission, apart from the general requirement to apply for permission to build, have to be made for extensions and renovations, work on house facades and roofs, repainting and demolition. In addition, building permission is required for building or altering outhouses. The purpose is to protect the valuable cultural environment.

The Future of the Cultural Landscape — a Vision

Not every thought about the future need necessarily involve a landscape. Many thoughts and dreams see people without a landscape: people who are doing something, giving something, getting something, becoming something, experiencing something. Yet it is always there, in the background, always exposed, always affected — the ever-present cultural landscape.

I should like to present my vision, like Nils Holgersson, by trying to see my various cultural landscapes a little from above but also from inside! Let me start my visionary journey by quoting from Rolf Edberg's book "The Land of Glittering Water".

"Somewhere behind every person there is a landscape that determines his or her physical conditions of life. Somewhere inside every person there is a mental landscape. This physical and this mental landscape are joined by a web of fine threads. They give us our identity."

Bönhamn Fishing Village in 2009

I feel happy every time I look out of my kitchen window at Bönhamn. Out there lie the sea, rocks, islands, storms, the mist — and the silence. There is plenty to protect and care for out there. It is a part of Ångermanland that I have come to love, and where my identity has developed. I do not have all my roots here, but those that I have are strong.

People here live close to nature. They know how to make use of the renewable resources that nature provides. They nurture them with loving care. They know that they are dependent on them: forest, soil, water, fish, wild animals. They stand up to the storms. They know that these, too, have their ecological meaning.

If I climb the mountain above my house, I can see with satisfaction that the village has developed in a way that is positive for the environment and culture. It has grown in harmony with natural conditions and people's needs — in the form of cultural buildings on a small scale: small museums, a baking house for all to use, a sauna, a weaving room, a photo lab, carpentry shops, small cafés down by the harbour and up in the village. They cling tight to the rocky slopes. I see them as the realisation of one of Anders Åberg's famous wood sculptures — a world in miniature. These buildings have strengthened the cultural background of the people of Bönhamn — and their identity as well.

Tourists come to a living fishing village in continuous contact with the sea and the cliffs. Young people have moved here, and the village echoes with the shouts and laughter of children. There is talk of starting a part-time nursery school. The school at Näs, three kilometres away, has been reopened. Beyond the carpentry shop and in neighbouring villages both private houses and small firms have sprung up. Everything has been planned with loving care by the local population working in co-operation with the county antiquary and other experts. Here new generations are being brought up to learn about the sea, the mountains and the forests.

Höga Kusten — an Area of National Interest

If I move to Dalsberget, I can gaze in peace and quiet at more than a hundred lakes that shine like pearls among an even greater number of hills and mountains. In the mid-nineties people living in the parishes of Nordingrå and Nora decided to make a joint effort to develop their countryside. With the help of the municipality and the county they began to discuss how the district could develop on the basis of the use of the land. Principles for the division of real property, the utilisation of land and physical planning gave them the tools they required. They produced a con-

We have "got rid of" a growing amount of household rubbish by piling it up on municipal tips. In Sweden there is still perhaps space enough — but how about more densely-populated countries? We also know that environmentally-harmful substances leak out of these tips. The tip at Sofielund in Stockholm, 1991.

tingency plan for the changes that the new Höga Kusten bridge would bring. Those who were hesitant about the bridge in the beginning have now started to work out how the new opportunities can be utilised; some of them are now enthusiastic supporters of the district development plans.

When the bridge was opened, people came from near and far to look at this beautiful great structure. They saw not just a bridge but a living rural district at Nora and Nordingrå, well able to look after large numbers of overnight visitors and give them good food and relaxation; but above all they met people who could talk about their history and their local culture.

Häggvik, with its Café Mannaminne, throbs with life. I can see the new lock being used by boats and leisure craft, bringing them closer to services, the community centre, the church, businesses and people. The old steamboat jetty is back in service again, so people can sail to and from Nordingrå and Häggvik.

The landscape has changed, because grazing cattle are once more a natural feature in the fields. Here small-scale, efficient farms, together with small firms, have created the basis for ecological tourism in harmony with the biological diversity that characterised the older cultural landscape. A small-scale wood-processing industry based on forestry has achieved good export results. The use of biofuel for vehicles has led to the creation of a distribution network controlled by the local industry, making it possible to provide various kinds of services in rural districts. The use of biofuel for heating has strengthened both forestry and agriculture. Modern telecommunication systems are available. The construction of the Bothnian railway line has helped to make the whole of the area between Sundsvall and Umeå more attractive to work and live in. Young people can commute by train between their university and their home and not lose contact with their roots. This favourable development is proof that it is possible to manage an area of national interest so that local and regional development is encouraged. Nowadays people realise that an area of national interest does not necessarily impose a ban on positive development.

Towns in 2009

Where I travel between towns in the south I can see that a totally new planning philosophy has struck root. There are living towns, where green belts are valued highly. Private cars have become less important as public transport systems have been developed. The focus is now on interplay between people, and I can see that several natural meeting places have grown up. Land use has changed from being a series of continuously expanding concentric suburbs to being efficient, economical and characterised by recycling.

The location and design of roads and industries is determined by strict environmental constraints. This has made it possible to integrate districts, thus lessening the demand for transportation, since work places and homes have once again come closer to each other.

In combination with conscious efforts to encourage cultural activities and services, planning has led to a stronger sense of identity for town dwellers. I see small squares, promenades, traffic-free areas. Sorting rubbish, composting and ecological building, together with kitchen gardens round apartment blocks, have increased biological diversity. Here and there I see courtyards where rainwater is used for fountains and springs. Street benches have reappeared, so that people can sit down for a few moments and give themselves time to think. Social discipline has improved, making society more secure and less anonymous. Towns have recovered their souls.

Stockholm—My Capital City in 2009

From Vita Bergen in the south of Stockholm I can see most of the city. All the flashing mirrors of water—lakes and the sea—make a magnificent sight. The water has been allowed to spread out; Slussen (The Lock) has changed and one of the bridges across Strömmen has been removed. I am glad to see that there is no Österled urban highway, nor

Recycling is the start of the natural-cycle economy. Here tyres are recycled at the Hagby tip in Stockholm. Scrap iron was the first material to be recycled, followed by newspapers and glass.

a Västerled either. Studies designed to adapt transport systems to the environment showed that the need for urban highways for long-distance through traffic could be better met by building motorways outside the Stockholm region. Instead of bypasses and urban motorways there is now a system of water transport—shuttle boats, taxi boats and ferries—that complements rapid urban railways, underground railways and trains.

Stockholm—a beautiful city, friendly to the environment, that has found its role through flourishing co-operation with all the Baltic countries.

From the Kaknäs Teletower I can look out over the first urban national park in the world: Haga-Brunnsviken and Djurgården.

Ever since Stockholm was nominated as a cultural capital city, the eyes of the world have been turned towards this park. It is proof that serious threats to the environment can be avoided, if only there is strong enough political willpower. The urban national park is to a far greater degree than ever before a meeting place for people of all ages and interests. The development of the park is watched closely and is decided by the Djurgården Council and various non-profit associations. The building projects that have been discussed over the years have been trimmed and adapted to preserve.

Fisksjöäng is once again a splendid park. The old gasworks facing it has been restored. I note that Husarviken has not been developed as some Olympic Games organisers had planned. Over by the Natural History Museum the Roslagen road has been lowered and the barrier effect removed. Instead, the University campus, together with the Natural History Museum's grounds, has attracted international attention because of the urban national park. There were no high ventilation towers built for the North Link Road. New technology made it possible to clean the exhaust gases. The politicians decided to accept the extra cost of de-pollution, which gave them the support of Stockholmers for building the Link Road.

My Sweden in 2009

The first national vision, which I helped to launch, has begun to achieve results. The proposal that the National Housing Board sent out for public comments led to a new attitude towards housing development. After the Board had been moved from Stockholm to Karlskrona, it saw Sweden in a broader perspective and shook off the "Stockholm blinkers" it had been said to have in the 1980s and 1990s.

Thus the Swedish vision became a powerful document that paved the way for a new dynamic regional-political era. It was also a model for the Baltic dream which is also on the way to becoming reality.

These visionary ideas raised the level of social planning as a democratic process in which the people's needs were more clearly defined. Once again local conditions are at the centre of things; development is based on them. The sense of purpose in rural districts, town districts, villages and towns now forms the foundation for development.

I consider how important it is that our common vision has its starting point in everyday life, in the close interplay between people in a neighbourhood. Only then can the vision we create together become reality.

Land and water have become increasingly valuable in a world whose population is growing amd where there is a growing need for clean air, unspoilt land and fresh water. The need to regulate the use of land and water has grown by leaps and bounds. Legislation concerning physical planning, environmental protection and the conservation of nature has also increased in importance for society and the cultural landscape—a trend that is evident internationally.

The human scale of villages and small towns has become a model for large towns and cities, contributing to a necessary survival programme.

Many people have escaped from the giant metropolises that have not succeeded in developing small-scale community life. The countryside with its villages and small towns appears in this light as a goal for migrants looking for a good place to live in. Telecommunications have made it possible to run knowledge-based in-

New technology is needed for more recycling. Here at Lövsta in Stockholm refrigerators are awaiting a technique to dispose of CFCs safely. New technologies are being developed in many parts of the world.

The fishing village of Bönhamn on Höga Kusten, with its old buildings and 17th-century chapel —
a setting worth preserving, but what about the job opportunities?

Industrial construction work under the pressure of the wave of urbanisation that led to severe housing shortages after the Second World War finally resulted in the mass building programmes of the 1970s. These led to social problems and unoccupied flats. This was true not least at Hallunda in Botkyrka, south-west of Stockholm, which signalled the final phase of the Million Programme.

dustries a long way from cities; but it is the use of bio raw materials like wood products in the form of biofuels and sawn wood, as well as grain products, energy forests, the cultivation of grass (*Phallarius arundinacea*) and the like that has resulted in a new industry based on forestry and agriculture.

The transportation infrastructure has also been extended so that small towns form networks with each other and their surrounding countryside. This has created opportunities for co-operation in various fields as well as reducing vulnerability.

Small schools have been reopened, this time from another viewpoint than before. Small industrial towns, bio mill towns, have replaced the large old mill towns. People are better organised, so they find it easier to cooperate and share services of various kinds. In my vision people have recreated more stable social networks, which means they are less liable to move all the time in search of a new, successful future.

Small-scale technology has developed into a strategy for survival. Biological and social diversity has increased in our society. Society is no longer controlled by technology for its own sake, but for the needs of mankind. This humanistic perspective completes the three-dimensional vision of the cultural landscape.

SHALL WE BE ABLE TO HARMONISE OUR PHYSICAL AND MENTAL LANDSCAPES?

The future of the cultural landscape, the physical landscape, will be determined by the developments that mankind's mental landscape undergoes. Our knowledge of nature and people is increasing; ecological links are becoming clearer and clearer. Our built-up environment and our management of natural resources will determine the success of our whole life environment. When mankind's physical environment is in tune with its mental environment, we may have reached the ecological and humanistic goal that many of us speak so warmly for today.

Finally, a few more lines from Rolf Edberg's book "The Land of Glittering Water":

"Nowhere does the world end and the ego begin. Mankind has to be seen in an environment — an environment that is never static. It has to be seen in a context — a context that is a process."

Literature and references

Alla tiders landskap, 1994, Swedish Touring Club. Stockholm.

Allhems Publishing, books about the provinces. Malmö.

Aronsson, K.-Å., 1991, Forest Reindeer Herding A.D. 1–1800. An Archaeological and palaeoecological Study in Northern Sweden. *Archaeology and Environment 10*, Umeå University.

Baudou, E., Nejati, M. (eds), 1981, Luleälvssymposiet 1–3 juni 1981. Papers of the Lule älv project 1, Umeå University.

Bebyggelsehistorisk tidskrift, 1-, 1981-

Berglund, B. E. (ed), 1988, The cultural landscape during 6000 years in southern Sweden—The Ystad Project. *Ecological Bulletins No 41*. Lund.

Bodvall, G., 1959, Bodland i norra Hälsingland, *Geographica no 36*. Uppsala.

Borgegård, L. E., 1973, Tjärhanteringen i Västerbottens län under 1800-talets senare hälft. *Kungl. Skytteanska Samfundets Handlingar nr 12*. Umeå.

Brink, S., 1979, Bodlanden i Järvsö socken. *Ortnamn och samhälle 5*. Uppsala.

Brink, S., 1983, *Ortnamnen och kulturlandskapet. Ortnamnens vittnesbörd om kulturlandskapets utveckling och dess utnyttjande i södra Norrland*. Uppsala.

Bylund, E., 1956, Koloniseringen av Pite lappmark t o m år 1867. *Geographica 30*. Uppsala.

Bylund, E., 1988, Inlandets bebyggelseutveckling på 1800-talet. *Västerbotten*. Magazine of Västerbottens läns hembygdsförbund.

Culture Heritage Preservation Programs, different counties.

Edestam, A., 1955, Dalslands folkmängd år 1880 och 1950. *Svensk Geografisk Årsbok*.

Egerbladh, I., 1987, Agrara bebyggelsprocesser. Utvecklingen i Norrbottens kustland fram till 1900-talet. *Gerum 7*, Umeå University.

Elert, C.-C., 1989, *Allmän och svensk fonetik*. Stockholm.

Ene, S., Persson, C., Widgren, M., 1991, Markdatabas Gotland, Department of Human Geography, Stockholm University.

Enequist, G., 1937, Nedre Luledalens byar. En kulturgeografisk studie. *Geographica 4*, Uppsala University.

Erixon, S., 1932, Byar, *Svenska kulturbilder XI–XII*. Stockholm.

Erixon, S., 1960, *Svenska byar utan systematisk reglering I–II*. Stockholm.

Forsberg, L., 1985, Site Variability and Settlement Patterns. An Analysis of the Hunter-Gatherer Settlement System in the Lule River Valley, 155 B.C.-B.C./A.D. *Archaeology and Environment 5*, Umeå University.

Forsström, G., 1973, *Malmberget—malmbrytning och bebyggelse*. Gällivare municipality.

Gårding, E., 1977, Variationer kring ett tema. Språket i utveckling, edited by Å. Pettersson, L. Badersten, Lund.

Göransson, S., 1971, Tomt och teg på Öland. Om byamål, laga läge och territoriell indelning. *Research reports from Department of Human Geography*, Uppsala University.

Hall, T., 1984, *Städer i utveckling. Tolv studier kring stadsförändringar*. Stockholm.

Hall, T., (ed) 1988, *Planning and urban growth in the Nordic countries*. London.

Hallerdt, B. (ed), 1988, Stad i förvandling. *Samfundet S:t Eriks Year Book*.

Hallerdt, B. (ed), 1992, Det nya Stockholm. *Samfundet S:t Eriks Year Book 1991/92*.

Hannerberg, D., 1977, *Kumlabygden IV. By, gård och samhälle*. Kumla.

Heddelin, B. (ed), 1991, *Vägar, dåtid, nutid, framtid*. National Road Administration, Stockholm and Borlänge.

Helmfrid, S., 1962, Östergötland "Västanstång". Studien über die ältere Agrarlandschaft und ihre Genese. *Geografiska Annaler*.

Historisk geografi, 1986, *Ymer*, Svenska Sällskapet för Antropologi och Geografi, Year Book.

Hjulström, F., Arpi, G., Lövgren, E., 1955, Sundsvallsdistriktet 1850–1950. *Geographica no 26*. Uppsala.

Hoppe, Gunnar, 1945, Vägarna i Västerbottens län. *Geographica no 16*. Uppsala.

Hoppe, Göran, Langton, J., 1986, Time-geography and economic development: the changing structure of livelihood positions on arable farms in nineteenth century Sweden. *Geografiska Annaler Vol 68B, no 2*.

Hough, M., 1989, *City Form and Natural Process*. Routledge, London and New York.

Hägerhäll, B. (ed.), 1988, *Världskommissionen för miljö och utveckling. Vår gemensamma framtid*. Prisma, Tiden.

Hägerstrand, T., 1979, Tankegångar bakom "intensivdataområden". *Arkiv 7, Bind no 4*.

Hägerstrand, T., 1993, Samhälle och natur. *Region och miljö*. In NordREFO.

Jansson, A.-M., Zuchetto, J., 1978, Energy, Economics and Ecological Relationships for Gotland, Sweden—a Regional Systems Study. *Ecological Bulletins No 28*.

Jensen, R. (ed), 1994, *Odlingslandskap och fångstmark*. A book to Klas-Göran Selinge. Central Board of National Antiquities.

Johansson, I., 1991, *Stor-Stockholms bebyggelsehistoria. Markpolitik, planering och byggande under sju sekler*.

Jonsson, M., Lindquist, S.-O., 1987, Vägen till kulturen på Gotland. *Gotländskt arkiv*.

Jonsson, U., 1985, Godsens förändring under 1800-talet: omvandlingsmönster och effekter på befolkningsutvecklingen. *Bebyggelshistorisk tidskrift 9*.

Jämtland County Museum, 1984, Inventering av fäbodar i Härjedalens kommun. *Kulturhistorisk utredning 28*.

Kvist, R., 1987, Luleälvsbibliografi. *Miscellaneous Publications 2*. Center for Arctic Cultural Research, Umeå University.

Layton, I., 1981, The evolution of Upper Norrland's Ports and Loading Places 1750–1976. *Geographical Reports No 6*. Umeå.

Lindgren, G., 1939, Falbygden och den närmaste omgivningen vid 1600-talets mitt. *Geographica no 6*, Uppsala.

Markanvändningen i Sverige, 1993, Second edition. Statistics Sweden.

Martinius, S., 1982, *Jordbrukets omvandling på 1700- och 1800-talen*. Malmö.

Människan, kulturlandskapet och framtiden, 1980, Konferences 4. Bibliography, Konferences 5. Royal Academy of Letters, History and Antiquities.

Möller, J., 1989, *Godsen och den agrara revolutionen. Arbetsorganisation, domänstruktur och kulturlandskap på skånska gods under 1800-talet.* Lund University Press.

Nilsson, B., 1972, "Barrskogslandskapets ekologi"—samhällsorienterad grundforskning. *Sveriges Natur.*

Nordberg, P.-O., 1977, Ljungan. Vattenbyggnader i den näringsgeografiska miljön 1550.1940. *Kungl. Skytteanska Samfundets Handlingar no 18.*

Nordström, O., 1991, *Lessebo.*

Olsson, R., 1981, *Helårsboendet på Glesbygd i Göteborgs och Bohus län. Chronos.* Department of Human Geography, Göteborg University.

Odum, H. T., 1973, Energy, Ecology and Economics. *Ambio.* Royal Academy of Science.

Pamp, B., 1978, *Svenska dialekter.* Stockholm.

Persson, C., 1992, *Jorden, bonden och hans familj. En studie av bondejordbruket i en socken i norra Småland under 1800-talet.* Department of Human Geography, Stockholm University.

Pomeroy, L. R., Alberts, J. J. (ed), 1988, *Concepts of Ecosystem Ecology. A Comparative View.* Springer-Verlag, New York etc.

Rosander, G. (ed), 1976, Nordiskt fäbodväsende. Förhandlingar vid fäbodseminarium i Älvdalen. Nordiska museet.

Rudberg, S., 1957, Ödemarkerna och den perifera bebyggelsen i inre Nordsverige. *Geographica no 33.* Uppsala.

Sporrong, U., 1985, *Mälarbygd. Agrar bebyggelse och odling ur ett historisk-geografiskt perspektiv.* Department of Human Geography, Stockholm University.

Sporrong, U., 1991, Jordinnehav och social legitimitet. Om gårdsstrukturer och arvsregler i övre Dalarna. *Royal Academy of Letters, History and Antiquities, Year Book.*

Stephansson, O. (ed), 1986, *Landet stiger ur havet.* Luleå.

Swedish Touring Club, Year Books

Svenskt glas, 1992.

Wikström, P.-O., 1994, *Spår i Mälardalen. En samling texter om människorna, landskapet och bebyggelsen.* Office of Regional Planning and Urban Transportation, Stockholm.

William-Olsson, W., 1984 (1937, 1941), Stockholms framtida utveckling. Bilaga: Huvuddragen av Stockholms geografiska utveckling 1850–1930. *Stockholm Monographs edited by Stockholm city 1.*

Åström, K., 1993, *Stadsplanering i Sverige.* Trelleborg.

Acknowledgments for Illustrations

Permission for distribution of maps approved by the Security Officer. The National Land Survey 1994–08–25. Permission 94.0345.

EK = Economic map
GK = Yellow map
GR = Green map
KB = Royal Library
LMV = National Land Survey
N = Naturfotograferna
RAÄ = Central Board of National Antiquities
SCB = Statistics Sweden
SGU = Geological Survey of Sweden
SNA = National Atlas of Sweden
Tio = Tiofoto AB
TK = Topographic map

Page	
Cover	Claes Grundsten/N
2	LMV
6	Avena
7	Helle Skånes
8	Drawing Nils Forshed, Photos LMV
9	Nils Forshed
10	Nils Forshed
11	Nils Forshed
12	N1 SNA, Drawing Nils Forshed, Map bottom SNA, data Swedish Touring Club, drawing Katarina Strömdahl
13	N2 SNA, Photo Arne Schmitz/N
14	Map SNA, data Bylund 1956, Photo left Claes Grundsten/N, Photo right Pål-Nils Nilsson/Tio
15	N3 SNA, data Ministry for Foreign Affairs, N4 SNA
16	Drawing Nils Forshed, Diagram SNA, data Björn Berglund
17	Drawings Nils Forshed, N5 SNA, data Björn Berglund, Roger Engelmark, Karl-Dag Vorren
18	SNA, data Björn Berglund
19	SNA, data Björn Berglund
20	Nils Forshed, SNA, data Björn Berglund
22	Photo top Tore Hagman/N, Photo centre Axel Ljungquist/N, Diagram SNA
23	Drawing Nils Forshed, Photo Evert Baudou, Map SNA, data Inez Egerbladh
24	Photo top K Lundholm, Diagram centre SNA, data Lennart Lundmark, Diagram bottom SNA, data N G Lundgren, Drawing Nils Forshed, Photo bottom Torbjörn Lilja/N
25	Diagram top SNA, data Ian Layton, Diagram centre SNA, data N G Lundgren, Photo top G Holmström/Norrbotten Museum, Photo centre Lars Bergström/RAÄ, Photo bottom SOU 1976:28
26	Photo top left Carl-Åke Eriksson, Photo top Avena, Photo bottom KB, Drawing Nils Forshed
27	Photo top LMV, Photo bottom Ulf Sporrong
28	Photo top LMV, drawing Catharina Mascher, Photo bottom Jan Norrman
29	Photo LMV, Maps SNA, drawing Katarina Strömdahl
30	N6, N7 SNA, data Ulf Sporrong, drawing Katarina Strömdahl
31	Drawings Katarina Strömdahl, N8 SNA, data Ulf Sporrong, drawing Katarina Strömdahl, Photo top Uggla/Nordiska Museet, Photo centre privately owned, Photo bottom KB
32	N9 SNA, data Ulf Sporrong, drawing Katarina Strömdahl
33	Photo top LMV, Photo centre Ulf Sporrong
34	Photo top Staffan Nyblom, Photos bottom Krigsarkivet
35	LMV
36	Photo top LMV, Maps bottom SNA, data Staffan Helmfrid, Göran Hoppe, drawing Katarina Strömdahl
37	Photo Avena, Map bottom SNA, data Göran Hoppe, drawing Katarina Strömdahl, Diagram SNA, data Göran Hoppe, N10 SNA, data Staffan Helmfrid
38	Nils Forshed
39	Drawing Nils Forshed, N11 SNA, data the Emigration Commission 1910, Diagram SNA, data Christer Persson
40	N12 SNA, data Jonsson 1985, Photos KB
41	Photo Mats Riddersporre, Diagram SNA, data Jens Möller
42	Photo KB, Drawing Nils Forshed
43	Photo top LMV, data Kersti Morger, Map SNA, data Kersti Morger
44	N13 SNA, data Kjell Haraldsson
45	Photo Svenska Sågverks- och Trävaruföreningen, N14, N15 SNA, data Kjell Haraldsson
46	N16, N17, N18, N19 SNA, data Göran Hoppe
47	Photo Avena, Map SNA, data Göran Hoppe
48	Photo top A Boström/Nordiska Museet, Photo bottom Stockholms stadsmuseum
49	Black-and-white photos Nordiska Museet, Photo map Sture Ekendahl
50	Photo, black-and-white, Stockholms stadsmuseum, Photo, colour, Nils-Johan Norenlind/Tio, N20, N21 SNA, data SCB
51	Drawings Nils Forshed, Photo, black-and-white, Nordiska Museet, Photo, colour, P Roland Johansson/N
52	Nils Forshed
53	Photo top Stockholms stadsbyggnadskontor, rina Strömdahl, Photo, black-and-white, Stockholms stadsmuseum, Photo, colour, Hans Wretling/Tio
54	Nils Forshed
55	N22, diagram, SNA, data SCB
56	N23, diagram SNA, data Hans Ylander/SCB
57	Photo top SCB, Aerial photograph LMV, N24 SNA, data Hans Ylander/SCB
58	N25 SNA, data SCB, Photo Nils-Johan Norenlind/Tio
59	Photo top Bertil K Johansson/N, Photo centre Göran Hansson/N, Photo bottom left Uppsala University, Photo bottom right Sture Karlsson/Tio
60	N26, N27 SNA, N28 SNA, data SCB
61	N29, N30 SNA, N31 SNA, data Elert 1989, N32 SNA, data Lars-Erik Edlund, Photo Per-Olov Eriksson/N
62	Lars Bygdemark
63	Photo top Jan Töve J:son/N, Photo centre Lars Bygdemark
64	Lars Bygdemark
65	Lars Bygdemark
66–73	N33 SNA, data Ulf Sporrong, drawing Katarina Strömdahl
66	Photo Lars Bygdemark
67	Photo top Lars Bygdemark, Photo bottom Bertil K Johansson/N
68	Photo Lars Bygdemark
69	Photo Lars Bygdemark
70	Photo Lars Bygdemark
71	Photo Lars Bygdemark
72	Photo Tore Hagman/N
73	Photo Lars Bygdemark
74	Pål-Nils Nilsson/Tio
75	Lars Bygdemark
76	Photo top Lars Bygdemark, Photo centre Klas Rune/N
77	Claes Grundsten/N
78	Bottom left KB, Bottom right Land Survey, Malmö
79	Top and bottom left KB, Top and bottom right Land Survey, Malmö
80	Photo top Nils-Thore Andersson, Photo bottom Lund University Library
81	Photo top Malmö city, Map SNA
82	Top EK 4C3f, LMV, Bottom EK 5B2j, LMV, Photo centre KB, Photo bottom Stig T Karlsson/Tio
83	EK 3F5d, 3F6d, LMV, Photo Armed Forces Archives
84	Map top SNA, Left EK 4D3c, 1949, LMV, Right EK 4D3c, 1984, LMV

85	Top EK 4F8d, LMV Photo LMV Map bottom SNA, data Olof Nordström	
86	Photo top left Lars Bygdemark Photo top right G82–13:3, LMV Photo bottom left KB Photo bottom right LMV	
87	Centre EK 5G4h, LMV Bottom TK 4GSV, LMV	
88	Regional Archive in Visby	
89	Photo top Arne Philip Photo centre Tommie Jacobsson/N Map SNA, data Ene, Persson, Widgren 1991	
90	Photo top G Schmidt/Skokloster Photos bottom LMV	
91	GR 7ESV, drawing Katarina Strömdahl	
92	Photo top Torleif Svensson/Tio Photo centre Lars Bygdemark Map left SNA, data Staffan Helmfrid Right GK 8E:26	
93	Top left EK 8F4d, 8F4e, 8F3e, LMV Top right KB Photo LMV	
94	SNA	
95	Photo top Allan Olsson Photo centre Magnus Waller/Tio Photos bottom LMV	
96	Three maps top left SNA, drawing Katarina Strömdahl Top right EK 9 Öckerö SO 1934, LMV Bottom GK 6A:99, LMV	
97	Maps SNA	
98	Photo top left Göran Olofsson Photo top right LMV Photo centre Magnus Waller/Tio Photo bottom KB	
99	Photo top left LMV Photo top and bottom right Göran Olofsson Bottom left GK 7B:24, LMV	
100	Top EK 8C3g 1961, LMV Drawing Nils Forshed Bottom GK 8D:05 1986, LMV	
101	Top GK 6C:83, LMV Bottom EK 7C5b, LMV	
102	Top GK 12C:06, LMV Centre LMV Bottom TK 10BSO, LMV	
103	Photo top left LMV Top right GK 13C:07, LMV N34 SNA	
104	Map SNA	
105	Top left GK 12H:01, LMV Photo top right Avena Bottom left GK 9G:80, LMV Bottom right EK 10F0c, LMV	
106	Photos Claes Grundsten/N Bottom GK 11I:20, LMV	
107	Top EK 11I3d, LMV Bottom GK 11I:22, LMV	
108	Top Red map 8, LMV Centre GK 9G:49, LMV Bottom left GK 9G:66, LMV Bottom right KB	
109	Top EK 10I2a 1951, LMV Centre EK 10I2a 1982, LMV	
110	KB	
111	Map KB Photo top Lennart af Petersén Photo bottom Göran Sehlstedt	
112	Maps of Stockholm with suburbs, 22nd ed., 1954–55, Stockholms adresskalender	
113	Top KB Centre Sundbybergs stadsbyggnadskontor Photo Stockholms stadsmuseum	
114	Top and centre Stockholms stadsbyggnadskontor Photo Leif Strååt/Bildmedia/Stockholm Konsult	
115	Järfälla municipality	
116	Top EK 10I9i 1952, LMV Bottom EK 10I9i 1980, LMV	
117	Photo top Tore Hagman/N Centre left EK 11J3f 1942, LMV Centre right EK 10I6b 1950, LMV Bottom left EK 11J3f 1976, LMV Bottom right EK 10I6b 1976, LMV	
118	GK 11E:43, 11E:63, LMV	
119	Top EK 11F5d, LMV Centre EK 12F5j, LMV Photo left Nils Ahlberg Photo right Jernkontoret	
120	Top SNA Centre EK 12I5c, LMV Photo bottom left Lars Bygdemark Bottom right EK 12I5d, LMV	
121	Photo top and bottom Göran Hansson/N Photo centre LMV	
122	Top EK 14E1j, LMV Bottom left EK 14E5f, LMV Photo Lars Bygdemark	
123	Top GK 15F:09, LMV Photo Jan Rietz/Tio	
124	Top left Red map 12, LMV Top right EK 13E4i, LMV Bottom EK 15D0j, LMV	
125	Top GR 15GNV, LMV, data Stefan Brink, drawing Katarina Strömdahl Bottom left GK 15G:83, LMV Photo Tyko Olofsson/MYRA	
126	Photo Nils-Johan Norenlind/Tio Diagram SNA	
127	Top left LMV Top right TK 17HSO, 17HNO, LMV Photo SCA	
128	Photo Pål-Nils Nilsson/Tio	
	Map SNA, drawing Katarina Strömdahl	
129	Map Ak6 part 1, Ak5 part 1, SGU Photo left Jan Lindmark Photo right LMV Drawing Nils Forshed	
130–131		
130	Photo centre Bertil Ekholtz Photo bottom Erik Bylund	
132	Top EK 28L6e, 28L7f, LMV Photo bottom Pål-Nils Nilsson/Tio	
133	Drawing Nils Forshed Photos Jan Elveland	
134	Ca 45, SGU	
135	Top EK 18C0e, 18C1f, LMV Photo LMV	
136	Top left Department of Human Geography, Stockholm Top right EK 19E0j, LMV Bottom LMV	
137	Top left EK 17E6c, 17E7d, LMV Top right Land Survey, Östersund Photo LMV	
138	EK 28K2–3 a-b, 28K2–3 c-d, LMV	
139	Photo top LMV Photos Nordiska Museet	
140	Armed Forces Archives	
141	Top LMV Bottom Gävle municipality	
142	Top Gävle municipality Photo Gävle municipality	
143	Gävle municipality	
144	Diagram, SNA N35 SNA, data Central Board for Real Estate Data	
145	Top Eskilstuna municipality Photo Lars Eisele	
146	N36 SNA Photo centre Bo Brännhage/N Photo bottom Tore Hagman/N	
147	Top Eskilstuna municipality Photos Lars Eisele	
148	Sydvästra Skånes kommunalförbund	
149	Skövde municipality	
150	Photo top Lars Bygdemark Photo bottom Norrköping municipality	
151	Top Lidköpings municipality Photo Lidköpings hantverks- och sjöfartsmuseum	
152	Kersti Rasmusson	
153	Kersti Rasmusson	
154	Kersti Rasmusson	
155	Drawing Gunnel Eriksson	
156	Photo Nils-Johan Norenlind	

Thematic Maps

MAP	SCALE	THEME	PAGE
N1	1:10M	Natural resources for early settlers	12
N2	1:10M	Permanent settlement Late Iron Age—Late Middle Ages	13
N3	1:10M	Sweden's borders	15
N4		Sweden's borders i 10th and 15th century, 1660 and from 1814	15
N5		Cultivation of cereals during Early Neolithic Age, Late Neolithic Age, Roman Iron Age and Viking Age	17
N6	1:10M	Rural settlements, ca. 1750	30
N7	1:10M	Crop-rotation	30
N8	1:10M	Field division systems	31
N9	1:10M	Cultural landscapes, ca. 1750	32
N10	1:10M	"*Enskifte*" or "*laga skifte*"	37
N11	1:5M	Percentage of "family farms" in Southern Sweden 1902	39
N12	1:10M	Large-scale farming 1862	40
N13	1:5M	Handicraft regions, ca. 1850	44
N14	1:10M	Proto-industry, 1750–1850	45
N15	1:10M	Manufacturing industry, 1850–90	45
N16	1:10M	Engineering industries with more than 100 employees, 1870	46
N17	1:20M	Cotton weaving mills, 1875	46
N18	1:10M	Breweries, 1875	46
N19	1:10M	Paper mills	46
N20	1:10M	Numbers employed in agriculture per county, 1920	50
N21	1:10M	Numbers employed in agriculture per county, 1990	50
N22	1:5M	Population within 30 km	55
N23	1:10M	Percentage population in urban areas per county, 1990	56
N24	1:10M	Changes in places defined as urban areas (>200 inhabitants), 1980–90	57
N25	1:5M	Employment by industry and county, 1990	58
N26	1:10M	Settlement regions	60
N27	1:10M	Physical regions	60
N28	1:10M	Natural agricultural areas	60
N29	1:20M	Demographic regions according to G Sundbärg, 1910	61
N30	1:10M	Industrial areas, 1960	61
N31	1:10M	Regional variants of standard spoken Swedish	61
N32	1:10M	Dialects in Swedish exemplified by "*idissla*" (ruminate)	61
N33	1:1,25M	Cultural landscapes—a regional description	66–73
N34	1:5M	Finnish colonisation and Finnish farmsteads	103
N35	1:10M	Number of building plans, town plans, district regulations and detailed plans in force on 20 october 1993, by county	144
N36	1:5M	Landscapes protected by law	146

Authors

Améen, Lennart, 1926, Reader of Human Geography, Lund University

Baudou, Evert, 1925, Professor Emeritus of Archaeology, Umeå University

Berglund, Björn, 1935, Professor of Quaternary Geology, Lund University

Bladh, Gabriel, 1959, Senior Lecturer of Human Geography, Karlstad University

Bylund, Erik, 1922, Professor Emeritus of Human Geography, Umeå University

Carlsson, Dan, 1946, Ph.D. of Human Geography, Visby

Castensson, Reinhold, 1943, Reader of Human Geography, Linköping University

Gelotte, Göran, 1936, Municipal Custody Antiquarian, Södertälje

Göransson, Sölve, 1925, Reader of Human Geography, Uppsala University

Hall, Thomas, 1939, Reader of Art History, Stockholm University

Haraldsson, Kjell, 1950, Senior Lecturer of Human Geography, Uppsala University

Helmfrid, Staffan, 1927, Professor Emeritus of Human Geography, Stockholm University

Hoppe, Göran, 1946, Reader of Human Geography, Stockholm University

Hyenstrand, Åke, 1939, Professor of Archaeology, Stockholm University

Hägerstrand, Torsten, 1916, Professor Emeritus of Human Geography, Lund University

Layton, Ian, 1938, Reader of Human Geography, Umeå University

Lewan, Nils, 1929, Reader of Human Geography, Lund University

Lindquist, Sven-Olof, 1933, Reader of Human Geography, County Custodian of Antiquities, Visby

Lundén, Thomas, 1943, Reader of Human Geography, Head of Division, Swedish Institute, Stockholm

Mascher, Catharina, 1963, Ph.Lic. of Human Geography, Stockholm University

Morger, Kersti, 1938, Ph.D. of Human Geography, 1st Antiquarian, Central Board of National Antiquities, Stockholm

Möller, Jens, 1956, Ph.D. of Human Geography, Länstrafiken, Lund

Nordström, Olof, 1921, Reader of Human Geography, Lund University

Olsson, Ragnar, 1931, Senior Lecturer of Human Geography, Göteborg University

Persson, Christer, 1957, Ph.D. of Human Geography, Stockholm University

Ponzio, Mario, 1936, Lecturer, Department of Human Geography, Stockholm University

Roeck Hansen, Birgitta, 1937, Ph.D. of Human Geography, Stockholm University

Sporrong, Ulf, 1936, Professor of Human Geography, Stockholm University

Thurdin, Görel, 1942, Cabinet Minister, The Ministry of Environment and Natural Resources

Tollin, Clas, 1945, Antiquarian, Central Board of National Antiquities, Stockholm

Tonell, Lennart, 1944, Senior Lecturer of Human Geography, Stockholm University

Widgren, Mats, 1948, Reader of Human Geography, Stockholm University

Ylander, Hans, 1930, Ph.Lic., Statistics Sweden, Stockholm

Öberg, Sture, 1942, Professor of Human Geography, Uppsala University

Index

ABC town 114
abrasion 91
agglomeration 56
alvar 87
Ancylus 65
area of national interest 146, 148
avvittring 37

bar-iron 118
Bergslagen 76, 118
blast furnace 42, 118
bloomery furnace 137
blooming steel process 118
bodland 32, 76, 124
boulevard 112
brewery **46 (N18)**
building plan **144 (N35)**
building regulation 141

Cambro-Silurian 76, 122, 136
Captain's House 64
carved stone 28
cattleyard 87
cavalry 34
central district 17
charcoal analysis 17
"church town" 133
city 112
city lights effect 54
claim 138
clay 65
clay till 100
cliff 65
clustered village 30, 31
colonisation 14
common plot 124
commuting 78
commuting distance 74, 75
concentration plant 118
cot 36
cottage industry 101
cotton weaving mill **46 (N17)**
craftwork for sale 44
croft 36
crop rotation **30 (N7)**
Crown land 38, 138
Crown unit 89
Crown works 118
cultivation **17 (N5)**
cultural landscape **66–73 (N33)**

demographic region **61 (N29)**
detailed plan **144 (N35)**
dialect **61 (N32)**
district regulations **144 (N35)**
division of farms 38, 42, 96, 124
donation land 81, 97
drumlin 63, 128

embankment 32
emigration 75
employed in agriculture **50 (N20, N21)**
employment **58 (N25)**
engineering industry **46 (N16)**
enskifte 14, 36, **37 (N10)**, 78, 141
Erik Tour 93
esplanade 141
ethnicity 22
étoile square 112

fallow system 30
falor 101
"family farm" **39 (N11)**
farmyard 87
field 30
field division system **31 (N8)**
Finnish colonisation **103 (N34)**
Finnish settlement 32, 76
fiscal 88
fissure valley 65, 104
fossilised cultural landscape 26

general plan 142, 148
geometric land register 88
grain-drying hut 103
grazing land 36
green-village 30
guild 44

handicraft region **44 (N13)**
high land 32
highest shoreline 62, 65, 76, 77, 128, 132
home shealing 124
hook and line fishing 94
hummocky landscape 18
hunting culture 23
hydrology 17

infields 74
inland cliff 87
ironmaster 118

job-seeking journey 122

kin village 31

laga läge 30, 33
laga skifte 36, **37 (N10)**, 141
land register 29
land tax 88
land uplift 12
landscapes protected by law **146 (N36)**
landshövdingehus 97
lappmarksgränsen 77
large-scale farming **40 (N12)**
limit of cultivation 77
linear village 30, 31
Littorina 65
Low farm 40, 41

manor farm 108
mantal 88
manufacture 42, 46, 47, 90
manufacturing industry **45 (N15)**
marginal district 17
marklej 88
mill 46
Million Program 109, 115, 150
mine manager's report 118
mine master 118
mine shaft 120
multi-crop system 32
municipal district 56
municipal reform 93

National Physical Planning 146
natural agricultural area **60 (N28)**
natural resources **12 (N1)**
The Natural Resources Act 144, 146
new town 114
nobleman's unit 89
nomadic reindeer husbandry 24
Norrland terrain 126
nucleated village 31. 32

old town centre 112
one-field system 30
osteological analysis 26
outfields 33
overshot water wheel 130

paper mill **46 (N19)**
parcel 32, 87
partially divided farm 31
pedlar 74, 101
permanent settlement **13 (N2)**
permission 144
phosphate analyse 28
physical planning 144
physical region **60 (N27)**
The Planning and Building Act 143, 144
pollarded trees 64
pollen analysis 17
pollen diagram 16

population **55 (N22)**
population in urban areas **56 (N23)**
Property Plan 144
proto-industry 43, **45 (N14)**
puddle iron 47

quarrying village 94

railway town 78
regional plan 148
rural district 56
rural settlements **30 (N6)**

sauna 103
seine net 94
semi-urban zon 74
settlement region **60 (N26)**
sherd 28
shore settlement 94
Siljan Ring 122
slag heap 137
slash and burn farming 32
smoke-curing hut 103
solskifte 30, 32
standard spoken Swedish **61 (N31)**
statare 41
storskifte 36, 122, 141
stängskifte 31
Sweden's border **15 (N3, N4)**
system of cultivation 30

tax-paying farm 89
Thomas process 138
town plan 141, **144 (N35)**
trawl 94
tresäde 30, 32, 74, 88
tvåsäde 30, 32, 35, 88

urban area 55, 56, **57 (N24)**, 97
urban district 56
urban sprawl 74
urbanisation 54, 78, 126

valley site 10
"vassal state" 87
visual misunderstanding 51

Walloon mill 120
"water alley" 112
water-washed slope 132

159

National Atlas of Sweden

A geographical description of the landscape, society and culture of Sweden in 17 volumes

MAPS AND MAPPING
From historic maps of great cultural significance to modern mapping methods using the latest advanced technology. What you didn't already know about maps you can learn here. A unique place-name map (1:700,000) gives a bird's-eye view of Sweden. Editors: Professor Ulf Sporrong, geographer, Stockholm University, and Hans-Fredrik Wennström, economist, National Land Survey, Gävle.

THE FORESTS
Sweden has more forestland than almost any other country in Europe. This volume describes how the forests have developed and how forestry works: ecological cycles, climatic influences, its importance for the economy etc. One of many maps shows, on the scale of 1:1.25 million, the distribution of the forests today. Editor: Professor Nils-Erik Nilsson, forester, National Board of Forestry, Jönköping.

THE POPULATION
Will migration to the towns continue, or shall we see a new "green wave"? This volume highlights most sides of Swedish life: how Swedes live, education, health, family life, private economy etc. Political life, the population pyramid and immigration are given special attention. Editor: Professor Sture Öberg, geographer, Uppsala University, and Senior Administrative Officer Peter Springfeldt, geographer, Statistics Sweden, Stockholm.

THE ENVIRONMENT
More and more people are concerning themselves with environmental issues and nature conservancy. This book shows how Sweden is being affected by pollution, and what remedies are being applied. Maps of protected areas, future perspectives and international comparisons. Editors: Dr Claes Bernes and Claes Grundsten, geographer, National Environment Protection Board, Stockholm.

AGRICULTURE
From horse-drawn plough to the highly-mechanized production of foodstuffs. A volume devoted to the development of Swedish agriculture and its position today. Facts about the parameters of farming, what is cultivated where, the workforce, financial aspects etc. Editor: Birger Granström, state agronomist, and Åke Clason, managing director of Research Information Centre, Swedish University of Agricultural Sciences, Uppsala.

The work of producing the National Atlas of Sweden is spread throughout the country.

THE INFRASTRUCTURE
Sweden's welfare is dependent on an efficient infrastructure, everything from roads and railways to energy production and public administration. If you are professionally involved, this book will provide you with a coherent survey of Sweden's infrastructure. Other readers will find a broad explanation of how Swedish society is built up and how it functions. Editor: Dr Reinhold Castensson, geographer, Linköping University.

SEA AND COAST
The Swedes have a deep-rooted love for the sea and the coast. This volume describes the waters which surround Sweden and how they have changed with the evolution of the Baltic. Facts about types of coastline, oceanography, marine geology and ecology, including comparisons with the oceans of the world. Editor: Björn Sjöberg, oceanographer, Swedish Meteorological and Hydrological Institute, Göteborg.

CULTURAL LIFE, RECREATION AND TOURISM
An amateur drama production in Hässleholm or a new play at the Royal Dramatic Theatre in Stockholm? Both fill an important function. This volume describes the wide variety of culture activities available in Sweden (museums, cinemas, libraries etc), sports and the various tourist areas in Sweden. Editor: Dr Hans Aldskogius, geographer, Uppsala University.

SWEDEN IN THE WORLD
Sweden is the home of many successful export companies. But Sweden has many other relations with the rest of the world. Cultural and scientific interchange, foreign investment, aid to the Third World, tourism etc. are described in a historical perspective. Editor: Professor Gunnar Törnqvist, geographer, Lund University.

WORK AND LEISURE
Describes how Swedes divide their time between work and play, with regional, social and age-group variations. The authors show who does what, the role of income, etc, and make some predictions about the future. Editor: Dr Kurt V Abrahamsson, geographer, Umeå University.

CULTURAL HERITAGE AND PRESERVATION
Sweden is rich in prehistoric monuments and historical buildings, which are presented here on maps. What is being done to preserve our cultural heritage? This volume reviews modern cultural heritage policies. Editor: Reader Klas-Göran Selinge, archeologist, Central Board of National Antiquities, Stockholm. Ass. Editor: 1st Antiquarian Marit Åhlén, runologist, Central Board of National Antiquities, Stockholm.

GEOLOGY
Maps are used to present Sweden's geology—the bedrock, soils, land forms, ground water. How and where are Sweden's natural geological resources utilised? Editor: Curt Fredén, state geologist, Geological Survey of Sweden, Uppsala.

LANDSCAPE AND SETTLEMENTS
How has the Swedish landscape evolved over the centuries? What traces of old landscapes can still be seen? What regional differences are there? This volume also treats the present landscape, settlements, towns and cities, as well as urban and regional planning. Editor: Professor Staffan Helmfrid, geographer, Stockholm University.

CLIMATE, LAKES AND RIVERS
What causes the climate to change? Why does Sweden have fewer natural disasters than other countries? This volume deals with the natural cycle of water and with Sweden's many lakes and rivers. Climatic variations are also presented in map form. Editors: Birgitta Raab, state hydrologist, and Haldo Vedin, state meteorologist, Swedish Meteorological and Hydrological Institute, Norrköping.

MANUFACTURING, SERVICES AND TRADE
Heavy industry is traditionally located in certain parts of Sweden, while other types of industry are spread all over the country. This volume contains a geographical description of Swedish manufacturing and service industries and foreign trade. Editor: Dr Claes Göran Alvstam, geographer, Göteborg University.

GEOGRAPHY OF PLANTS AND ANIMALS
Climatic and geographical variations in Sweden create great geographical differences in plant and animal life. This volume presents the geographical distribution of Sweden's fauna and explains how and why they have changed over the years. There is a special section on game hunting. Editors: Professor Ingemar Ahlén and Dr Lena Gustafsson, Swedish University of Agricultural Sciences, Uppsala.

THE GEOGRAPHY OF SWEDEN
A comprehensive picture of the geography of Sweden, containing excerpts from other volumes but also completely new, summarizing articles. The most important maps in the whole series are included. Indispensable for educational purposes. Editors: The editorial board of the National Atlas of Sweden, Stockholm.